MONTGOMERY
and the FIRST WAR ON TERROR

What a British Military Hero
Can Teach Those Fighting Today's
War on Terror

Robert Oulds

First Published 2012
Copyright © Robert Oulds 2012

Bretwalda Books
Unit 8, Fir Tree Close, Epsom, Surrey KT17 3LD
www.BretwaldaBooks.com

To receive an e-catalogue of our complete range of books
send an email to info@BretwaldaBooks.com

ISBN 978-1-907791-73-4

Bretwalda Books Ltd

'War is merely the continuation of policy by other means. We see, therefore, that war is not merely an act of policy but a true political instrument, a continuation of political intercourse, carried on with other means.'
Carl Von Clausewitz – Military Philosopher

'If you wish for peace, understand war, particularly the guerrilla and subversive forms of war.'
The British Military theorist Basil Liddell Hart, 1967

CONTENTS

6   Introduction - Two Definitive Guerrilla Wars

Part I Before the War on Terror

16   Chapter 1 - Theories on Guerrilla Warfare

21   Chapter 2 - Montgomery's Formative Years

Part II Ireland

31   Chapter 3 - Montgomery and the Anglo-Irish War

39   Chapter 4 - The Rebellion Begins

46   Chapter 5 - The opposing forces in Ireland

76   Chapter 6 - Enter Montgomery

114   Chapter 7 - Aftermath

122   Chapter 8 - Montgomery after Ireland

Part III Palestine

131   Chapter 9 - Montgomery and the Arab Revolt
      in Palestine 1936 – 39

136   Chapter 10 - The opposing forces in Palestine

149   Chapter 11 - The fighting begins

161   Chapter 12 - Enter Montgomery

188   Chapter 13 - Aftermath

Part IV Lessons to be Learned

201   Chapter 14 - Assessing Montgomery in Action

217   Chapter 15 - Northern Ireland, Iraq and Afghanistan
       in the modern era

262   Chapter 16 - Conclusion

268   Appendix 1- Timeline:
       Montgomery's Career at a Glance

278   Appendix 2 - Endnotes

284   Appendix 3 - About the Author

286   Index

Introduction

TWO DEFINITIVE GUERRILLA WARS

'War is too serious a matter to entrust to military men'
Georges Clemenceau, French Prime Minister, who was known
for his successful and robust leadership of France at the close
of World War One

Bernard Law Montgomery, later to become Field Marshal Viscount Montgomery of Alamein, was certainly one of the UK's most adored and controversial soldiers whose fame was assured by his victories in World War Two. A ComRes poll from 2008 asking who was Britain's greatest military hero found that in the public eye Montgomery, also nicknamed Monty, was ranked second only to Nelson; putting him above the Duke of Wellington.

Montgomery's enduring legacy is the subject of much interest and debate. His victories over Nazi Germany, most notably at El-Alamein and through his commanding of the land forces on D-Day and in the Normandy campaign, won him a place in our national hearts. What is much less well known is that Montgomery in the earlier part of his career was an accomplished opponent of guerrilla forces; those elusive combatants some would call terrorists and others freedom fighters.

Between the First and Second World Wars the Britain Empire faced two major challenges from two very different guerrilla wars. These not only threatened the standing of the United Kingdom in the wider world but in the case of one it actually threatened the British state's territorial integrity. These conflicts were the war against the Irish Republican Army (IRA) during the Anglo-Irish War which happened after World War One. The second conflict was a fight which took place in the Middle East on the eve of World War Two. This latter conflict took place in Palestine and is known as the Arab Revolt; it lasted from 1936 until it was finally crushed in 1939. Here the British authorities were facing a serious challenge from a predominantly Muslim guerrilla army, which was also involved with acts of what were viewed by the British as terrorism.

Bernard Law Montgomery was at the heart of both these conflicts.

For the first time this military history book tells the full story of Montgomery's involvement in tackling two insurgencies against the British authorities as well as looking at the wider political and strategic situation. Monty also came to some insightful realisations about the nature of these wars and how the political authorities should handle them.

The lessons that he drew from these conflicts are especially relevant in this day and age and to the latest wars that Britain has become involved in.

The latter stage of the last century and the early part of this new millennium has been characterised by bloody ethnic conflict in parts of Europe. This era has also been the victim of acts of terror affecting many nations from as far afield as the United States of America to Spain and to nations in Africa. These have driven the United Kingdom and many members of the Western NATO alliance to become involved in peacekeeping operations and in actions known as liberal-interventionism.

These military ventures have in some cases descended into full-blown guerrilla wars; particularly in Afghanistan where the UK is involved in its bloodiest conflict since the Korean War of the early 1950s.

This has put the United Kingdom and its armed forces at the forefront of what has become known as the "War on Terror". What is more, Britain has traditionally had its own home-grown terrorist problem in Ireland which although generally quiet still has its troubles to this day. It is also likely that the British military will be facing continual pressures to become involved in other conflicts around the globe. Conflicts where a large, high-tech armed force is pitched against a smaller, low-tech insurgency are today dubbed "asymmetric conflicts".

The implications of the two main conflicts examined in this book, the Anglo-Irish War and the suppression of the Arab Revolt in Palestine, are still with us today. What is more, they have remarkable similarities to the military challenges facing Britain in the second decade of the 21st Century. And due to the UK's military alliances, historic interests and permanent position on the Security Council of the United Nations, British armed forces are likely to remain involved with many asymmetric wars around the globe for some time to come, even continuing to take preventative measures. The UK's British Defence Doctrine (BDD) officially recognises the UN's 'Responsibility to Protect' agenda contained within the UN paper A more secure world: Our shared responsibility. The BDD also states that British military policy should focus on, 'preventative and developmental lines of activity (including pre-emptive action)'. As such military intervention around the globe, be that supporting lawful governments against an insurgency or fighting against the trade in illegal drugs, is an international duty which will see the UK involved in more conflicts oversees. As such Britain must be prepared for them.

Learning the lessons of Montgomery and the counter-insurgency operations that he led takes us right back to the start of his military career when, before the First World War, he served on India's North-West Frontier. Here on the edge of the British Raj he was facing hostile Afghan tribesmen. During this time in Britain's imperial history there were then, as there still are now, punitive expeditions against rebellious Pashtun tribesman, whose descendants make up the backbone of the Taleban. Montgomery's skills were recognised even then at the age of 23; he was given the task of training specialist scout troops in mountain warfare. In the 1930s Montgomery again served on the North-West Frontier, ironically in the exact region that is now a home of the modern Pakistani Taleban.

The two main conflicts that will be examined, the Anglo-Irish War and the rebellion against British rule in 1930s Palestine, will look not only at Montgomery's involvement but will also explore the political conclusions which he reached and look at the political background at the heart of those guerrilla wars. The changing fortunes of war will also be analysed as will the military strategies, weapons and tactics.

Bernard Law Montgomery, with some success, organised the fight against the original IRA in their Republican heartland. An Irishmen by heritage, Montgomery not only organised an effective counter-insurgency campaign, he also reached some very profound and interesting conclusions about how this war on terror should be handled. It was his first major counter-insurgency. Montgomery's fight against the Arab Revolt in Palestine was his *tour de force*. He described it as 'a task greatly to my liking'. This book will explain how the UK secured victory over the Arab insurgents. Montgomery's conclusion as to the nature of the conflict and how it should be handled were also prescient and insightful.

Historians and biographers of Montgomery have usually

focussed on analysing his actions during World War II without looking at his role in the guerrilla wars and what he can teach us today. However, the lessons from these conflicts are far more relevant to the challenges that the UK will face in the modern era. This is especially the case regarding the on-going, but currently low level, troubles in Northern Ireland, as well as the conflicts in Afghanistan, Libya and elsewhere in the Arab and Muslim world that the UK has become involved in.

The striking similarities between the first and modern wars on terror

In British Law, as tested in the case of Regina v Gul, the Criminal Division of the Court of Appeal ruled on 22nd February 2012 that those taking part in or actively supporting the insurgents in both Iraq and Afghanistan are subject to the Terrorism Act 2000. A key passage from the judgment reads 'Insurgents who acted against the armed forces of a state anywhere in the world and who sought to influence a government for political purposes were committing acts of terrorism.'

Montgomery's historic conflicts in Ireland and Palestine share many similarities with the current challenges that the UK faces in Afghanistan. A large part of the fighting in both Ireland and Palestine was a direct military challenge to British authority in those countries. Yet those conflicts were not just driven by a desire for national political control. They were also part of the socialist and anti-imperialist radicalisation of politics which occurred at the end of the First World War. The fight against British and American involvement in Iraq and Afghanistan has also been driven by a reaction to the western world; namely radical Islam. And by a yearning to avenge the perceived wrongs of western dominance over the belligerents national homelands.

Just as the radicals in Ireland wanted to re-create the apparent 'Golden Age' of an independent Gaelic and Roman Catholic Ireland the Islamists that are today fighting Britain also wish to create an Islamic State known as a Caliphate and restore Muslim pride, liberate a land called Palestine and re-establish their own 'Golden Age'.

There are also other dynamics at work which drive the conflicts – religious and ethnic tensions. Ireland, Palestine, Iraq and Afghanistan are all divided along traditional sectarian lines. And this religious inter-communal hatred is a major cause of the fighting. Ireland has its ancient enmity between its Roman Catholic and Protestant communities. What is more, members of those groups often have different national origins. The Arab Revolt in Palestine grew out of clashes between the local Arabs and recent Jewish settlers. They had different cultural and religious backgrounds but share a mutual claim on the land. The conflict in Afghanistan also has linguistic, ethnic and sectarian divisions at its heart. On one side, backing the foreign intervention in Afghanistan, are the Durrani's who are wealthier and have traditionally formed the ruling class. On the other side, from where the Taleban receive most of their support, are the Ghilzai who have traditionally been less settled and more fundamentalist in religion. There are also a multitude of other groups. In all those conflicts the UK has found itself in the middle of different warring sects.

The political position of Ireland has for centuries been a source of concern to those on mainland Britain who felt that the western island had to be kept politically close to the British authorities. In the 17th and 18th centuries, there was the very real fear that it would become a base for the descendants of the deposed Stuart dynasty. And then in the early part of the 20th Century, due to the Republican ideological alliance with radical socialism, there was the fear that Ireland would become the base for a British Bolshevik revolution. Many Republicans in Northern Ireland to this day retain their links with militant Marxist organisations.

The question of strategic alliances has also been a dilemma for Britain in the conflicts in both Ireland and Palestine. There had been a deeply problematic relationship with the Loyalists from the north-east of Ireland who within the space of a few years were seen as both foes and friends. The contradictions between Jewish and Arab demands presented a quandary for the British authorities, who were unsure as to whose demands should be met and whether or not it was in the UK's interests to serve one group or another. The Arabs were more numerous in number and had kin who lived, as they still do today, in oil rich areas. Conversely, Jewish people at the time were perceived by some in the British Government to be of greater international political significance. Likewise, today's conflicts are not without their own complex strategic considerations.

Palestine in the 20th Century was also strategically positioned and a key part of British interests in the region. The territory, which had been "mandated" to Britain by the League of Nations, was the link in a crescent that joined Mesopotamia (now Iraq) and the British controlled Kingdom of Jordan with Egypt and the vitally important Suez Canal. In Palestine there was also an oil pipeline which linked Britain's Middle Eastern oil interests to an easily accessible port in the Mediterranean. The construction of this had been attacked repeatedly by Arab Palestinian militants.

Modern day Iraq is strategically positioned as a buffer between the Islamic Republic of Iran and the American-friendly Kingdoms of the Arab Gulf States, two of which had Iraqi troops enter their sovereign territory in recent memory. The importance of Iraq's natural resources does not need further explanation.

Strategic issues go beyond territorial integrity and the secure supply of natural resources. In Palestine in the 1930s, as war clouds loomed over Europe with threats to British dominance of the Mediterranean Sea, it was important not to be seen to be defeated by the German-backed Arab rebels. In the modern era, where Britain has been engaged with battling Islamic militants who have supported attacks against the UK and her allies, there is the need not to be seen to be defeated by our ideological enemies. Some of whom have committed atrocities from the West to Africa and to the Middle-east.

The occupation of Iraq after the 2003 Gulf War was officially sanctioned by United Nations Security Council Resolution 1483. This gave the forces of the United States, the United Kingdom and many other countries the legal cover for the military occupation of that land. This made the country between the rivers in effect a mandated territory with the western powers having responsibility over the territory's administration. This echoes the legal situation regarding Palestine after the British Army drove out the forces of the Ottoman Turkish Empire during World War One. There is a similar situation in Afghanistan. The NATO led military involvement in Afghanistan and the influence over the government of that land began as part of the effort to oust the ruling Taleban from power. The Islamic Emirate of Afghanistan had been providing a safe haven for Al-Qaeda terrorists. This action and the continuing war has been officially endorsed by Resolution 1386 of the UN Security Council. This makes Afghanistan, like Iraq,resemble a mandated territory.

Afghanistan, where Montgomery began his soldiering, was then as it is now a threat to the stability of parts of the Indian Sub-Continent. Then incursions threatened the British Raj and now the ethnic links which straddle national borders threaten the stability of a long standing Western ally, Pakistan. The influence of Russia in Afghanistan and throughout Central Asia has also been a continual issue for centuries. In Montgomery's day the Russians were in competition with the British Empire while today they face the *Pax Americana*.

There are also two other striking similarities between the past and present conflicts. One element of the recent troubles in Northern Ireland as well as the terror in Afghanistan and Iraq which is remarkably reminiscent of the historic fighting in Palestine in the 1930s is that some of the belligerents did not come from where the fighting was taking place. Some fighting men crossed porous borders to fight alongside those with whom they shared ethnic or religious sympathies and who actually lived within the battle space. The second striking similarity is the level of criminality. The tensions in those nations provided excellent opportunities for unscrupulous young men to make money. Criminal actions came to dominate the conflicts. In Palestine during the last century, just like in Iraq and Afghanistan today, there were a spate of kidnappings and many extortion rackets. The drug trade in Northern Ireland and Afghanistan have also been a significant source of financing for the armed groups. This banditry feeds and funds the fighting and adds to the state of lawlessness.

To fail to understand the numerous origins of the fighting and not to understand the wider political and strategic issues will be to fail adequately to counter Britain's military opponents. The guerrilla wars in Ireland and Palestine and Montgomery's conclusions about those strangely modern conflicts give policy makers in this era the opportunity to learn from history.

This book will also assess Montgomery as a military commander in his two guerrilla wars; a unique type of armed conflict that requires special solutions.

Part I

Before the War on Terror

Chapter 1

THEORIES ON GUERRILLA WARFARE

'The element of resistance will exist everywhere and nowhere.'
Carl Von Clausewitz on The People in Arms in his renowned book *On War*

The military term "Guerrilla War" derives from the Spanish for 'little war.' During the French occupation of Spain during the Napoleonic wars small bands of Spanish resistance fighters fought against the much larger conventional French army. The guerrillas, as they became known, used their knowledge of the terrain and above all their mobility to mount fast hit-and-run attacks against the massed French forces.

Guerrilla warfare is asymmetric in nature. This means that the opposing sides are not equally matched in either tactics or resources. The guerrillas, who may often be little more than armed civilians known as irregular soldiers, will be small in number and lightly armed. They will be pitted against a numerically superior and often heavily armed conventional army. However, the guerrillas will often have greater freedom of movement and will further enhance this by conducting acts of sabotage that will impair the conventional army's communications and transport links as well as restricting their supply routes.

As the fighting is often not between legally defined states many of the laws of war as codified in the Geneva Convention are not followed. And as such guerrilla conflicts have historically become synonymous with vicious fighting where no quarter is given. In fact it is an established aim of a guerrilla army to make the conventional army pay an unacceptably high price in manpower. At which point either the occupying army or its political masters will wish to extricate themselves from the conflict handing the rebels a strategic victory. The rebellion may also contain what the opposing state forces consider to be acts of terrorism. This can be a strategy aimed at killing and maiming military personnel and civilians alike as well as destroying property and infrastructure in the hope that it will create a change in government policy. This can also involve the terrorists seeking to achieve a dramatic and shocking success; the so-called 'Spectacular'.

Guerrillas need to receive shelter and supplies from the local population, from whom they will often be indistinguishable. The bloodiness of the conflict will be enhanced as the conventional forces will often try to end the public's assistance to the guerrillas by employing collective punishments against those it suspects of supporting the rebellion. In the hope of cutting-off the insurgents from their civilian base of support a conventional army may also take the step of moving the residents of an area into militarily protected areas and even into internment camps. Another stratagem employed to split the guerrillas from their base of support is known as the 'winning of hearts and minds'. This will seek to win over the local population to the cause of the conventional army. Such an approach will have two main methods; one is the use of propaganda and the other is to supply services to the civilians. The guerrillas will also look to use the same methods and will seek to incite the non-combatants to back their cause.

The respected Prussian soldier and military philosopher, Carl Von Clausewitz, categorised how a successful guerrilla war was to be waged in his posthumously published book from 1832 titled *On War*. In that famous work he wrote about 'The People in Arms' in opposition to a conventional army. According to Von Clausewitz a well organised guerrilla war is, 'Like smouldering embers, it consumes the basic foundations of the enemy forces.' He also wrote that if the guerrilla forces are not quelled the insurrection will enter a new phase becoming, 'a crisis' where according to Von Clausewitz, 'a general conflagration closes in on the enemy, driving him out of the country before he is faced with total destruction.'

The Prussian theorist listed five requirements for an insurgency to be victorious. These are;

1. The war must be fought in the interior of the country.
2. It must not be decided by a single stroke.
3. The theatre of operations must be fairly large.
4. The national character must be suited to that type of war.
5. The country must be rough and inaccessible, because of
mountains, or forests, marshes, or methods of cultivation.

Carl Von Clausewitz thought that the socio-economic conditions of the population was also a factor, he declared that 'poor men, used to hard, strenuous work and privation, are generally more warlike.' And in scantly settled rural areas the isolated farming communities can become ungovernable. The conventional forces in those areas will have difficulty policing and punishing the insurgents, 'the element of resistance will exist everywhere and nowhere.'

There have been many famous guerrilla leaders throughout history. Some have not only become established theorists about the conduct of such conflicts but also cultural icons. One such leader of the people in arms against the conventional forces of a state was Ernesto 'Che' Guevara, the Argentinian who took part in the Cuban revolution as well as other guerrilla conflicts in Africa and in South America. He wrote a book that he intended to become a manual for those who wished to defeat an imperial occupation or western backed dictatorship. Che Guevara also recognised that a guerrilla force needs a host population to supply its operations. He hoped that small and mobile guerrilla forces could become the vanguard of a popular revolt against those of the state that he wished to defeat.

It is interesting to note that Che Guevara was partly of Irish ancestry. His father. descended from settlers from Ireland whose surname was Lynch, said of his famous son that "the first thing to note is that in my son's veins flowed the blood of the Irish rebels." And it was in Ireland in the earlier part of the twentieth century that the definitive guerrilla war was waged.

It is one of history's ironies that Montgomery, one of the twentieth century's most able opponents of guerrilla forces, should in his later life meet and strike-up a rapport with famous guerrilla commanders who also became statesmen.

Monty met Mao Zedong the leader of Communist China who before he took over that nation had been a guerrilla commander. He led the Communist guerillas against the Japanese occupiers of Chinese land and against the conventional army of China led by its military ruler, Chiang Kai-Shek. Kai-Shek's Kuomintang Party, otherwise known as the Nationalist, ran the Chinese state until being forced out of power by the communists. Mao was not only a guerrilla leader but was also a military theorist who authored the work known as *On Protracted War*. In that text Moa advocated the use of small revolutionary bands operating out of an area where the cadres had popular support. The irregular forces could then take the war to a conventional army in hit-and-run raids. The guerrillas would in time become the masters of the countryside and isolate the conventional army in the cities and their bases. Starved of supplies the conventional army would become little more than prisoners in their own military camp. Eventually the guerrillas would, Mao said, become strong enough to face the occupying power in open warfare. At which point the conventional army can be defeated decisively in a major military confrontation.

Another communist guerrilla commander turned national leader that Montgomery was to meet was Josip Tito the President of Yugoslavia. Tito, a Croatian by birth, led the Yugoslav Partisans against the German occupiers of Yugoslavia. His allied backed guerrilla forces not only survived against the German army but also succeeded in tying up many Axis divisions that could have been used elsewhere. The actions of Tito's partisans were an important factor in the liberation of Yugoslavia from the Nazis.

Both Moa and Tito were ruthless revolutionary leaders who successfully used guerrilla tactics to defeat their opponents. Bernard Law Montgomery was a soldier who was equally ruthless in his task of using a conventional army to take the fight to guerrilla forces and through his aggressive approach to warfare he triumphed against an insurrection. In fact he began his military career facing irregular forces.

Chapter 2

MONTGOMERY'S FORMATIVE YEARS

'Peshawar was a good station in those days with plenty of training, [and] the ever present chance of a frontier expedition to keep us up to scratch... Indeed it is his keenness that seems to stand out most in my memory.'

Memoir by Brigadier Clement Tomes on Montgomery's time on the North-West Frontier facing Afghan tribesmen; where Monty started his army life.[1]

At a young age Montgomery had decided on a career in the army. In 1907 he joined the Royal Military Academy, Sandhurst. This is the British Army's initial officer training centre; it is styled as a national centre of excellence for leadership. In September 1908 Montgomery, having successfully completed his training, joined the Royal Warwickshire Regiment; a regiment with which he was to have a long association.

Modern deployments of the British Armed Forces echo the initial steps taken by Montgomery at the start of his career. His first posting would prepare him for a career in unconventional warfare.

Montgomery on the North-West Frontier

The tribal lands which mark what can only be loosely described as the 'border' between Afghanistan and India, now Pakistan, remains even to this day a land that has on occasions tested the British Army to destruction.

Montgomery's service in this unforgiving area which had worn out other less determined British officers began at the age of just 21. In December 1908 he was posted to the 1st Battalion of the Royal Warwickshire Regiment who were based in Peshawar on the North-West Frontier of India facing Afghanistan and the buffer-zone between British interests in the Sub-Continent and those of the Russian Empire which had been steadily encroaching into that area as both powers vied for supremacy in Central Asia in what was known in Britain as *The Great Game*. This *Tournament of Shadows* as it was known in Russia mostly amounted to what can now be best described as a regional cold-war, which included some conflicts, between those two great imperial powers.

The heirs of Montgomery's Royal Warwickshire Regiment now amalgamated with other regiments to form the Royal Regiment of Fusiliers have also served with distinction in Britain's latest entanglement in the troublesome and deadly fighting with the Pashtun tribesman who belong to the Taleban in the Helmand Province of Afghanistan. During Montgomery's time serving on this frontier there were then, as still exist today, punitive expeditions against the rebellious Pashtun tribes whose descendants make up the backbone of today's Taleban.

Montgomery's training was almost exclusively in the harsh discipline of mountain warfare. It is interesting to note that Montgomery's great adversary from World War II, Erwin Rommel, made his name by successfully leading troops in mountain warfare against the Italians during the bitter fighting in the Alps during the First World War.

Much of Montgomery's training in combat in the mountains took place in an area called Cherat. This is a strategically located hill station close to the Khyber Pass which links modern day Afghanistan and Pakistan. From Cherat the Peshawar valley, some of the Khwarra valley and much of Kohat District can be monitored.

Just as it was then the Cherat fortification is still a place where elite soldiers are trained. It is now the base for the Pakistan Special Services Group, an independent commando division of the Pakistan Army similar to the US Green Berets and the British Army's SAS. The Cherat military base is not only used for training Pakistan's elite soldiers. It has also been used to host joint courses for the American, Turkish, German and the Azeri military in conjunction with those from Pakistan. What is more, Cherat in Montgomery's day was in the heart of unstable tribal lands and the territory surrounding it remains an explosive area where conflict and the threat of fighting is still ever present. Just as this area keeps the military forces from many nations skilled and effective in the art of mountain warfare the demands of this tinderbox region and the likelihood of a frontier expedition kept Montgomery and his men skilled soldiers.

Montgomery's commanders almost immediately recognised his abilities as an organiser and trainer of men; key characteristics that he would be famous for in his later military career. It was decided that 50 selected men from each battalion would be trained as mountain warfare scouts and it was Montgomery, still only in his early 20s, who was selected to organise and train these troops. His contemporaries considered that he did a good job and, as his record from the Second World War shows, Montgomery as a trainer of men was second to none.

It is usually thought that Montgomery developed his key military skill – the effective communication with the troops making sure that they knew their commander and the role he expected of them – was developed after the First World War where he witnessed the failures brought about by absentee generals. However, on the North-West Frontier Montgomery was already living this doctrine well before World War One. Montgomery's military professionalism and desire to communicate even went as far as learning the languages of the native troops under his command and that of the local inhabitants. In the short time he served on the politically unstable frontier territory he learnt Urdu, passing an examination in that language in 1910. He also learned Pashtu, the main tribal language of the people of the Afghan border region. Incidentally this is the language spoken by the modern Taleban insurgents of Afghanistan and Pakistan. Montgomery understood the need to be able to communicate effectively with the local population who could turn into his enemies if another Anglo-Afghan War erupted.

Iron sharpens iron. And the continual challenge of having to be prepared for conflict with Afghan tribesman helped make Montgomery an exceptionally dedicated soldier. In particular the grounding he received in combating irregular forces in the extreme conditions of the Hindu Kush Mountains on the North-West Frontier impressed upon the young Montgomery the importance of physical fitness, attentiveness and the need for organising troops effectively. He even learnt the Field Service Regulations off by heart and took an examination in specialist mule transportation. At this time he realised that to be successful 'one must master one's profession.'[2] In April 1910 Montgomery was promoted to the rank of Lieutenant, his rise in Britain's armed services was underway.

Montgomery completed his tour of service on the North-West frontier in October 1910 when his Battalion moved to a new posting in Bombay, now known as Mumbai, in India. Monty left

India in the autumn of 1912 and in January 1913 he became the Assistant Adjutant of the 1st Battalion of the Royal Warwickshire Regiment. This gave him responsibility for some of the battalion's organisation. Montgomery was becoming recognised for his military professionalism and this dedication to mastering the discipline of the battlefield was to show itself during the great conflict which was soon to engulf Europe and other parts of the globe; a conflict that would, like others of his generation, leave a lasting impression on the young soldier.

Montgomery in the First World War

In August 1914 Montgomery and the Royal Warwickshire Regiment were sent to France as part of the British Expeditionary Force to face the German army invading France and Belgium. Monty soon proved himself to be courageous under fire as he saw battle that very same month and repeatedly distinguished himself in combat. On 13th October, after fighting in France and Belgium where his brave actions stood-out, Montgomery was seriously injured by a German sniper while leading his platoon in an attack on the Germans in Belgium. His near life threatening injuries included being shot several times through the lung and in the knee. Captain Montgomery was awarded the Distinguished Service Order for, according to the London Gazette published on 1st December 1914, 'Conspicuous gallant leading on 13th October, when he turned the enemy out of their trenches with the bayonet. He was severely wounded.'[3]

Montgomery's skills as an effective trainer of soldiers were also evident during the First World War. In February 1915, although recovering from his wounds, he was still not fit for overseas service. Montgomery was given the task of instructing the British volunteer army, the 91st Infantry Brigade, in the art of war. Montgomery was given the rank of Brigade Major to match his new duties.

After being declared fit to be sent back abroad, Montgomery was posted to France in January 1916. He was to be sent to the centre of the conflict and took part in the Battle of the Somme. On 26th July during this clash Montgomery was injured during an artillery attack but not hurt seriously enough to be withdrawn from combat.

During the fighting Montgomery proved that he was a brave soldier; yet it was as a Staff Officer that his exceptional talent really stood out. In 1917 Montgomery received the rank of Major and joined the staff at his division's headquarters. Monty was given the task of helping with organisation and training and he excelled in these roles becoming a real asset to the British army. In 1918, after receiving a further promotion in July of that year to the rank of Brevet Lieutenant Colonel, he helped plan and organise the successful British offensives. These decisive attacks on the Germans broke the deadlock and finally opened up the German lines. From August to the close of the war on 11th November the so-called Hundred Days Offensive reintroduced mobile warfare back to the Western Front and drove back the German army.

Monty was marked out for high rank during this conflict, his potential had been spotted and he was not to disappoint. Montgomery's career continued to flourish after the Great War had concluded. On 5th September 1919 he was promoted to Lieutenant Colonel and was given command of part of the British occupation forces of Germany, known as the British Army of the Rhine where he commanded the 17th Battalion of the Royal Fusiliers.

Montgomery received a host of awards from the fighting during the First World War. On top of his Distinguished Service Order, Montgomery was also Mentioned in Dispatches on eight occasions, a rare achievement, and he received the French *Croix de Guerre*; an award given to those who distinguish themselves by acts of heroism in combat. Medals, honours, promotion and the loss of half a lung were not the only legacies that Montgomery took out of World War One. He came out of this first great conflict having learned a great deal about how leadership in the army could be improved. The lessons that Montgomery drew from the bloody conflict that was then known as the Great War were to shape his generalship throughout his military career.

Lessons from World War One

In January 1920 Montgomery sought to further his career by entering the British Army Staff College in Camberley; he enrolled after being nominated to join the course which he successfully completed. Montgomery's military skills had been recognised and as another conflict spiralled out of control he was sent to the heart of the violence to restore law and order and supress a vicious guerrilla war being waged by the Irish Republican Army against the authorities of the United Kingdom. Here he would begin to put into effect some of what he had learned.

During the last six months of the war on the Western Front he developed what was then a unique system where the advanced troops in an attack were given wireless transmitters so that news from the front could reach the generals straight away so that they could then adjust their tactics accordingly.[4] Montgomery introduced the very same system during the fighting in Ireland which also paid dividends during the Second World War.

The conclusions that Montgomery drew from the First World War went beyond battlefield tactics. Monty was scathing of the Army leadership during the Great War. In that conflict he felt that, 'The higher staffs were out of touch with the regimental officers and with the troops.' Montgomery wrote that,

'There was little contact between the generals and the soldiers. I went through the whole war on the Western Front, except during the period I was in England after being wounded; I never once saw the British Commander-in-Chief, neither French nor Haig, and only twice did I see an Army Commander.' [5]

The generals were also often not aware of the terrible conditions in which the men had to live and all too often die. What is more, the soldiers in the British army during the First World War were not adequately motivated by their superiors and neither were they properly told of their strategic and tactical aims and objectives. Nor were they fully informed by their senior commanders of their role and what had to be achieved in an operation. When Montgomery was in command he went to great lengths to make sure that the shortcomings he saw amongst Britain's generals on the Western Front were not to be found in his own leadership. In the fields of training, motivation and the issuing of clear and precise instructions Montgomery, as a commander, was second to none. He would repeatedly prove this throughout his career in battles ranging from Ireland to El Alamein and in the preparation for the D-Day landings which took place on 6th June 1944.

In his *Memoirs* Montgomery also criticised what he saw as, 'The frightful casualties… ' And he thought that the more aggressive generals during the Great War, '… had a complete disregard for human life.' [6] During Montgomery's later career he made the welfare of the soldiers one of his top concerns.

While he cared about the lives of his men he did not, however, show the same regard towards the lives of the forces opposing his troops. In the counter-insurgency conflict in Ireland, and in the later fighting in Palestine supressing the Arab Revolt, Monty was to employ another lesson that he would have learned during the First World War. He saw at first-hand how the

German Spring Offensive of 1918 known as the Kaiser's Battle and as the Ludendorff Offensive succeeded in capturing a great deal of French territory but nothing that was strategically significant. The uncoordinated German army advanced into terrain that was not of military importance and crucially the German attacks had failed to destroy the forces of both France and Britain which were in the path of the German onslaught. So although the British army in the field had been rocked and forced to retreat it stayed intact within the theatre. Thus it was able to fight another day and take the war back to the Germans.

Montgomery recognised the fatal flaw of a strategy where the capture of terrain was the only goal. He wrote about these battle tactics at length in the British Infantry Training Manual. Montgomery could make his point very directly. He thought that soldiers should, 'Aim always to bring enemy to battle, and attack, and kill as many as possible...' Montgomery concluded that it is, 'No good manoeuvring enemy out of his position.'[7]

Montgomery, as a scholar of the military theorist Carl von Clausewitz, recognised that although capturing ground looked good on paper it was not the be all and end all of military operations. Many politicians and generals throughout the First World War hankered after territorial gains and desired the aesthetic pleasure this gave them when reviewing a map, but to merely capture terrain is not enough for strategic success. To win decisively the opposing forces must be eliminated. This is especially the case when combatting a guerrilla war where ground is of little interest to the insurgents. Guerrilla forces are fluid and will gladly give up terrain to avoid being drawn into an open fight; these were exactly the tactics used by the Irish rebels. Montgomery's perception that the destruction of an enemy force was the most important military objective was to reveal itself in the fighting in Ireland where he would take the fight to the IRA.

Part II

Ireland

Chapter 3

MONTGOMERY AND THE ANGLO-IRISH WAR

'My own view is that to win a war of that sort you must be ruthless; Oliver Cromwell, or the Germans, would have settled it in a very short time. Now-a-days public opinion precludes such methods; the nation would never allow it, and the politicians would lose their jobs if they sanctioned it.[8]

Montgomery writing to a British Army Major, Arthur Percival, who was based in County Cork

Bernard Law Montgomery was of Irish ancestry; his family seat was at New Park near the town of Molville in County Donegal. This land was later confiscated from his family by the government of the Irish Free State. His personal connection to the conflict meant that he was a soldier defending the integrity of his national heritage. Just a few weeks before Montgomery arrived in Ireland in January 1921, the fighting had impacted on his family in the most direct way when his cousin was killed by the IRA.

Such bloody behaviour and the additional violence that they in turn begot was not just restricted to the isolated and lawless County Cork where Montgomery took up his command. Dublin was also the scene of high levels of violence. On 21st November 1920 an IRA assassination "Squad" commanded by senior IRA leader Michael Collins had murdered a policeman, an Irish informer and shot a dozen British intelligence officers. Among the latter was Lieutenant-Colonel Hugh Montgomery, Monty's cousin, who finally died of his wounds in December 1920. As part of the hunt for the IRA killers that followed, a force of the Royal Irish Constabulary and members of their Auxiliary Division raided a Gaelic football match held at the Croke Park stadium in Dublin. In circumstances that remain controversial to this day, fighting broke out that killed twelve civilians, including one player. Two further civilians died at Croke Park in the stampede which began either when the police opened fire or when the IRA members who were claimed to be hiding amongst the crowd attempted to escape and started to fire on the security services. Three IRA prisoners were later killed whilst in captivity.

A wreath was laid to the victims of this massacre by the British monarch Queen Elizabeth II during her recent visit to Ireland in May 2011. The British press erroneously reported that British troops killed the civilians. Yet the facts are that responsibility rested with the police. What is more, the British Army condemned the actions of the police.

Two courts of inquiry were instituted and they concluded that;

'The fire of the RIC was carried out without orders and exceeded the demands of the situation.'

Furthermore, Major-General Boyd, Commander of the British forces in the area of Dublin, was of the opinion that;

'The firing on the crowd was carried out without orders, was

indiscriminate, and unjustifiable, with the exception of any
shooting which took place inside the enclosure.[9]

Clearly the authorities were well aware that brutality would be counterproductive.

In response to the events in Dublin, Tom Barry's Flying Column of the IRA in County Cork ambushed and killed 17 members of the Auxiliaries on 28th November 1920 at Kilmichael. It is thought that some of the 17 surrendered but were later killed in cold blood. One Auxiliary police officer that Barry alleges was drowned in a bog was actually an escapee who was captured and eventually put to death. Barry consistently denied these claims.

Following other killings of members of the RIC and its Auxiliaries on 11th December 1920, the Police took what they perceived to be revenge against the civilian population. The Auxiliary Division of the Royal Irish Constabulary (ADRIC) burnt out the city centre of Cork, County Cork's capital. This action did however succeed in killing two IRA operatives. It was in this tense and deadly environment that Montgomery had to operate.

Background to the conflict

The Anglo-Irish War, also known as the Irish War of Independence, began in early 1919 with the attempted formation of an independent Irish state. The conflict exploded into a pattern of guerrilla warfare with an all too familiar mix of inter-communal violence, terrorism and assassination. The roots of the conflict were, however, much older and while some blamed the events of the 1916 Easter Uprising, where a small number of Irish nationalists declared an independent Ireland, however the tensions were old even then.

Ireland had been an integral part of the United Kingdom since 1801. Despite a number of rebellions against the Union with

Great Britain; rule by the institutions of Britain did receive the tacit, and often overt, support of many Irishmen and women. Many Irishmen participated in the institutions which governed Ireland from the seat of power in Dublin Castle. This institution, known to many as the Castle, centrally oversaw the running of Ireland and its 32 administrative subdivisions called Counties. What is more, many Irishmen, be they Unionist or Nationalist and regardless of religion, had volunteered to fight for King and Country during the Great War. That became part of the problem; John Edward Redmond the moderate leader of the nationalist Irish Parliamentary Party thought that Irishmen supporting the war effort against Germany would guarantee the enactment of home rule for Ireland. Unionists, however, who had also fought for Britain in the Great War felt that their loyalty should be rewarded by having their position in the United Kingdom safeguarded. Compromise was going to be difficult. Redmond died in March 1918.

The genesis of the still on-going conflict in Ireland has roots which go back far into the historical memories of the different cultural traditions on that island. The crisis which led to the guerrilla war against the British presence in Ireland began to emerge when the moderate Home Rule League and later the Irish Parliamentary Party (IPP) managed to place the issue of some form of Irish home rule firmly into the British political lexicon; a task which they had been seeking since the 1870s. However, the first two attempts were defeated in the British Parliament; the first in the House of Commons and the second by Conservative Peers in the House of Lords.

Over time there was a gradual hardening of opinion. In 1905 a new and more radical political party was formed by an Irishmen of Welsh ancestry by the name of Arthur Griffith. This new party was called Sinn Féin, a Gaelic word which translates as Ourselves Alone. Although they were socialist, this organisation did not begin as a militant movement; in fact its original aims can be viewed as moderate. A key aim of this political party was for Ireland to become self-governing from the British political system based in Westminster and Whitehall in London. However, this did not mean full independence from the Crown. Far from being a Republican organisation, Sinn Féin initially favoured a constitutional, limited, monarchy shared with Great Britain. What is more, it should be noted that Ireland as a constituent part of the United Kingdom enjoyed the same limited democratic rights within the British political system as other constituent parts of the UK.

In one sense Sinn Féin's desire for constitutional reform of Ireland's relationship with the rest of the UK was not just an end in itself but it was also seen as a means to developing Irish cultural life and identity and, through a socialist ideology, they sought to improve the standard of living in Ireland. This is despite the fact that driven by a labour shortage wages in Ireland rose sharply from 1916 until the end of the First World War making the last few years of the Great War, as it was then known, a time of prosperity in Ireland.

Before the First World War Sinn Féin was not a significant force in Irish politics, yet home rule was still a possibility. In 1912 the Liberal Government, successfully introduced the Third Home Rule Bill and Irish self-government was not only back on the political agenda but also a real possibility. However, the issue of Home Rule was controversial not only on the British mainland but especially so in Ireland itself. The prospect of Irish self-government alarmed Ireland's Unionists who supported the island remaining a full constituent part of the UK. Particularly worried were the Protestants who feared that they would lose their religious freedoms, and their British citizenship. They also feared that it would damage the material well-being of all those who lived on the island of Ireland. As will be shown the tensions began to spiral out of control. By 1913 opinion had become so polarised that armed groups were openly being formed.

The alarming situation, along with the Third Home Rule Bill, was suspended as a result of outbreak of World War One. But during that conflict two significant events took place. One was the 1916 Easter Rising in Dublin and the execution of some of those involved. This rebellion used arms smuggled into Ireland from Britain's wartime enemy, Germany, and was to prove an abject military failure but eventually it became a propaganda triumph. The Easter Rising was carried out by a small clique of militants acting against the wishes of most Irishmen and women; especially in Dublin where the rebellion took place. The bemused citizens of that city actually jeered the would-be revolutionaries when, after their surrender, they were marched into captivity by the forces of the Crown. The British soldiers actually had to protect the militants from attack by some locals. Later opinion would change dramatically, making the men who were executed into martyrs.

The second significant event was the massively unpopular attempt to introduce conscription into Ireland in 1918 to aid the war effort against Germany. These events both succeeded in hardening opposition amongst Ireland's Roman Catholic population to British rule. And this in turn led to more support for Sinn Féin which was becoming increasingly radicalised. These events made it very difficult for a compromise agreement to be reached. Nevertheless, further attempts at a settlement were made.

An Irish Convention was held in Dublin from 1917 to 1918 but the talks failed to achieve a harmonious settlement to the growing crisis. The Convention was boycotted by Sinn Féin, while Unionists from the north-east of Ireland continued to oppose any move that would give a single Irish government too much power over the affairs of the whole island. However, even the Unionists from Ulster were beginning to look favourably upon a compromise deal where they may have become willing to accept home rule without partition as long as financial independence was temporarily limited. However, Republican hardliners opposed this compromise and the moderate Irish nationalist leader John Redmond withdrew the motion in order not to split the nationalist movement.

The growing conflict was not just a matter of political independence and self-government. There was also the aim of creating a Roman Catholic, socialist and culturally Celtic society. This was a reaction against the perceived predominance of protestant Anglo-Saxon culture in the United Kingdom. This movement had begun during the Victorian era. There was also a socio-economic background to the fighting. The conflict in the south of Ireland was largely a class war against the protestant elite. In the north of Ireland, Protestants were often no better off than their Roman Catholic neighbours who also found employment in Protestant owned industries.

Nonetheless, religious tensions had existed on the island for centuries. Despite the fact that Roman Catholic forces had been used to suppress rebellions such as the 1798 United Irishmen revolt led by the Protestant Wolfe Tone, many Roman Catholics did not see their Protestant neighbours as true Irishmen. Some disparagingly described Protestants as 'British' or 'English'. Some Republicans were happy to conduct a sectarian conflict and ethnically cleanse their future independent state of the descendants of the settlers who had arrived centuries before. Yet not all settlers were Protestant and not all Protestants were settlers. This sectarian conflict even continued in parts of the south after British forces had withdrawn from Southern Ireland. And likewise it continued in the north-east with Protestants attacking their Roman Catholic neighbours.

This potent mix of nationalism, revolutionary socialism, and sectarianism made the Anglo-Irish War a multi-dimensional conflict with many different and powerful drivers that would spur the Irish Republican Army and its supporters to continue waging a bloody war against the forces of the Crown.

Chapter 4

THE REBELLION BEGINS

The 14th December 1918 General Election to the British House of Commons based in Westminster saw Roman Catholic Ireland elect the radical Sinn Féin politicians on mass and heralded the political defeat of the moderate Irish Parliamentary Party. Out of 105 parliamentary constituencies in Ireland the Republicans won 73 in Ireland. The election, however, did further expose the growing splits evident in Ireland with more Irish Unionists being returned particularly in the north-east of the island.

The newly elected Sinn Féin MPs refused to recognise the legitimacy of the UK Parliament and did not take up their seats at Westminster. Instead they chose to form their own Parliament known as the *Dáil Éireann* which translates as Assembly of Ireland. It first met openly in Dublin's Mansion House on 21st January 1919. The Sinn Féin MPs also set about the task of building a Republican government with ministries of state which would take over the functions previously undertaken by the British government. Although, Sinn Féin did not advocate explicitly the use of force to achieve an independent Ireland it did imply that they would take whatever action they deemed to be necessary.

Echoing the words of the 1916 Easter Rising declaration of

independence the *Dáil* reconfirmed the 'independence' of the Irish Republic on 21st January 1919. The Irish Volunteers were officially reconstituted as the Irish Republican Army, which then became the sanctioned armed forces of the newly created republic. The war, which had been brewing for some time as tensions increased, had finally begun in earnest with the killing of police constables as soon as the Republic had been declared.

Alongside the alternative parliament, government and army; Sinn Féin also began establishing a substitute system of law and order which eventually grew to operate in 21 of Ireland's southern counties; it included its own courts, called the *Dáil* Courts, and its own police force known as the Irish Republican Police. As British legal authority broke down in the face of IRA violence the rebel alternative stepped in to fill the gap. This Republican system of justice mainly resulted in offending parties being sentenced to a punishment beating, exile or execution. Some criminals, however, were sent to the Republic's rudimentary prisons.[10]

In line with the socialist tendency of many Irish Republicans a number of trade unions went on strike in protest against the perceived occupation of Ireland by the forces of the British Crown. Sinn Féin also used its political domination of many of Ireland's Counties to further undermine the British state. These county councils no longer recognised the writ of Dublin Castle and instead threw their weight behind the *Dáil*.

The Republican political leadership ordered the IRA to kill the Crown security services making the Royal Irish Constabulary (RIC) who, along with anyone who associated with them, the main targets of Republican violence. The RIC were to suffer greatly from the IRA's campaign and within a short period of time law and order broke down. Many police stations were quickly abandoned and their men evacuated. After just a year and a half of the troubles 15 manned posts had been seized and more than

350 abandoned ones were destroyed. By the end of the conflict over a third of the RIC's police stations had been vacated.[11]

This violence was condemned by the press, some of whom were then subject to intimidation, and from the Roman Catholic Church. Nonetheless, the Republican Sinn Féin leadership did not submit to these appeals.

The Republican Leaders

The military and political leadership of the Republican movement were closely intertwined. Michael Collins, a key organiser of the IRA and head of its intelligence network with his own assassination squad, was also the Minister for Finance in the alternative Republican government set up by Sinn Féin. Following the Anglo-Irish Treaty of which he was a signatory, Collins became the Chairman of the Provisional Government of the Irish Free State and Commander-in-chief of its armed forces. He would later be killed on 22nd Auguest 1922 by the IRA during the Irish Civil War.

Other prominent figures in the Irish Republican Army included Richard James Mulcahy, who served as the IRA's Chief of Staff. He was also a politician and prominent member of the *Dáil* and the Republican shadow Irish government. After the conflict with Britain ended he used repressive measures to stamp out his former colleagues in the IRA when they rebelled against the government of the Irish Free State.

There were a number of Presidents of the *Dáil* during the Anglo-Irish War. The first was called Cathal Brugha. He was instrumental in the development of the IRA, he opposed the peace treaty with Britain and was killed by the forces of the Irish Free State who were commanded by his bitter political rival Michael Collins. Cathal Brugha was, however, only in post until 1st April 1919 when he was succeeded by Éamon de Valera, who later styled himself as President of the Republic. After the War

41

with Britain de Valera became the Taoiseach, Prime Minister, of Ireland. de Valera kept Ireland neutral during the Second World War and upon learning of the death of Adolf Hitler in 1945 he sent his condolences to the German Ambassador in Dublin. During the Second World War more than 10% of soldiers in the Irish Army, a number in excess of 4,000 men, deserted to join the British Army's fight against Hitler. Upon their return to Ireland they suffered terrible treatment. de Valera had them placed on a blacklist where they were denied public employment and pensions. Their children were often taken into care where they were singled out for abuse.[12]

. Arthur Griffith, the founder of Sinn Féin, replaced de Valera on 10th January 1922. Éamon de Valera, an opponent of the peace treaty with Britain, resigned the Presidency after a majority of *Dáil* members backed the agreement. Griffiths held the post of President of the *Dáil* until he died on 12th August 1922. Griffiths' death was partly caused by the strain involved in establishing the Provisional Government of the Irish Free State.

Significantly these rebel leaders were members of a secret organisation known as the Irish Republican Brotherhood.

The Irish Unionist Leaders

The *de facto* leader of Unionism within southern Ireland was William St John Fremantle Brodrick, the 1st Earl of Midleton, a town in County Cork in the south-west of Ireland. As tensions grew between the opposing sides in 1918 he and John Redmond tried to broker a deal at the Irish Convention that would bring in home rule without partition, but this did not receive the support of the Republicans.

Two of the prominent opponents of Irish home rule were Sir James Craig and Edward Carson. Both were instrumental in forming the loyalist militia known as the Ulster Volunteers. Edward Carson, who had served in the British War Cabinet during World War One, was from Dublin which he had previously represented in the House of Commons. Carson was also the leader of the Irish Unionist Party. As a prominent unionist he not only fought against home rule for Ireland but also championed the cause of Ulster remaining within the United Kingdom. Craig, from Northern Ireland, also fought against home rule. He became the first Prime Minister of Northern Ireland.

The British Political Leaders

David Lloyd George was the Prime Minster of the United Kingdom during the entirety of the Anglo-Irish War. During his time in office from 1916 to 1922 he made repeated attempts by both negotiations and by force of arms to end the political crisis in Ireland. The minster responsible for administering Ireland was known as the Chief Secretary for Ireland. The incumbent sat in the Cabinet of the British Government. The politicians that held this post during the conflict in Ireland were, like David Lloyd George, members of the Liberal Party which had consistently supported Irish self-government.

The first Chief Secretary for Ireland during the conflict, Ian Stewart Macpherson, came into office on 10th January 1919; just as the conflict was about to erupt. He was removed on 2nd April 1920 and became the Minister for Pensions. Sir Hamar Greenwood, from Canada, replaced Macpherson as the Chief Secretary. He was appointed on 2nd April 1920 and remained in post until the 26 counties of the south became independent of the United Kingdom government.

British Military Leaders

Straddling the link between Britain's political leadership and the senior ranks of the military was the position of Chief of the Imperial General Staff (CIGS), the professional head of the

British armed forces. Throughout the conflict until the initial stages of the British withdrawal from most of southern Ireland this post was held by Field Marshal Sir Henry Hughes Wilson. He was an Irishmen from County Longford in the approximate centre of the island, part of the traditional province of Leinster. Field Marshal Wilson stood down from the Army in February 1922 to pursue a career in Northern Irish politics. He was replaced by Wilson's fellow Irishmen General Frederick Rudolph Lambart; the 10th Earl of Cavan, which is now in the Republic of Ireland. General, later Field Marshal Lambart, then oversaw the eventual disengagement from the conflict in Ireland's southern counties.

The Officers Commanding British forces in Ireland during the Anglo-Irish War were two soldiers who had previous experience of not only serving in the First World War but also tackling an earlier guerrilla war. The two generals that held this post had both fought in the earlier Second Boer War which was successfully waged by Britain against rebels in South Africa and had concluded less than two decades before the fighting got under way in Ireland.

At the start of the conflict the Commander-in-Chief of British forces in Ireland was Lieutenant-General Sir Frederick Shaw. He served from 1918, before the conflict began, until his replacement in 1920; upon his dismissal he retired from the Army. Shaw's successor was General Sir Cecil Frederick Nevil Macready. He remained in post until 1922 when the war had concluded. As such he was the last to hold this appointment. Nevil Macready, whose wife was Irish, was not a stranger to the troubles in Ireland. He was sympathetic to the principle of home rule and in March 1914 he had been sent to Belfast in the north of Ireland as the commander of British forces in that city. Macready was tasked with keeping the peace in Belfast in the event of fighting if the Unionists revolted against the imposition of Irish home rule. General Macready was also very familiar with policing issues. Macready was the Commissioner of the London Metropolitan Police, the head of the British Capital's police service, from 1918 until 1920.

In May 1920 another veteran of both the Second Boer War and the First World War became the police advisor to the Dublin Castle administration. This was Major-General Henry Hugh Tudor. In November 1920 he also became the final Inspector-General of the Royal Irish Constabulary when his predecessor retired; Tudor also became the commander of the Dublin Metropolitan Police. This made him Ireland's Chief of Police and their supporting units of Auxiliaries and Temporary Constables – who were dubbed "Tudor's Toughs". Following the Anglo-Irish War Tudor took up a command in the British Mandate territory of Palestine.

The Battlefield

Ireland consisted of many cities as well as a large number of small rural communities connected by narrow lanes which snaked through the countryside. Many of Ireland's rustic settlements were surrounded by hills and bogs which made movement of large scale conventional forces difficult. What is more, the travel and transportation difficulties were compounded by there being an insufficient rail network. Airfields were even sparser and proper airstrips were few and far between. Both town and country contrived to offer the rebels excellent opportunities for both concealment and attack.

The fighting, however, was mainly restricted to Dublin and the countryside and the cities of South-Western Ireland. These areas were the key to victory or defeat. In other parts of the island the fighting was only sporadic and at times even non-existent.

Chapter 5

THE OPPOSING FORCES IN IRELAND

The Crown Forces

The British Army

At the height of the fighting there were in excess of 50,000 troops in Ireland, many of them in Irish Regiments.[13] The British army was well trained and was the best equipped of all the belligerents. At its disposal were a myriad of weapons, including artillery, and transports which ranged from bicycles to armoured cars and aeroplanes.

The Army's official role was to support the police and the civil authorities in their task of restoring law and order and protecting Ireland's administrative infrastructure from IRA attack. However, in those areas of Ireland where martial law was introduced the army did take over the function of the courts in prosecuting Republican rebels and the task of policing Ireland's most lawless areas.

The Police

In total there were around 17,000 policemen in Ireland at the start of the Anglo-Irish War. These were divided between two main branches; the Dublin Metropolitan Police and the Royal Irish Constabulary.

In 1814 Sir Robert Peel, during his time as Chief Secretary in Ireland, founded a Peace Preservation Force to deal with rural disorder, factional infighting, crime and violence which Ireland's original Baronial Police were ill-equipped to deal with. In 1822 this police force which predates the London Metropolitan Police was reformed into a series of county constabularies whose administration was based around the four traditional provinces of Ireland. In 1836 the county police forces were run from the seat of Irish administration in Dublin becoming the Irish Constabulary. The Royal Irish Constabulary (RIC) received the epitaph 'Royal' for its role in suppressing a Republican revolt in 1867.

The RIC was Ireland's police force and it carried out policing duties like any other force. It was, however, an armed service; its weapons were light firearms such as rifles and pistols. It had jurisdiction across the island, outside Dublin, and it was to suffer greatly at the hands of the IRA. The men were based in small rural isolated police stations which were often little more than converted houses. These posts later had their defences improved and Defence of Barracks Sergeants were employed to help protect them from Republican attacks.

A Special Branch of the Royal Irish Constabulary also existed which dealt with intelligence and security issues. There was also a mounted division. The RIC wore green uniforms and had the Irish harp in its insignia, after partition was finalised in 1922 it operated only in the North-east and changed its name to the Royal Ulster Constabulary.

The unarmed Dublin Metropolitan Police (DMP) was based on London's Metropolitan Police. It sought to protect law and order in Dublin and its surrounding area. The DMP consisted of over 1,200 policemen. It suffered less than their fellow officers in the RIC. The DMP also had a small armed and plain-clothed special branch known as G-Division whose officers were meant to be involved with the fight against the insurgents. However, a small number were active IRA sympathisers who assisted the rebels with their work.

Throughout both services the overwhelming majority of policemen were Roman Catholic, the senior officers were, however, mostly of Protestant descent but there were Roman Catholics in senior positions.[14]

As the conflict intensified in June and July of 1920, there were many resignations from the Royal Irish Constabulary. This was largely due to the threats and the violence, including the fear of assassination, which members of the RIC suffered at the hands of the IRA., Some 560 policemen left the service in just eight weeks.

This led to the deployment of more members of a security service called the Royal Irish Constabulary Temporary Constables which received the nick-name the Black and Tans and the creation of a new force known as the Auxiliaries. These units were formed to support the police and fill the gaps created by the resignations in the RIC and directly take the fight to the IRA and its supporters.

The Black and Tans and the Auxiliaries
Sir Hamar Greenwood announced to the British Parliament in Westminster in August 1920 that more Black and Tans, officially known as the Royal Irish Constabulary Special Reserve, were to be sent to Ireland. He also announced that the newly created Auxiliary Division Royal Irish Constabulary (ADRIC) or Auxiliaries, also described as Auxies, were being recruited and would be deployed to Ireland's most troubled areas in the South-West and Dublin.

Republican propaganda depicted these entrants into Ireland's bloody conflict as the inmates of prisons and other assorted scum of mainland British society who had been enlisted to oppress the Irish fight for national freedom. In reality, the ADRIC were recruited mainly from the ranks of former officers who had served the British Army in World War One and had been demobilised after that conflict. What is more, a significant proportion of these recruits did come from Ireland. What is true that they were sent to Ireland deliberately to take the war to the IRA and its supporters. The Black and Tans were often ex-soldiers many of which had served their country with honour during the Great War.

The Black and Tans, named after their uniforms, came into the conflict in Ireland in March 1920 after the British government advertised for men who were prepared to 'face a rough and dangerous task'. Many joined to escape from the unemployment which dogged their lives after the fight against Germany had ended. In all, approximately 8,000 served in Ireland. Their role as Temporary Constables in the Royal Irish Constabulary was to help the regular RIC with guard duties and maintaining law and order. The Black and Tans also operated as a counter-insurgency force which took the war to the IRA and those they suspected of supporting the guerrillas. Such was their front-line role that the Anglo-Irish War is also known in some Republican circles as the Black and Tan War.

The men of the ADRIC, who numbered just over 2,200, were mostly deployed to Dublin and its surrounding area and the rebellious province of Munster, in particular County Cork where Montgomery was to be based. Their arsenal consisted of rifles and hand-guns. The tactics of the Auxiliaries consisted of fast aggressive patrolling, using their quick armoured cars to race into towns where there were thought to be IRA suspects. The ADRIC would then order all present to come out of their homes and submit to being searched for weapons. Intimidation and violence was a large part of their repertoire. At the start of the fighting the ADRIC nearly cowed the Republicans into submission and throughout the conflict they had a reputation as dangerous opponents of the IRA. They were respected and feared for their martial qualities, and were sometimes described by Republicans as 'super-fighters'.

Members of these forces later joined the British colonial police in Palestine.

Loyalist Militia

There were people throughout Ireland who supported that land remaining a constituent part of the United Kingdom; these "Loyalists" as they became known were usually from Ireland's Protestant tradition. However, in Ireland's southern counties they were isolated and heavily outnumbered by the majority Roman Catholic population. In such circumstances many Loyalists would not take the risk of becoming engaged in the conflict but there were those that provided support and information to the British forces.

In Ireland there was one significant and substantial area that had a Protestant majority, this was Ireland's north-eastern province of Ulster. The bulk of its population remained fiercely loyal to the Crown; and they were as equally determined to fight to stay part of the UK as the Republicans were to end British rule.

In 1912 the Loyalists in the north of Ireland, alarmed at the prospect of the Protestant population becoming a minority in a Roman Catholic independent Ireland, established a popular militia, known as the Ulster Volunteers. This group was formed to fight against home rule. Many loyalists from Ulster declared their opposition to the 3rd Home Rule Bill and nearly half a million signed what is called Ulster's Solemn League and

Covenant. This declaration proclaimed their desire to stay within the United Kingdom and was presented on 28th September 1912. It read;

Being convinced in our consciences that Home Rule would be disastrous to the material well-being of Ulster as well as of the whole of Ireland, subversive of our civil and religious freedom, destructive of our citizenship and perilous to the unity of the Empire, we, whose names are underwritten, men of Ulster, loyal subjects of his Gracious Majesty King George V, humbly relying on the God whom our fathers in days of stress and trial confidently trusted, do hereby pledge ourselves in solemn Covenant throughout this our time of threatened calamity to stand by one another in defending for ourselves and our children our cherished position of equal citizenship in the United Kingdom and in using all means which may be found necessary to defeat the present conspiracy to set up a Home Rule Parliament in Ireland. And in the event of such a Parliament being forced upon us we further solemnly and mutually pledge ourselves to refuse to recognise its authority. In sure confidence that God will defend the right we hereto subscribe our names. And further, we individually declare that we have not already signed this Covenant.

God Save the King

In January 1913 following this declaration, the Ulster Volunteers were reorganised into the Ulster Volunteer Force (UVF). Tensions between the British government in Westminster and the UVF steadily grew and by 1914 the government considered crushing the UVF by force of arms if they resisted the imposition of home rule. However, both home rule and the suppression of the Ulster Volunteer Force was abandoned as World War One approached. In the face of the threat posed by the loyalist militia and the difficulty in overpowering the Loyalists, especially as some leading figures in the British Army sympathised with the UVF, it became clear that a self-governing Ireland was no longer feasible. The UVF had succeeded in stopping, for the time being, home rule for Ireland.

In the autumn of 1920, during the later battle with the IRA when the issue of home rule was firmly back on the agenda, the British authorities formed the men of the UVF into a police force known as the Ulster Special Constabulary (USC). This organisation operated in the north of Ireland as a police force that would guard against IRA attacks. The USC freed up resources that could be used in other parts of the island. The weapons used by the UVF and the Ulster Special Constabulary were similar to those of the Royal Irish Constabulary, notably hand guns and rifles. Their training was also along the same lines as other police units. Many in the army later regretted the use of the loyalist militia as a police force.

Although the British government at first viewed the conflict as a police matter, the British Army was to be thoroughly drawn into the crisis sparked by the tensions between these loyalists and the forces fighting for an independent Irish republic.

The Republican Forces

The Republican Potpourri
There was a myriad of organisations dedicated to establishing by force an independent Irish Republic. The rush to arms in Ireland had even led to the creation of a group known as *Na Fianna Éireann*, meaning Warriors of Ireland, which became a paramilitary youth organisation. This organisation was founded in the early 20th century and taught young boys basic military skills upon the lines of the Boy Scouts. It also sought to indoctrinate its members into the Republican military cause and over time it became a training ground for potential paramilitary

recruits when its members reached manhood. Many of its members later transferred to the guerilla forces that were taking the fight for an independent Ireland to the forces of the British state.

Another organisation was The Irish Citizen Army, known in Gaelic as *Arm Cathartha na hÉireann*. This was the military wing of the Irish Socialist Republican Party; which was a Marxist/Republican political organisation that sought to create an independent and socialist Ireland. One of its most prominent members was the Scottish born, to Irish parents, Marxist politician James Connolly; who is still iconized in Republican murals in parts of Republican West Belfast to this day.

The various paramilitary groups combined their operations under the stewardship of members of another group called the Irish Republican Brotherhood to stage the ill-fated 1916 Easter Rising in Dublin.

The Irish Republican Brotherhood (IRB) otherwise known as the Fenians were amongst the most important, but relatively little known, organisations fighting against the British presence in Ireland. It was founded as long ago as 1858 as a hierarchical part political, part paramilitary secret society whose members were bound by oath to keep it an anonymous organisation, to obediently follow orders and fight to 'establish and maintain a free and independent Republican Government in Ireland.' The Brotherhood also followed a strategy of entryism which not only saw the infiltration of other nationalist organisations but also included the subversion of groups that originally simply sought to promote Gaelic culture and Irish sports. Over time IRB members became prominent in Irish political life and helped radicalise many organisations.

The IRB had a Supreme Council which acted as the Brotherhood's governing body. Their constitution considered that the Supreme Council was the government of a future Irish

Republic. There was also an Executive composed of a Secretary, Treasurer and President. It was also hoped that in time the President of the IRB would become the head of state of an independent Ireland.

The IRB's organisation reflected the county structure of Ireland and was divided along those lines. The basic units consisted of 10 men or less and were led by a Section Leader. He was responsible to what was known as Chief of the Circle, he along with a Secretary and a Treasurer, were elected by the members of the Circle; which itself comprised a number of Sections. Each county was divided into two, sometimes more, districts. The Chief of the Circle was responsible to the Chairman of the District, along with his deputy, secretary and treasurer. All of which were again elected by the grassroots activists. Similarly, further up the command chain was the County which had similar internal structures. The highest regional part, known as the Division, was based loosely on Ireland's four traditional provinces of Ulster, Leinster, Munster and Connacht.

To accommodate the large Irish diaspora within the United Kingdom and the Republican sympathisers it contained; Scotland, Northern England and Southern England were included in the IRB's divisional structure.

Over time, despite Sinn Féin and its creation the *Dáil* sharing a genesis that began with the influence of the Irish Republican Brotherhood, these organisations began to become independent of the IRB. With the growing political strength of an increasingly independently minded Sinn Féin, and the influence it had over the development of Ireland's guerrilla armies, there was a decline in both the military and political importance of the Irish Republican Brotherhood. In an act of political petulance the IRB leadership, committed to creating an independent Ireland, refused to submit to the authority of the

Dáil on the grounds that British forces were still in occupation of Ireland, and therefore there was not as yet a full and functioning independent Irish Republic to which the IRB should submit to and therefore the IRB did not give their allegiance to the *Dáil* even though most Republicans viewed this body as Ireland's true and lawful government. The IRB did, however, offer this alternative Irish government its best wishes. Although the IRB as an organisation did become politically marginalised the Irish Republican Brotherhood still had a unique part to play in the unfolding conflict; its secret nature lent itself to the task of assassinating the enemies of the Republican cause.

Furthermore, many of the IRB's members were also prominent in the other Republican organisations and its leadership did achieve the notable success of helping to establish the Irish Volunteers; the force that would in time lead part of the island into a new and independent chapter in its history. It became a requirement that all physically fit members of the Brotherhood should join the Irish Volunteers and subsequently the Irish Republican Army which the volunteers evolved into when the Republic was declared in January 1919 and the rebellion began in earnest.[15] There was a great deal of cross fertilisation between these different groups but in time one began to dominate the drive to establish an independent Irish state. This group was known as the Irish Volunteers.

The movement called the National Volunteers which eventually became the Irish Volunteers, known in Irish as the *Óglaigh na hÉireann*, was founded in 1913. Its initial impetus came from the formation of the Loyalist Ulster Volunteers which emerged in 1912 out of the growing Home Rule crisis. Some split off from the Volunteers over the issue of its leadership supporting Britain in the fight against Germany. The more militant and radical members of the Irish Volunteers quickly became infiltrated by the IRB who came to command the militia.

In due course the Irish Volunteers were not just part of the growing militarisation of Irish politics; it was now intended that this force would become a mass popular army that would fight against the British presence in Ireland. The Irish Volunteers had in effect become the Irish Republican Brotherhood writ large; they shared the same aims and objectives, notably the separation of Ireland from the United Kingdom. With the growth of Sinn Féin and its political influence over Ireland the Irish Volunteers became the military wing of the main Republican political party.

The Irish Volunteers had a women's auxiliary wing called *Cumann na mBan*, meaning Irishwomen's Council. The members of this paramilitary group provided support to the militia men of the Irish Volunteers, and later the IRA, which included; looking after the ill and injured, relaying information, spying, fundraising, and organising shelter and supplying food for the guerrillas. In time the women of the *Cumann na mBan* were to become indispensible to the IRA.

Overtime it was the IRA, which incorporated the many anti-British forces, which became the main foe that the police and the British army faced in Ireland.

The Irish Republican Army

At its height it was estimated that the IRA may have consisted of over 120,000 activists; a significant number in a population of just over 4 million. However, some were more active than others. Many IRA members led normal family and professional lives, taking part in occasional training and acts of sabotage. More dedicated men took part in deadly attacks on police stations and military patrols. It is likely, that the number of Republican guerrillas who were committed to the conflict counted in just the thousands rather than the tens of thousands.

Men were encouraged to join by radical elements in Irish

Roman Catholic society and many former soldiers from the First World War joined the IRA. Sinn Féin political clubs also played an important part in recruiting soldiers to the newly formed army and gave basic military instruction.

Not only was there an active campaign of recruiting new volunteers, there were also localised attempts to conscript young men into the IRA. However, this was not a centralised policy and came from the actions of fanatical elements. New recruits were also reared from the ranks of the Irish National Boy Scouts, the *Fianna Éireann*.

The Republican Parliament, the *Dáil Éireann*, awarded funding for the IRA following a vote. This money was primarily raised through fundraising in America. Sinn Féin also held appeals for money raised through its Self-Determination Fund and even from fêtes which were held outdoors. Money was also collected from IRA activists in the form of an annual membership fee. This entitled the brigade to be officially regarded as a unit of the Irish Republican Army.

There also existed a special assassination unit which operated under the direct command of the IRA leader Michael Collins. This was known as the Squad, and its actions not only hampered British intelligence but also sparked a cycle of violence that led to some of the worst atrocities and loss of life in the conflict.

IRA organisation

The IRA's supreme command was based in Dublin. To reduce the chances of detection by the forces of the Crown it regularly moved its location to different parts of the city. Its Commander-in-Chief was the President of Ireland's shadow government. It had a Chief of Staff and a Quartermaster-General, a post which had the responsibility for procuring and securing both arms and ammunition. It also had a President and two Treasurers. These most senior officers were not distant from the men they were commanding; some in fact were commanders of individual units operating in the Dublin area.

Like any modern regular army the IRA had a clearly defined hierarchical structure. A collection of squads made up a company, companies were part of battalions and these in turn were grouped into Brigades which operated under the command of the Dublin HQ. Each of these different building blocks had its own officers who answered to more senior ranks further up the structure.

Operational squads of the IRA, including the commander, usually consisted of between 19 and 25 men but were sometimes much larger. Four of these units comprised an IRA Company. These companies were run on democratic lines. The commander and his two subordinate officers were elected, subject to the approval of IRA Headquarters, by the members of the company. The IRA's senior commanders also had the power to dismiss officers that they or the individual members no longer had confidence in.

Each squad was divided up into two sections each with its own section commander appointed by the Company Commander who would also appoint people to other positions such as a Quartermaster who would be responsible for the unit's weapons and would make sure that arms were kept in good working order. This person would often take on the dual role as the squad's intelligence officer.

Through his officers the company commander would have ultimate responsibility for training, equipping and organising IRA companies. It was also the company commander's duty to keep an attendance record of those who had, or had not, attended training sessions. The senior officers in a Company formed an advisory council to the company commander.

Enforcing discipline was also part of the Company Commander's remit and he had the power to suspend a volunteer pending a Court Martial which according to the rules should be held as soon as was practicable. In the interests of justice the trial itself was meant to be as fair as was possible within the company. Evidence had to be submitted in writing and the accused had the right to choose his own defence counsel. The commander would nominate the prosecutor. If it was the commander or the company's senior officers who had brought the charge the case would be heard by officers from another company. If it was the commander who had an allegation of misconduct or insubordination against him the matter would be heard by senior officers further up the IRA's hierarchy.

In the case of guilty verdicts sentences would usually range from a reduction in rank to dismissal. If there was an appeal against the decision the case would be taken up the chain of command to the senior officers in the County where the company operated. Furthermore, sentences had to be confirmed by the Battalion Council. If the court martial took place at the Battalion or Brigade level an appeal against a sentence would be heard by the central command based in Dublin.

Between four and seven companies, but occasionally more, formed an IRA Battalion. The size of the Battalion depended upon the number of recruits that came forward to join the Republican forces. Each Battalion had senior officers that oversaw the roles of each officer within the company.

Similar in fashion to the Company, the Commander of a Battalion was responsible for disciple within his battalion, however, there was a Council which consisted of the senior officers which would act as an advisory committee and considered directives that came down from the IRA leadership. The Battalion Council also had a role in hearing the appeals of those who had faced a Court Martial.

Three to six battalions, but occasionally more depending upon the number of recruits available, formed a Brigade. In theory there was one brigade to each of the 32 counties of Ireland. However, where there was little support for the IRA in a county a Brigade could hardly be said to exist as a viable unit. The counties of Antrim and Down, because of a lack of support for the Republican cause in those areas, made up one Brigade. Where a significant number of recruits were available, such as in the South-western counties of Cork and Limerick, three Brigades operated in just one county.

Continuing with the IRA's quasi-democratic structure, Brigade officers were elected by the senior officers in the Battalions which made up the Brigade. The elections did not take effect until they were ratified by headquarters and all Brigades took their orders from the IRA HQ based in Dublin.

IRA Brigades had individual officers under the Brigade Commander that, like the army they were facing, were responsible for overseeing the Battalions operations. They had a Quartermaster responsible for weaponry plus Captains of Engineers, Signallers, Intelligence and a Chief of Medical Services.

Each Brigade also had a Council which advised the Commander. This mirrored the body that would advise the commanders of the Battalions and would consist of the Brigades senior officers. The organisational culture of the IRA was one where discipline was enforced and subordination was not tolerated. The executive staff of the IRA based in its Dublin HQ would also support senior officers when they were conducting court martials. This gave this guerrilla army a reasonable standard of disciple which was naturally reinforced by the fact that its volunteers shared a similar cultural background and were ideologically committed to creating by force of arms a new nation.

The IRA was not only well organised and disciplined but was also well trained. Training was based upon British Army instructions. A rebel training manual was developed which gave instruction which ranged from drill to shooting, engineering and first aid. All IRA members were trained in the many aspects of warfare they would need to employ against the forces of the Crown and experts in each of those many areas were also trained and developed. Whereas the British Army would take many months to train a soldier before it was felt that he was ready to take to the field, the IRA were able to make a willing volunteer ready for combat in Ireland's guerrilla war after as little as one week of shared training with other men in their unit.

As training took place outside only small groups took part so that they could avoid being detected. As a further security measure look outs were posted to warn of any approaching police patrols. As the police were gradually forced to withdraw from large parts of Ireland's isolated countryside the IRA found they were able to train in larger numbers.

Through a secret newsletter, the An *TÓglach* which means *The Volunteer*, the central commanders made sure that the IRA's operatives were kept informed of military techniques. The guerrillas were also kept up-to-date with policy developments and notified of the actions that they should be taking. To deliver communications from the IRA's headquarters a network of dispatch riders and supporting teams of aides to supply food and accommodation for the couriers was established. The assistants would also be able to help with repairs to the messenger's bicycles or cars.

IRA units were well equipped with shotguns and revolvers. Rifles were held but were fewer in number. The IRA acquired a number of Lewis machine guns, however, the .303 calibre ammunition required by these automatic weapons was in short supply. Explosives, for sabotage and other acts of terrorism, were a key part of a brigade's arsenal. Hand grenades were greatly sought after and when they could not be obtained they were manufactured by local volunteers. To obtain more weapons attacks on police stations, army barracks, people's homes and military patrols were carried out. Attempts were also made to buy arms from the British troops, some of whom could be bribed to sell weapons to the IRA. The smuggling of armaments from as far afield as the British mainland, America and Continental Europe was also a major source of resupply.

From November 1919 the IRA concentrated on building up an intelligence network. The role of coordinating the intelligence was given to the brigades Quartermaster's. The IRA's intelligence gathering took on the form of a bureaucratic, yet effective, form filling exercise where operatives would fill-in information sheets that would then be returned to IRA headquarters. These recorded details which ranged from the strength of the British army and the police force to the number of suspected British agents and even the amount of people in a brigade's area that were available for recruitment into the rebel forces. To prepare the way for an IRA attack women and children were often used to observe police stations and army barracks to record the numbers and movements of government forces. Whereas the IRA had an active and effective intelligence network, intimidation of the general population by Republicans meant that the British forces found covert information increasingly hard to come by.

Each IRA battalion had a medical officer who used supplies that were often purchased on the British mainland. This officer was usually a local medical student or doctor who was a supporter of the Republican cause. The medical assistance came from women who were trained and recruited by the Women's Branch of the Republican movement, the *Cumann-na-mBan*. Their nursing of wounded IRA guerrillas and their help with the evacuation of injured guerrillas made them to all intents and purposes part of the IRA's military machine. If the IRA's medical services in the field could not provide sufficient help the wounded were often sent to hospital in Dublin were they would receive better care from other sympathetic physicians. A doctor with sympathy towards the rebels would usually provide false medical papers as to how the injuries were caused; this would make it difficult for the British authorities to detect wounded IRA operatives.

The tactics of the IRA

The basic military strategy of the IRA was to attack, assassinate and intimidate the forces of the British state until Ireland was made ungovernable. Because the *Dáil* was seeking to establish its own system of governance for an independent Ireland it was the aim of the IRA to eliminate the existing institutions of British rule. They could not exist side-by-side and one had to be destroyed. As such; judges, magistrates, public administrators and anyone else who was seen as part of the existing system was targeted for assassination.

At a local level, the IRA favoured the principle of Mission Command. This meant that each unit commander was given the objectives and aims that his men were intended to achieve, but the way in which he fulfilled his mission was left up to him. It allowed for the man on the spot to act as best fitted local conditions and the skills of his men without being hindered by precise orders from a senior commander based many miles away.

IRA Brigades would often operate in what were dubbed Flying Columns. These were small fast moving and flexible units of guerrillas who operated independently of one another. Although the idea of a massed attack was toyed with in South-Western Ireland where IRA numbers were greatest, the IRA continued throughout the conflict to operate in relatively small units.

These Flying Columns were the Active Service Units of the IRA and the principle strike weapon of the Republican forces. And they had the responsibility of taking the fight to the British forces in a given area of operations. However, the primary aim of any Flying Column was not to win a military victory in battle over the police and the army but simply to survive. The existence of armed rebels remaining at liberty who would be free to attack at any time and at any place of their choosing would both discourage the British authorities and force them to maintain massive numbers of troops in Ireland who would be attacked the moment the guerrillas thought that the odds favoured them.

The IRA received much more than moral support from among the Roman Catholic civilian population; in fact they provided a ready supply of new recruits to replace those killed or wounded in combat. Furthermore, according to one IRA commander, the line between a soldier and a civilian became increasingly blurred. Some civilians, though not part of a flying column, became active opponents of British rule and would assist the guerrilla bands. Those volunteers,

'... did not simply stand and wait until called on, but were actively engaged in harassing the enemy in their Company areas. Some attacked and sniped enemy posts, arrested spies, burned so-called Loyalist houses, trenched roads, scouted, guarded and arranged billets for the Flying Columns.'[16]

According to the British army the IRA stratagem consisted of their operatives, usually dressed in civilian clothes, using three main elements surprise, silence and previous preparation. The IRA used different tactics for different targets. Police stations, for instance, would come under sustained attack by large numbers of rebels working in well organised pre-planned operations. Often the cover of a Gaelic football match organised by the Gaelic Athletic Association, an organisation which had links to Sinn Féin, would be used to bring people into the area of the specified police station. The arms to be used would be brought in the accompanying motor vehicles.

These attacks were usually carried out at night but as the conflict developed daylight assaults became more frequent. For a radius of anything between 5 and 20 miles all roads to the police station, bar one, would be blocked with barricades to prevent reinforcements staging a rescue. IRA spotters would also be active on the roads approaching the police station and would warn of any rescue party. Telegraph lines to the whole area would be cut to prevent any word of the attack reaching the army.

These assaults were often successful in isolating the police station. Other tactics might include waiting until a patrol had left the station, these would then be ambushed and their uniforms taken. The rebels would then don the uniforms and attempt to gain access to the station, while the other rebels would then rush the post.

Another successful method of attack was used against police stations that were adjoined to another building. IRA men would get into the adjacent building, then use explosives to blow a hole in the wall through which the rebels could enter. Alternatively, a hole was drilled in the party wall through which petrol was pumped into the police station and ignited, thus burning the policemen out.

However, the police were alert to such tactics. Because IRA attacks often followed a set pattern, it was on occasions possible for the British security services to detect the attacks in advance by observing that trees by the road had been earmarked for felling. It soon became clear that the assailants were averse to taking casualties so if the police officers put up a determined resistance the rebels would often retreat. If a rescue party did manage to reach the besieged police station the IRA operatives would make their escape via the one road that was still open.

The IRA guerrilla forces also developed tactics to ambush army and police patrols and military convoys. Here bands of armed rebels, ranging in numbers from 6 to as many as 60, would first block a road with a fallen tree or other obstruction, then strike from roadside ditches or from behind walls. In a double-whammy against British forces, a second ambush would be prepared on the route that the relieving force would be expected to take. This second ambush would be sprung when the government patrol was at its most vulnerable, that is when it was on the road.

Lone policemen out on the beat would be targeted by attacks carried out by brazen individuals behind the cover of a supportive crowd. The rebel would shoot at the troops or police and would then be shielded by civilians gathered around. Police bicycle patrols were a particularly favoured target.

Army Guards protecting public buildings and infrastructure such as railways and communications were observed by the IRA to learn their movements. When the rebels were confident of their success insurgents in civilian dress would approach the guard often using a ruse to distract the sentry's attention making him especially vulnerable. The building that was under the protection of the guards was then ransacked, weapons taken and communications cut.

A ruthless programme of assassinations was conducted against the police and officials of the government. Loyalists were also targeted for assassination. The IRA termed these murders "Executions". An IRA meeting would first be held and judgment would be passed on the individual under discussion; if found 'guilty' plain clothed IRA operatives would carry out the attack. A series of executions were carried out after a Republican sympathiser within Dublin's government buildings allowed the details of British agents to fall into rebel hands.

These agents were then subject to IRA assassination in what became a very effective counter-espionage strategy.

The Republicans made great efforts to appropriate the post in order to search for Government communications that might have offered some valuable snippets of information. Tactics for seizing the post included capturing mail cars and trains and even individual postmen. As part of its efforts to keep the sympathy of the local population, the IRA sorted the mail and made sure that non-Government mail was posted.

In an attempt to eliminate the British state from Ireland, Government buildings were targeted for destruction. And anything that may be of use to the security services, such as abandoned police vehicles were also destroyed.

When the IRA was not certain of the support of local people, a policy of intimidation ensured that witnesses were seldom forthcoming. What was apparent from the tactics of the Republican rebels is that they often depended upon the tacit and overt cooperation of the local population for their success. The rebels were not only aided and abetted by the local population but were in fact members of the local communities in which they fought. This not only made the IRA a deadly foe but made the task of rooting them out a very difficult one for the British army, the police and the loyalist forces to achieve. Especially as their ethos for preparation meant that they would strike when victory was likely.

This philosophy for organised and well thought out attacks is clearly shown in a set of captured instructions on planning for attacks on camps and barracks.

You will have all barracks, police and military, in your area examined and watched, with a view to raiding them. Some of the points to know are:-

1. Number in all barracks. Number who sleep in and are in at different times. Number who go out on patrol, to church, on outside duty, etc.

2. Time of leaving on patrol, routes taken, time of return.

3. Precautions taken at night in opening doors
(send someone to try).

4. Where arms are kept. If kept loaded.

5. Position of telegraph or telephone wires to barracks or local
Post Office.

6. Best way and time to take barracks by surprise.

Have report covering all above-mentioned points and any
other you may think necessary into Brigade Headquarters by
Sunday, 19th January 1919.[17]

The Republican guerrillas were clearly well organised by their senior commanders and an effective force. However, the coming battle was to be as much political as it was military. Therefore, the Republican leadership hoped to goad the forces of the Crown into an overreaction which would win the rebels more political support.

To turn the British public against the continued war and to seek revenge for reprisals carried out by the British forces in Ireland the IRA also extended its military operations to mainland Britain. They were primarily carried out by sympathisers drawn from the Irish population living in the English cities of London, Liverpool and Manchester. Their operations, which consisted of shootings as well as bomb and arson attacks on Britain's infrastructure, caused few casualties.

The Initial British Response to Rebellion

The reaction of the forces of the Crown were at first characterised by complacency and inactivity. The situation was so dire that on 27th August 1919 Lieutenant-General Sir Frederick Shaw, the General Officer Commanding the British army in Ireland, wrote to Brigadier-General Sir Joseph Aloysius Byrne, the Inspector-General of the RIC, that the army could not provide troops to protect isolated police stations.[18] Shaw did make amends for his earlier apathy by requesting that the RIC should be bolstered by the introduction of new volunteer units which became known as the Black and Tans and the Auxiliaries. However, the introduction of these forces and their conduct during the war provoked a great deal of opposition to the British authorities. As the situation in many parts of Ireland was out of control Lieutenant-General Shaw was replaced in 1920 by General Macready. The British Government also purged the seat of British rule in Ireland, Dublin Castle, of its ineffective administrators.

In August 1920, along with a steady increase in troop numbers, the British Parliament approved the Restoration of Order in Ireland Act 1920. This law gave the Crown authorities extra powers in Ireland's most lawless areas and the ability to prosecute IRA activists without a jury trial; jurors could be subject to Republican intimidation. The Act of Parliament did lead to an increase in the conviction of rebels, yet it was not enough to restore law and order.

The British authorities responded to the IRA attacks on the UK's mainland by arresting hundreds of suspected IRA sympathisers and by killing 5 IRA terrorists. Parliament also introduced the Emergency Powers Act 1920 which gave the Government and the Privy Council the power to introduce special powers to restore order.

There was also an attempt at a political settlement to end the fighting. This was the 1920 Government of Ireland Act, it is also known as the Fourth Home Rule Bill. This effort at a compromise peace passed through both Houses of the British Parliament and received the Royal Assent as early as November 1920.

Contrary to popular opinion the constitutional division of Ireland came about not as a result of the 1922 Anglo-Irish Treaty but from the Government of Ireland Act 1920. This created two parliaments in Ireland whose areas of responsibility roughly reflected the political and religious divide on that island. One was based in the north-east, with its seat in Belfast governing the territory of the counties of Antrim, Armagh, Down, Fermanagh, Londonderry and Tyrone. This area was to be known as Northern Ireland. It has often been termed "Ulster", though the original Irish province of that name included three other counties Cavan, Donegal and Monaghan. This political institution received the support of the inhabitants who lived within its boundaries, however, its sister Parliament did not.

The other Parliament in theory would govern the south, this was based in Dublin; but its writ did not run far and there was little to no support for it amongst the Roman Catholic population. It was intended that over time the whole of the island of Ireland would be governed by a Council of Ireland and powers would be transferred from the Southern and Northern Ireland Parliaments until the council became in effect a legislature governing all 32 of Ireland's counties. There would also be a High Court of Appeal for all of Ireland.

The Parliament of Southern Ireland would consist of a Senate and a Southern Irish House of Commons. Those institutions would produce a government which would run the affairs of Southern Ireland. There would also be a separate judicial system for the south with a High Court, Court of Appeal and Supreme Court. The Lord Lieutenant of Ireland would become the Crown's representative in the two regions of Ireland.

It is not inconceivable that the provisions of the Government of Ireland Act would have led to a process of greater, and perhaps eventually full, Irish political independence from the UK. However, the creation of two home rule parliaments was rejected out of hand by the Republicans. The Irish elections to the Southern parliament of May 1921 were held against a background of violence and intimidation. Sinn Féin candidates stood unopposed and as such the 'election' returned an overwhelming Sinn Féin majority whose members boycotted the Southern House of Commons just as they refused to attend the British Parliament in Westminster. The Southern institutions were therefore still born and they were abandoned and more power was awarded to Ireland's Crown Representative, the Lord Lieutenant.

he feeling amongst Ireland's Sinn Féin politicians had by this date shifted towards favouring the establishment of a Republic that enjoyed full and immediate independence. This allowed for little room for a compromise solution to be developed with the British Government and perhaps more importantly Ireland's Protestant and Unionist community.

Thus, Britain's proposed political solution had failed and the British government had to continue with the strategy of suppressing the revolt by force of arms.

The imposition of Martial Law

The situation in the Province of Munster that consisted of South-West Ireland, the region which included the area that would later become the responsibility of Montgomery, had deteriorated to such a degree that in September 1920 the Government of the Liberal Prime Minister, David Lloyd-George, and his Cabinet decided to agree to the proposals from Dublin Castle, where the government institutions were based, to impose Martial Law on that troublesome corner of the island. Munster consisted of six counties one of which, the County of Waterford, was deemed not to warrant martial law being imposed as the situation was relatively calm. Eventually, a quarter of Ireland's 32 counties would be placed under martial law.

The Proclamation also gave the British authorities based in

Dublin Castle the power to extend martial law to other areas on the island if the military situation warranted it. Strangely for such an apparently extreme measure the cabinet decision which established the principle of martial law also ruled that Republicans who were being detained may be freed from prison to attend a meeting of the *Dáil Éireann*, and could only be re-arrested if they committed a new criminal act.[19] This decision effectively decriminalised the rebel parliament; the very same body that was awarding funding to the IRA and working towards establishing a shadow Irish state whose immediate reason for being was to wage war on the British presence on the island of Ireland. Furthermore, the members of the Dáil were naturally leading Republicans who were now legally at large and able to re-join the war.

The announcement to proclaim martial law, which came into force in December 1920, began with detailing a series of terrorist outrages with particular focus on the murder and mutilation of sixteen cadets by Republicans. It then appealed to people to;

'Obey and conform to all orders and regulations of the Military Authority issued by virtue of this Proclamation.'

It also called on the loyal and law abiding residents of Ireland to help the Crown Forces in upholding law and order. Key passages from the proclamation read;

'IRISHMEN!

Understand this:

Great Britain has no quarrel with Irishmen; her sole quarrel is with crime, outrage and disorder; her sole object in declaring MARTIAL LAW is to restore peace to a distracted and unhappy country: her sole enemies are those who have countenanced, inspired, and participated in rebellion, murder and outrage.'

The proclamation then went on to explain that military governors were appointed in much of Munster and that the population were to obey them 'in all matters whatsoever'. A system of military courts was also established to try anyone found to be breaching the main orders in the proclamation. The main provisions were that it called on anyone who was not in the military or police to surrender arms, ammunition and explosives unless they had a permit for them. The ultimate punishment for failing to do so was that the Military Court could, upon conviction, impose the death penalty. The death penalty was also made the ultimate sanction for the unauthorised wearing of British police or military uniform and that anyone in possession of such uniforms could be sentenced to prison.

The proclamation also stated;

'That a state of armed insurrection exists, that any person taking part therein or procuring, inviting, aiding or abetting any other person to do so, or harbouring any such person, is guilty of levying war against His Majesty The King, and is liable on conviction to suffer DEATH'.

As the proclamation officially recognised that the situation was effectively a war it put all British forces in Ireland on active service. General Macready also declared that;

'No person must stand or loiter in the streets except in pursuit of his lawful occupation… All meetings or assemblies in public places are forbidden and for the purpose of this Order six adults will be considered a meeting… All occupiers of houses must keep affixed to the inner side of the outer door a list of the occupants setting forth their names, sex, age and occupation.'

This clearly affected the civil liberties of the population within the south-west. However, the imposition of martial law did not affect the running of the law courts and local government which was to continue with their functions as before until otherwise directed.

It was felt that martial law would be favoured by not only the troops and would make retaliatory incidents by the British army less frequent but also by the people of Ireland. Evidence was placed before the cabinet that suggested that even Nationalists would welcome such a policy if it brought an end to lawlessness. The reality, however, proved to be very different; the imposition of martial law proved to be a disaster and the intensity of the rebellion increased greatly.

Particularly unpopular aspects of Martial Law included the controversial internment without trial of suspected IRA activists. Other actions which further alienated the civilian population included the imposition of death sentences upon IRA guerrillas by the Military Courts. These non-judicial executions, like those given to many involved with the 1916 Easter Rising, merely acted as *cause celebres* for the Republican cause and stirred up the IRA guerrillas to further action as they sought to avenge their comrade's deaths.

Within large parts of the Martial Law area the British Army imposed night time curfews, restricting the movement of civilians. Although the curfews gave the British forces the opportunity to shoot anyone, presumably an IRA activist, who happened to be breaking the curfew; it proved to be a double-edged sword for the British Army. The restrictions meant that the streets were free from all apart from the forces of the Crown, thus giving the IRA the opportunity to strike at the security services safe in the knowledge that they would not kill their own people. If the British Army, however, killed or injured a civilian who broke the curfew even if they did so for a very good reason there was no recourse to the courts nor would any compensation be provided. This further alienated the local population of the Martial Law area.

Furthermore, there were instances, particularly in Cork, where the IRA would on occasions patrol the streets during the curfew. This act of bravado had the effect of raising the prestige of the IRA amongst the local population who were becoming increasingly frustrated and resentful towards the repressive measures that were being forced upon them by an army that came from what some perceived to be a foreign land.[20]

The cause of Irish nationalism, the opposition to Martial Law and the restrictions which followed, coupled with the increasingly deadly attacks by the Republican forces, who were harnessing the resentment towards the British and whipping up Ireland's ancient sectarian and class hatreds, combined with the IRA's ruthlessly efficient organisation created a very difficult situation for the forces of the Crown. As the guerrilla war developed the fighting appeared to be leading to a situation where the insurgents were on the verge of victory, particularly in South-Western Ireland. However, the IRA was about to encounter an opposing commander who made sure that his forces were equally prepared for their guerrilla operations.

Chapter 6

ENTER MONTGOMERY

In December 1920 Montgomery, was given the massive responsibility of becoming the Chief of Staff of the 17th (Cork) Infantry Brigade. He was given the rank of Brigade Major and was to head up the organisation, implementation and detailed planning of the brigade's combat operations and intelligence. He was also to manage the brigade's resources and administration. Montgomery's Brigade was the largest infantry brigade in Ireland. It was tasked with suppressing the revolt in County Cork where Republican violence was at its most deadly. This area was the most lawless in Ireland and the roads and communications were often in the hands of the IRA and its insurgent supporters. Furthermore, the atmosphere of hostility towards the British forces was palpable especially after the events at Croke Park and the series of bloody killings throughout Cork that followed.

Montgomery entered this conflict in January 1921 with gusto directing the fight against the IRA. One of Montgomery's soldiers, Douglas Neil Wimberley, who later rose to the rank of Major-General and served under Montgomery in North Africa and Sicily, held Montgomery in high regard. Assistant-Adjutant Wimberley of the Cameron Highlanders praised Montgomery's 'incisiveness'. According to Wimberley another junior officer said of Monty, 'Our new Brigade-Major is certainly a little tiger for work, and by Jove you have to jump when he gives you an order, and he is also a martinet as regards punctuality.'[21]

The 17th Infantry Brigade originally consisted of 7 battalions and was later increased to a total of 9. In time this force increased in size from around 9,000 soldiers to one that totalled approximately 12,570 men and by the height of the conflict in the summer of 1921 it included; 8,800 infantry troops, 2,080 artillery men and soldiers from machine gun and other units. Also at Montgomery's disposal were 540 Auxiliaries and 1,150 of the Black and Tans. Montgomery helped make the 17th Brigade a force to be reckoned with, yet they were to encounter a guerrilla leader of renowned genius called Tom Barry who commanded the IRAs West Cork Flying Column. Incidentally Tom Barry had served with distinction in the British Army during World War I and was the son of a Royal Irish Constabulary policeman.

Although the men under Montgomery's command managed to inflict heavy casualties on the guerrillas who made up the East Cork IRA unit, Tom Barry and his less well equipped insurgents, which numbered no more than 110 men, managed to evade capture and turn much of Western Cork into a bloody battle zone. Throughout the whole of County Cork, the IRA were outnumbered by a force in excess of 40 times their number. There were just 310 IRA riflemen in that lawless county, the numbers limited by the simple fact that the IRA only ever possessed three hundred and ten rifles held by the three IRA brigades operating in Cork. In that part of the country the rebels also had five machine-guns as well as some 350 pistols.[22]

Florence O'Donoghue, who was an important opponent of Montgomery serving as the Head of Intelligence in the IRAs 1st Cork Brigade and later a historian of that conflict and a Major in the Irish army, judged Montgomery to be a successful adversary. O'Donoghue wrote in his book No Other Law that Montgomery 'could to a large extent immobilise our basic organisation, disrupt communications, and add to our losses in men killed and captured.' Major O'Donoghue was not alone in holding Montgomery and most of his military actions in high regard. According to a senior Irish Army commander, Lieutenant-General Michael J Costello who as a young man was involved with the Anglo-Irish War, thought of Montgomery as an effective enemy. He wrote that Montgomery along with one of Monty's British Army intelligence officers, Major Arthur Percival, 'eventually developed towards the last months of the war the only tactics which seriously menaced the survival of the I.R.A. units.'

Costello also wrote that,

'Montgomery as Brigade Major of the 17th Brigade
was thought by his superiors and contemporaries to
"have done well in Ireland", and to have given promise
of the qualities admired by some when he later became
Britain's most famous field-marshall.'[23]

Before Montgomery arrived the morale of the British Army units based in Cork was not high. Furthermore, the forces of the Crown were finding it difficult to locate and engage in combat the IRA's flying columns, as on the British side the war was not being successfully administered and executed. The Republican guerrilla tactics of mobile units striking at a time of their choosing, backed by a sophisticated intelligence and supply network, was hampering the attempts of the sizeable British force in Ireland's South-West to restore the authority of the British state.

Monty changed all that.

Montgomery's tactics

Montgomery employed subtle command techniques in an

attempt to win a military victory over the IRA. In this conflict Montgomery put into practice one of his key conclusions from the Great War which had ended a little over two years earlier. This was making sure that everyone under his command knew what was expected of them both in terms of their conduct and the tactics to be used when on campaign. He observed that the British military leadership had failed to achieve this during World War I and he was determined to put this right. Such an approach was his signature leadership methodology throughout his military career. It paid dividends when he was rebuilding the shattered morale of the 8th Army prior to the pivotal second battle of El-Alamein in 1942 and again during his command of the land-forces during D-Day and the subsequent fighting in Normandy.

In June 1921 after assessing the tactics of the IRA and the military and political situation, Montgomery put together his guidance as to how what had become to all intents and purposes a war was to be fought. His instructions were set out at length in a document called *17th Infantry Brigade Summary of Important Instructions*.[24] Although this may have been blandly titled it covered everything his forces needed to know to enable them to combat the insurgency in Ireland. It also allowed newly arrived officers to hit the ground running and be fully prepared for the task in front of them. Montgomery took steps to make sure that these comprehensive instructions were to remain secret as their falling into the hands of his enemies would have jeopardised the fight against the IRA. Keeping operational as well as tactical secrecy was also to become a hallmark of his military career.

In 29 points the *Summary* thoroughly set out how the job of fighting the IRA was to be handled. Examples of the most salient points in his guidance, which are still as relevant in modern conflicts as they were then, included; not allowing civilians to approach armed cars as this gives undercover IRA operatives an opportunity to throw bombs into the car. There were also clear and precise instructions designed to make sure that convoys were protected from attack. These ranged from planning the journey to making sure that routes and times of travel regularly varied so as not to allow the IRA to predict the army's movements. There were also instructions on the spacing between different parts of the convoy, on the use of sentries and on the best tactics to use to fight off a rebel attack.

Montgomery even advocated the use of hostages to ensure that convoys were not attacked. He recommended that known Sinn Féin activists should be taken on each journey. In addition to motorised patrols he also gave advice on how best to organise cycle and foot patrols so that mutually supporting fire could be given and if attacked quickly turn defence into offence. Tactics for ensuring safe train travel were also specified at length. And to make sure that troops on patrol could always be in touch with Headquarters he emphasised the need for good communications. He mandated that carrier pigeons should accompany convoys and all detachments that are on the move.

In his instructions Montgomery also emphasised the importance of respecting religion by not interfering with those attending Mass. If there were to be searches at such a time they should be conducted when people were leaving a Church service and not when they were heading for one. Montgomery understood the damage that any allegation of British forces interfering with religion would have upon the British mission in Ireland. The negative propaganda was sure to have been used by Republicans as part of their campaign which whipped up religious conflict.

Montgomery also specified that no religious establishments were to be searched without prior approval from his Brigade Headquarters. He explained at length the techniques of how to conduct a successful search of individuals, such as those travelling by train and by wheeled transport. Montgomery was aware of the techniques used by the rebels to transport arms and ammunition; one of their favoured techniques was to hide them in coffins. He therefore told his men to search coffins – unless of course it was obvious that a funeral was taking place. Montgomery's men were expected to use their common sense.

He also stipulated that the homes of suspects should be checked often. He set out advice including making sure his men search for false linings of cloths and luggage, false rooms and compartments. This was very much a game of cat and mouse and Montgomery advised that;

'Nothing but the most careful, methodical, and lengthy
investigation will achieve success. The searchers must
have as much imagination as the other side.'

Monty did advise caution, these searchers were not to damage property and entry was not to be forced through the use of rifles. In an attempt to avoid any negative publicity arising from the search of private property, the householder was asked to sign a certificate stating that nothing had been stolen and no needless damage had been caused. The resident of the property was not to be forced to sign and if they did not do so a report had to be prepared and delivered to headquarters.

Although Montgomery recognised that women were increasingly being used by the IRA to carry dispatches and even arms, they were only to be searched by other women and should not be imprisoned apart from in exceptional circumstances. To address the problem he emphasised the need for his men to make sure that an adequate amount of female searchers and prison guards were available to meet the need posed by the IRAs use of the fairer sex.

Conduct on the conscription of civilian labour was also set out. This was a controversial subject, but Montgomery stipulated that it was permitted when used for removing obstacles made by the rebels and making repairs to damage caused by IRA attacks. Montgomery also sanctioned this as a collective punishment, especially after events such as a Police station being targeted, when it was deemed necessary to improve the post's defences. The British forces were instructed to do their utmost to make sure that the burden for this work fell on those with Republican sympathies.

To ensure that civilian casualties were kept to a minimum there were also orders as to when a sentry should and should not open fire. These orders emphasised that lethal fire should be used as a last resort and to prevent a position from being overrun or if a British Serviceman was actually being threatened. Ideally sentries should obtain permission from his commanding officer but of course this was not always possible. Montgomery gave instructions for all passes to be checked even of those purporting to be British officers.

On the issue of making arrests Montgomery emphasised the importance of quality over quantity. He wanted high value targets detained and not those of little importance as this would be counter-productive and just clog-up the prison system. However, he did set out at length the need to make sure that important rebels were arrested and detained – and not allowed to escape by use of an alibi backed up by sympathisers. He therefore advised that anyone captured who raised the slightest suspicion should be passed over to the Intelligence Department for assessment.

Although Montgomery recognised the need to shoot escaping prisoners he highlighted that ideally they would be shot to stop rather than kill them. Likewise he advised that when confronted by an aggressive mob soldiers should not open fire into the air or the ground but should single out fire towards the most hostile person and shoot them below the knee. Opening fire on those acting suspiciously was also sanctioned to enforce a curfew. In an attempt to totally eliminate the risk of what is now called collateral damage Montgomery urged British forces to make sure that if trouble was expected the public should be cleared from the streets to ensure their own protection.

Montgomery took advantage of the powers granted to him by the Martial Law proclamation and in an attempt to bring about law and order enforced increasingly strident measures to control the civilian population of Cork. The curfews that Montgomery imposed applied to all civilians and there were no exceptions. However, it was at times argued that this just had the effect of further alienating the general population.

Montgomery also stipulated intelligence gathering on the IRA and their activities was a major activity for his officers to undertake. He also held his Intelligence Officers of his espionage network personally responsible for the information affecting their units. Furthermore, foreign nationals who were associating themselves with Republicans had to be reported to senior officers as well as any evidence the army had on them. Just as Montgomery had his own intelligence network he recognised that the Republican forces had a highly effective information gathering arm and that steps had to be taken to make sure that IRA spies were not able to obtain information about the British forces and their operations. Measures were also undertaken to protect sources of information. Keeping an eye on future events to spot potential flash points was also a function which Montgomery gave to his officers; as such he advised them to monitor the press. This also allowed them be aware of reports that could incite trouble, if so this gave the army an opportunity to correct any misleading information. Montgomery also forbade any unapproved contact between his men and the media; and especially made sure that press photographers were usually forbidden and that any photos taken by his men were passed to Brigade HQ. Only his headquarters had contact with the press and thus controlled information leaving his army. This would give Montgomery a better chance of winning the propaganda war as well as keep the operational secrecy that he so cherished.

The element of surprise was another key factor that Montgomery instructed his officers to utilise. He advocated the use of stealth where operations would be conducted by soldiers on foot. Men in motorised vehicles might be slow to alight and the engine noise would give away the soldiers approach well in advance. To surprise the IRA Montgomery gave advice on how to use fast moving troops to outwit and outflank enemy detachments. He even advised that men chosen to act as scouts should be swift at running and ideally be in shorts to aid this purpose. In this vicious war Montgomery advised his officers to use cunning when combating the Republic forces.

On top of his belief in keeping operational secrecy Montgomery also understood code-breaking and how the IRA might crack British codes. He gave instructions to his Officers that uncoded communications needed to be carefully worded so that they would not compromise the ciphers being used to obscure a unit's messages from their IRA foes. He also stipulated that wireless communication was only to take place in an emergency. He emphasised caution when using telephones and telegrams. Montgomery's instructions again reminded his officers that the IRA had an extensive intelligence network and that they were highly likely to be eavesdropping on British communications. Montgomery's forces were told to exercise caution in all communications, but especially when documents were being transported.

He also set out instructions on the use of plain clothed soldiers. They were to mix with the general population.

Montgomery specified that they should be highly proficient in the use of hand guns. They were, however, not to take offence action unless it was deemed absolutely necessary such as if a civilian's or soldier's life was at risk. There were three areas of operation where plain clothes soldiers were to be used, these were; protective duties, as observers in operations and for intelligence work.

Montgomery was a fanatical teetotaller and specified that whilst they are out on duty none of the men under his command were not to consume any alcoholic liquor.

His instructions also sought to motivate his men to take the fight to the enemy, writing, 'It has been clearly proved that the rebels have no "stomach" for a fight as we understand it. A few determined soldiers, well led, will defeat 50 armed rebels with ease.'

This is just one small snippet of his inspirational words but it is the beginning of a remarkable career in his delivering words designed to encourage his soldiers to perform to their utmost. He also stressed the need for his officers to be alert to the danger of ambushes, a favoured IRA tactic, and have a secure defence. In his words, 'The principle of "protection" must never be disregarded, whether on the move or at rest.'

British forces, according to Montgomery should also be wise to the IRAs attempts to draw them into ambushes by mounting diversionary attacks on British forces and then launch the real attack on the relieving party who are rushing out in the mistaken belief that their comrades were under attack. As such they are not to rush to the scene of an attack without adequate precautions. Emphasising the need for proper precautions and planning was to be a trademark of Montgomery's military theory and practice and it found its first expression in the Anglo-Irish War.

Montgomery also recognised the importance of a factor that

went beyond the numbers of killed, captured and wounded and territory held. This was the intangible dynamic of morale. He understood that leaving troops vulnerable to attack would undermine this crucial component in military success and would likewise raise the morale of his Republican opponents. Montgomery also saw that having his officers make sure that their men were well protected from attack had another important benefit. This was that they would be less likely to carry out unofficial reprisals which would be used as part of Sinn Féin's anti-British propaganda war.

Montgomery was adamant that the reputation of the army must be beyond reproach. On this thorny topic he gave both official and unofficial advice. Officially he stated the policy that reprisals, even against property, were strictly forbidden. However, in his unofficial advice he tacitly admitted that the Royal Irish Constabulary were undertaking such punitive policies, of which he thoroughly disapproved, and he stressed that his officers must not allow the men to be led astray by the police.

Conversely, however, Montgomery did stress that on any and all areas there must be no public criticism of the police. This was to ensure that good relations with the Royal Irish Constabulary would be maintained which he saw as crucial. He also advised that it was a strategy of the Republicans to poison the minds of each service's personnel against the other. IRA men were in the habit of posing as civilians and engaging soldiers or policemen in conversation to spread information which would spread distrust or dislike, and so harm their mutual co-operation. The best way to undermine this IRA tactic, was by forming a high degree of personal teamwork. If difficulties in a joint operation did arise then he set out a formal complaints procedure which reported to his headquarters in Cork. This allowed a mechanism for distrust or disapproval to be expressed and defused.

It is clear that the conflict in 1920s Ireland was a deadly and vicious one where a soldier could be attacked by an apparently innocent looking civilian and had to be prepared for all eventualities. Montgomery's instructions were clearly multi-dimensional. He did his best to make sure that his men were ready for this conflict and their morale improved. Monty's effective training programme and his establishment of an effective intelligence unit were innovative measures, as was his use of his own mobile fast moving and flexible flying columns whose aim was to flush out and engage the Republicans. Nevertheless, these tactics met with only limited success. Their main effect was that they drove the guerrillas of the IRA underground where they would do their utmost to refuse and evade battle with the British forces.

This situation is described by the IRA commander Tom Barry, who wrote;

The British were now only emerging from their bases to conduct large-scale round-up operations. They would sally forth from three or four towns simultaneously, converge on particular districts, comb them and return to their fortresses. To meet this new situation our tactics were to evade encirclement, to destroy bridges and roads before and behind those rounding up units and to snipe their patrols and barracks, whenever possible. [25]

However, Barry and his 3rd West Cork Brigade of the IRA were nearly captured on 19th March 1921 but the rebels did manage to escape encirclement and survived to fight another day.

Yet Montgomery remained convinced that sweeps throughout the land by his own flying columns were the best way of militarily dealing with the forces of the Irish Republican Army. He wrote after the conflict that, 'I am certain that the best procedure was mobile columns mutually cooperating with each other.' There was, however, a caveat and this was that for the mobile columns to be successful effective intelligence had to be delivered. This required that the units on their sweeps of Ireland's countryside had what was then known as wireless telegraphy (W/T) so that they could be coordinated with each other from the brigade's headquarters and use the intelligence that was being gathered. Monty wrote that, 'We often found that the best intelligence was received by us in Cork, and if columns had no W/T we could not take advantage of it.[26]

Criticisms of his tactics did however exist. It has been argued that Montgomery's operations in Ireland did not make adequate use of airpower in his conflict with the Irish Republican Army. Instead he considered control of the ground to be of prime importance. Later in his career, as we shall see, Monty was to become one of the earlier advocates of the use of airpower in the elimination of ground forces which was to become a prerequisite for future success on the battlefield. Perhaps by not utilising this still relatively new technology to its utmost Montgomery was being short-sighted. However, it must be admitted that 1920s Ireland was still an underdeveloped country. There were few runways available and the technology, and its efficiency and effectiveness, was still in its infancy. So it is unlikely that a more aggressive use of airpower would have altered the outcome of this conflict.

In fact Montgomery wrote of his experiences with aeroplanes in the Anglo-Irish war that,

These were really of no use to use, except as a quick and safe means of getting from one place to another. Even then the landing grounds were few and far between. The pilots and observers knew nothing whatever about the war, or the conditions under which it was being fought, and were not therefore in a position to be able to help much.'[27]

Despite the fact that there was close co-operation between the IRA and the civilian population Montgomery did not seek to drive a wedge between them. His assessment of the situation was that there was little opportunity to do so. In fact he had developed a somewhat jaded attitude towards the bulk of Ireland's population and the possibility of winning over the general public to accepting British rule. He wrote; 'I think I regarded all civilians as "Shinners", and I never had any dealings with any of them.' The Irish Lieutenant-General, Michael J Costello, however thought such an attitude was counter-productive. He judged that Montgomery's attitude towards the civilian population, 'was conducive to providing the I.R.A. with recruits from people previously neutral or hostile.[28]

Montgomery also failed to cultivate links with loyalists who were rarely brought into close contact with him. Beyond the military opportunities that this may have presented it also meant that those who were loyal to British rule were subject to a great deal of intimidation from their Republican neighbours. Montgomery regretted what they had to go through, he wrote, 'I think that we did not appreciate their sufferings…'[29]

The suffering was felt by many on all sides. This was a vicious war and those who were thought to be IRA insurgents and those suspected of being engaged in aiding the guerrillas were liable to have their homes and property, including farms and shops, burned to the ground. After the conflict Montgomery wrote about house burning and his views on this thorny subject were uncompromising, 'Personally my whole attention was given to defeating the rebels and it never bothered me a bit how many houses were burnt.'[30]

This policy however met with a ruthless response from County Cork's IRA insurgents. They repaid the burning of property owned by Republicans with interest by embarking upon a campaign of burning the homes of those who supported British rule. The IRA made it known that for every Republican home burnt two loyalist homes would be attacked in revenge.

This warning was not heeded and after the British Army burnt the property of two Republicans, which consisted of a small farmhouse and the cottage of a labourer, retaliation followed and is described by Tom Barry,

'The following night the I.R.A. burned out four large Loyalists' residences in the same neighbourhood. The British countered this by burning four farmhouses and we promptly burned out the eight largest Loyalists' homes in that vicinity. And so the British terror and the I.R.A. counter-terror went on.'

As a consequence of the reprisals, described by the IRA commander Tom Barry as *'counter-terror'*, many loyalists sought to move away and sold their properties. The IRA's next step was to prohibit potential buyers and auctioneers from selling the homes of loyalists. This meant that those who supported British rule either had to stay in their vulnerable homes where they would remain as unwilling bargaining chips in the IRA's campaign of house burning reprisals or they would have to leave with no proceeds from a sale. In some of those instances the Republicans would take over the property and sell it to raise money to fund their campaign. This ruthless policy accomplished the goal of discouraging the British Army from burning the homes of the guerrillas and their sympathisers.[31]

Stalemate in Ireland

The heavy handed British response in many areas of Ireland coupled with Republican propaganda further radicalised public opinion against British rule in Ireland. However, there was another important factor at work that brought many Irish people behind the IRA's war effort. This was that they saw that the guerrillas were to a large degree holding their own and in some cases being successful; this encouraged more people to join and lend their support to the IRA.

The IRA was capable of driving out the Royal Irish

Constabulary, the police in Ireland, from many isolated and vulnerable posts. In some areas the IRA created a large degree of lawlessness and a power vacuum that was being filled by Republican forces. However, this situation was far from uniform across Ireland with many parts outside of the South and South-west remaining firmly in Crown hands. There was also no hope that a military victory would be won against the British army; yet that is not the aim of a terrorist and guerrilla campaign. There was little hope of the fighting ending because the IRA believed that the continual killing would intimidate the people of mainland Britain and the government into withdrawing from Ireland. Whilst this situation continued the likelihood of British soldiers committing atrocities increased and it was believed that if this happened the situation would be further inflamed to the benefit of the IRA.

British soldiers were often subject to attack and assassination. Yet, it was noted in advice to the British Government that despite this severe provocation there were no acts of retaliation by the army against the civilian population.[32] Even so this situation was causing a great deal of concern amongst the army's top brass.

The lack of troops meant that the soldiers were almost continually involved in operations, with those in the more lawless districts only spending two nights per week in bed. The demands on the soldiers were so great that they had to take part in operations that would keep them continuously awake for between 24 to 48 hours. This lowered morale and placed an enormous strain on the troops, particularly the young. What is more, as this was a guerrilla conflict without clearly defined front lines there were not any rear areas where the troops could be sent to find rest and recuperation away from the stresses and strains of the conflict around them.

The soldiers were also acutely aware that their efforts were not generally appreciated by the people of mainland Britain. They were disconcerted by the lack of anti-IRA stories in the media and thoroughly disheartened by the reports of attacks on their actions in public meetings and in the British Parliament.

Morale was further lowered by the soldiers having to be away from their wives and families for long periods of time. Furthermore, it was felt that the rural and isolated nature of much of Ireland meant that the unmarried men, apart from those posted to the cities, were unable to find any adequate entertainment to relieve the stresses and strains of conflict. The campaign of terror and assassination which they faced meant that,

'the strain upon them [the soldiers] from the junior to the highest ranks is incomparably greater than it would be in time of actual war. The lieutenant or captain in charge of a village or post not only has the hourly danger of assassination hanging over him, but has to be at any moment prepared to come to a decision in regard to the defence of his charge, or to act on a sudden call from the Police.'

It was sensed that the strain was greatest on the higher ranking officers. It was understood that the situation was at its most acute in Cork, which is where Montgomery managed the fight.

The officers were also being hamstrung by the political machinations that dominated the conflict in Ireland. As part of the Republican propaganda war complaints about the army were often brought to the attention of the officers by rebel sympathisers. The commanding officer would then have the difficult task of deciding what to do. On one hand the complaints may be spurious but on the other it may be necessary to address any wrong doing by the army. This was the dilemma of trying to enforce law and order amongst a civilian population. Furthermore, the officers were concerned that sympathisers with the Republican cause in the House of Commons would ask parliamentary questions about operational matter. These formal requests for information have to be answered, and the information obtained could be used to disparage the actions of the army. This was especially hard to bear when it was considered that members of the *Dáil Éireann* were at liberty to campaign against the British army.

The result of this remorseless and unappreciated work was that in the view of the army leadership, 'the men cannot be expected to go on indefinitely without the conditions under which they are serving having effect upon their morale, discipline, and future from the point of view of military usefulness.' [33]

The British army's proposed strategy

By the spring of 1921 it was clear to the leadership of the British army that the situation was most unsatisfactory. It was not only feared that the stalemate between the Crown forces and the IRA would continue throughout the summer and the autumn but also that winter would hand the advantage to the Republicans. The so-called 'Irish atmosphere', a term created to describe the psychological effects of operations in Ireland, was expected to break the British army's spirit so that the officers and men would have to be withdrawn. Clearly something had to change. The Generals thought that victory had to be achieved by October 1921.

Increasing the number of troops was not an easy remedy to administer. The British army was suffering from imperial overstretch with too many overseas commitments. To fulfil the demands for extra troops in Ireland the army leadership under Field Marshal Sir Henry Wilson pointed out that the reinforcements were only possible if there was a reduction in the numbers used in Britain's other commitments.

Throughout the summer of 1920 there was a rebellion against British rule in the important Mandate territory of

Mesopotamia, now Iraq. This revolt drew away from Ireland both political attention and military resources that should have been directed towards dealing with the revolt at home.

Throughout 1920 and 1921 another crisis began to brew on the continent of Europe. This was the growing international dispute between the German government and Polish nationalists in a region known as Upper Silesia. Ironically at this time British forces were being considered for peace keeping duties in Upper Silesia where they could have been acting in conjunction with Germany against ethnic Poles who were backed by the French. The Polish nationalists sought Upper Silesia's incorporation into the newly established Republic of Poland. This had the potential to engage the UK in yet another theatre of war.

As a result of this latest crisis in mainland Europe the army took the step of warning the government of British Prime Lloyd George that there was a risk that British policy was drawing the UK into a commitment which it most definitely did not have the resources to meet. This was a conflict too far and an adequate amount of resources were not available if the peace keeping mission dragged Britain into yet another war.

The Chief of the Imperial General Staff, Field Marshal Sir Henry Wilson who was from County Longford in Ireland and was assassinated by the IRA in 1922, and General Nevil Macready, the General Officer Commanding-in-Chief of British forces in Ireland, were becoming deeply concerned about the lack of troops in Ireland.

The diary entries of Field Marshal Sir Henry Wilson show the growing alarm. On 18th May 1921 he wrote;

'At 1.30 Curzon (the Foreign Secretary) rang me. He gave me a long sermon about the state of affairs in Silesia, ending by saying that Prime Minister and he had decided that five battalions should go to Silesia. I at once attacked. I said that,

directly England was safe, every available man should go to Ireland, that even four battalions now on the Rhine ought also to go to Ireland. I said that the troops and the measures taken up to now had been quite inadequate, that I was terrified at the state of that country, and that, in my opinion, unless we crushed out the murder gang this summer, we should lose Ireland and the Empire. I spoke in the strongest manner and I frightened Curzon, who said he must refer it all to the Prime Minister.'

What is more, in the view of Wilson, the personnel situation was also being made worse because of the growing problem of Irish soldiers in the British Army applying not to be sent to Ireland for fear that their families would become targets of the IRA.

On 23rd May Wilson also wrote in his diary about his discussions that day with the Secretary of State for War, Sir Laming Worthington-Evans. Wilson wrote;

'Macready absolutely backs up my contention that we must knock out, or at least knock under, the Sinn Féiners this summer or we shall lose Ireland, and he told S. of S. (Secretary of State for War) so in good round terms, and that it was not wise nor safe to ask the troops now in Ireland to go on as they are now for another winter. As there were no troops with which to relieve them, we must make our effort now, or else, tacitly and in fact, agree that we were beaten. S. of S. is really impressed and frightened.' [34]

Wilson and Macready proposed to the Cabinet on 24th May 1921 a series of actions designed to win the war in Ireland. The strategy they proposed mainly consisted of more drives through the Irish countryside to flush out the rebels and engage them in battle. Army operations were also intended to gather information that may be of use to the military.

The General and the Field Marshal also hoped that the

bringing together of all the security services; Police and Auxiliaries under the command of the Army and their forces would, in conjunction with the Navy, guarding the coast to prevent arms smuggling, offer an excellent opportunity of reaching a successful military conclusion to the conflict. However, they both stressed that they could not 'promise any definite result.' Yet every effort should be made to take advantage of the better weather which the summertime offered to 'break the back of the rebellion during the three months of July, August and September.'[35]

The tools that were requested by the Army leadership for their summer offensive, which was described as a supreme effort, included requesting an additional 20 battalions of infantry and a further 3 cavalry regiments. Airplanes were also requested as were wireless personnel and these forces were to be bolstered by the addition of extra armoured cars. The army leadership placed a particularly high value on armoured cars and the protection and offensive capabilities which they offered.

The army reinforcements and an increased role for the Navy were seen as absolutely necessary because there were insufficient numbers of troops to effectively deal with the threat posed by the Republicans. The additional forces would not only allow for the offensive sweeps to be firmly undertaken but would also enable the authorities to impose civil control measures such as enforcing travel and transportation regulations. It would also allow for the servicemen to get some adequate rest and give them a chance to recuperate.

Wilson and Macready also advised the Cabinet on 24th May 1921 that they were of the opinion that the introduction of Martial Law throughout Ireland, bar the counties of Ulster, and the subsequent clear message delivered through its proclamation would show to both the people of Britain and Ireland that the Government was committed to forcing a settlement to the conflict by the Autumn of 1921 and before the winter set in. Field Marshal Wilson did, however, recognise the importance of the wider political situation if and when and the British Army was given the green light to make the supreme effort that he was advocating. He wrote in his diary in June 1921 that;

'... unless we have England entirely on our side, I would strongly advise that we should not attempt martial law in all its severity, because I was sure it would not succeed, and failure meant disaster. If the soldiers knew that England was solid behind them they would go on till they won out; if on the other hand they found that this was not the case then we should have disaster.'[36]

The offensive action of the army would at first seek to quell opposition to the British Government in urban areas, it was thought that the rebels would then flee to the mountainous areas where it was hoped that they could be apprehended with relative ease. Before these drives would begin the newly arriving forces would be trained and informed of the particular military situation and tactics that were required in this conflict, the quintessential guerrilla war. It was then proposed that the battalions would then be moved to their respective operational areas. Of the 20 battalions of infantry, four were requested for operations in Dublin and its surrounding districts, nine battalions were intended to bolster the 5th Division which fought in Western-Central Ireland. The remaining seven battalions and the three cavalry regiments were earmarked for Munster, in the South-West of Ireland where Montgomery was operating. The three regiments of cavalry were seen as being of particular importance as they were one of the few ways in which swift offensive action could be taken against the IRA in the wilder rural areas were roads were few and poorly surfaced.

As part of the offensive drives it was planned that instructions would be given to the army to show the flag. This it was hoped would hearten those that remained loyal to the British Government and make sure that those who were sitting on the fence would not go over to the Republican side. It was also felt that showing that the army was in Ireland to stay and remained in control would discourage the rebels from further action by leading all but the most fanatical of them to believe that an IRA victory was out of the question. As part of the drive to regain control it was proposed that large mobile columns were to perpetually move around the country making sure that every village and farm was visited by the army. The police posts that were abandoned due to attacks from Republicans were to be re-established and re-occupied by the Royal Irish Constabulary, apart from those few which were deemed by the army to be unnecessary.

An effective and determined propaganda war was also seen by General Macready and Field Marshal Wilson as a key component of any victory. British propaganda primarily sought to undermine how the Republicans were perceived by highlighting the links between Sinn Féin and Germany which existed during World War One. It was hoped that this would not only harden opinion at home and motivate the troops in Ireland and improve their morale but also dishearten the Sinn Féiners, many of which had fought for Britain during the First World War. Accordingly 1,500 copies of a pamphlet exposing the links between the Republican leadership and the German military were distributed in Ireland.

This propaganda offensive was also intended to bolster political opinion in the United Kingdom Parliament, the House of Commons, where British involvement in Ireland and the actions of the army were drawing fierce criticism from some quarters most notably Oswald Mosley MP, the future leader of the British Union of Fascists. It was explained to the Government that criticisms made in Parliament of the British campaign in Ireland were harming the morale of the British forces.

The British propaganda offensive also sought to directly counter Republican misinformation which General Macready perceived was 'pursuing its course unchecked in the Press'[37]. The strategy which the army advised was that the Government should target important persons, particularly politicians, who were critical of the government approach and inform them of the facts as the army perceived them to be.

Stalemate continues

The army leadership perceived that troop numbers were still at the heart of the military's failure to restore the authority of the Crown and law and order; and more troops were put into the fray. Montgomery's force was increased to a total of 9 battalions. Yet the demands placed upon his force were still too great. They still had to police too large an area and the number of units which made up his force had become a complex administrative burden upon his HQ. There were two alternatives which Montgomery faced; either there had to be a greater number of brigades or he had to increase the number of staff within each brigade. As any new brigades would take time to learn to operate in Ireland's demanding theatre it was decided to increase the number of staff, and intelligence, officers at Montgomery's disposal. This innovative system proved to be unwieldy and later new brigades were added to Montgomery's 17th Brigade in Cork. The area each brigade operated in was redrawn and these new formations dealt with smaller and more manageable parts of Ireland's lawless South-West.[38]

Political interference and the continual need to seek approval for military actions from far away politicians based in London did little to improve operational effectiveness. This made the work of the commanders on the ground, who were already hamstrung by the unwillingness to commit enough resources to the task, even harder.

By June 1921 there were a total of 51 British army battalions operating in Ireland. 12 were protecting Dublin and its surrounding area; twenty battalions, consisting of approximately 25,000 men, were operating in the martial law area in Ireland's south and south-west. That force also included a number of cavalry regiments and machine gun corps. The pattern of the fighting is shown by the fact that just 14 battalions were allocated to the rest of Ireland. The guarding of internment camps was undertaken by the remaining five battalions. Despite the large number of battalions it was judged that these numbers were insufficient to fully quell the rebellion. From mid-June to mid-July 1921 a further 17 battalions were drafted into Ireland. Seven were sent to the south-west, five to the vicinity of Dublin and the remaining five battalions being distributed to the remainder of Ireland.

The military deadlock was unpalatable to all sides. The IRA was unable to drive the British Army out of Ireland and could not hope to win a conventional battle. Yet at the same time due to a lack of soldiers the British army was finding it increasingly difficult to maintain effective offensive action. What is more due to the growing opposition to British authority, and the non-cooperation which the Army received from much of the general public, the forces of the Crown could only enforce the bare resemblance of control throughout much of South-West Ireland. What is more, in County Cork the size of Tom Barry's IRA force facing Montgomery had not only doubled in size, but had tripled the amount of weapons from the number that it possessed a year before. What is more, its men had become much more experienced in the art of guerrilla war.

The killing was set to continue and the deaths of British serviceman were beginning to weigh heavily upon the government's thinking as to how the conflict should be handled. It was also the case that many British politicians no longer wished to govern that troubled land. Further violence was therefore deemed futile by many in the British government and the IRA leadership. A new way forward was needed to end the military deadlock.

War and Peace Talks

The perception that a negotiated settlement was needed steadily grew amongst all sides. King George V, who had criticised the actions of the Black and Tans and the semi-official policy of reprisals called for reconciliation in Ireland when he opened the Parliament of Northern Ireland in June 1921. To ease the path towards the beginning of negotiations the army sought to take a less provocative approach to its activities and scaled back the reprisals they took when attacked. However, as the British Army reduced its force, the IRA responded by increasing its attacks. And in this new phase to the war the number of British killed and wounded grew from thirty per week in March 1921 to sixty seven in June's first week.[39] Nevertheless, the ground was now clear to approach the Republican leadership to bring about a ceasefire. The Earl of Midleton and General Macready then began unofficial discussions with Republican politicians.

Following those talks on 24th June 1921 David Lloyd George, the Prime Minister of the United Kingdom, wrote to Éamon de Valera, the Sinn Féin leader and President of the Irish Republic. Lloyd George's letter read as follows;

'Sir,

The British Government are deeply anxious that, as far as, they can assure it, the King's appeal for reconciliation in Ireland shall not have been made in vain. Rather than allow

another opportunity of settlement in Ireland to be cast aside,
they felt it incumbent upon them to make a final appeal, in the
spirit of the King's words, for a conference between themselves
and the representatives of Southern and Northern Ireland.
'I write, therefore, to convey the following invitation to you, as
the chosen leader of the great majority in Southern Ireland,
and to Sir James Craig, the Premier of Northern Ireland: -
(1) That you should attend a conference here in London, in
company with Sir James Craig, to explore to the utmost the
possibility of a settlement.
(2) That you should bring with you for the purpose any
colleagues whom you select. The Government will, of course,
give a safe conduct to all who may be chosen to participate in
the conference.
(3) We make this invitation with a fervent desire to end the
ruinous conflict which has for centuries divided Ireland, and
embittered the relations of the peoples of these two islands, who
ought to live in neighbourly harmony with each other, and
whose co-operation would mean so much, not only to the
Empire, but to humanity.
'We wish that no endeavour should be lacking on our part to
realise the King's prayer, and we ask you to meet us, as we will
meet you, in the spirit of conciliation, for which His Majesty
appealed.
'I am, Sir,
Your obedient servant,
D. LLOYD GEORGE.'

de Valera at first did not want to compromise and Lloyd
George's request was not initially accepted. However, on 8th
July 1921 he wrote back to the Prime Minister accepting the
idea of attending a peace conference and a truce was agreed
which came into force at noon on Monday 11th July 1921. The
terms of the truce were intended to create a state of peace

between the warring parties. Nevertheless, whereas the British were not permitted to reinforce its security services in Ireland the IRA used the temporary respite to regroup and rearm.

In due course formal negotiations opened between the British Government and Éamon de Valera and the other leaders of the Republican movement. These developments were claimed by both sides as a victory. The reality was that neither side had achieved their military objectives. Yet, it may have been the case that the British forces were on the verge of temporarily quashing the IRA's guerrilla activity in the period before the truce was declared. However, there was still much fighting to be done.

Despite the negotiations being undertaken under the cover of a truce the reality was that the Irish Republican Army continued some of their operations and attacks on the forces of the Crown; this pattern of repeated attacks lasted for nearly a year after the war had officially ended. The IRA used this time to strengthen their military forces and they were duly aided by many new volunteers to their ranks who came forward once the fighting had formally ceased. Though welcome recruits these late comers were derogatorily called the 'Trucileers' by those Republicans who had actually taken part in the conflict when it was at its height.

The IRA was not the only side to be seeking the military upper hand. The British Army also kept up its pursuit of working out a plan as to how it can impose its will on Ireland. The army saw that it had the duty to restore law and order and make sure that the 'official', as a Unionist would perceive them, organs of the state should be reinforced and returned to their position of authority. As such they were still considering an offensive if the 'peace' broke down.

Already by 16th August 1921, when the summer offensive should have been fully underway Field Marshal Wilson wrote to the Secretary of State for Defence to complain that troops were being withdrawn from Ireland to meet other commitments overseas. At the rate that troops were being taken out of the theatre Field Marshal Wilson predicted that by the end of 1921 13,500 soldiers will have been withdrawn; clearly no way to quash the continuing attacks on British forces. The reduction of men from Ireland meant that by 1st December 1921 infantry battalions would be ration strength numbering on average just 495 soldiers. This effect of this was that the British army was incapable of adequately prosecuting the summer offensive and unable to deal with the conflict in the winter months; a time when the military initiative would switch back to the IRA allowing them to seize back the political initiative in the negotiations.

The army leadership again emphasised the need for more numbers; requesting an additional 40,000 trained soldiers who could be committed to the conflict straight away. These extra troops would allow for the infantry battalions to be brought up to an adequate strength of 800 and ideally 1,000 men. Only through these reinforcements was it felt that the military could meet the challenge of the winter months and take the offensive to the rebels.

The army made the case that if the government decided to continue with military operations then, 'our best chance of a success is to carry them out with the maximum strength which we can possibly attain; this will be cheaper in lives, both for ourselves and for the rebels, and infinitely more certain of successful issue, and in much shorter time that if we attempt such an operation with weak units and bad weather.'[40]

Monty and the Political Settlement

The political 'solution' that was finally achieved from the peace talks pleased few if any but on 6th December 1921 the terms of the Anglo-Irish Treaty was agreed between the representatives of the British Government, the Unionist leadership in Northern Ireland and the representatives of the *Dáil*. However, the Sinn Féin leadership signed only after David Lloyd George warned the Republican delegation that if they did not agree to the terms the war against the IRA would be taken to a new level and the Republicans would face an even more severe crackdown from the British forces.[41]

The main provision of the agreement was that Ireland would become a self-governing dominion within the British Empire along the lines of Canada and Australia. This new nation would become known as the Irish Free State. Although the Irish Free State would be to all intents and purposes an independent nation-state, it would, like other dominions, retain the British monarch as its Head of State. This was a controversial aspect for many within the Republican movement. It is important to note that the peace agreement did not formally partition Ireland between the six northern-eastern counties whose population was mostly Protestant and Unionist and the southern and mostly Roman Catholic 26 counties where a majority of the population had become Republican. Northern Ireland was formally included as a part of the Irish Free State.

The Anglo-Irish Treaty was the conclusion to a long series of discussions on Irish Home Rule which had been overshadowing British politics since the late Victorian era. The idea of a self-governing Ireland was not new and had been accepted by many in the British establishment most notably by the Prime Minister of the United Kingdom, David Lloyd-George. Indeed, the terms of the agreement were not too dissimilar to the provisions of the Government of Ireland Act which had created the Northern and Southern Parliaments. However, the Anglo-Irish Treaty had an important constitutional difference; this was that instead of there being a gradual coming together of the Northern and

Southern Parliaments the North would have the option to secede from the Irish Free State. This they did within one month of the establishment of the Irish Free State. And thus Northern Ireland, which was initially included as part of the Irish Free State, withdrew and remained an integral, but self-governing, part of the United Kingdom.

In this respect the years of fighting and the bloodshed had produced a political settlement that was less favourable to the broader Republican desire of a united Ireland than had previously been on offer by the 1920 Government of Ireland Act, with its Council of Ireland, which was intended to become a legislature for the whole island. Although the 1920 act would have initially brought about devolution within the United Kingdom the constitutional changes may have been the formal beginnings of an amicable parting of the ways between Great Britain and Ireland in its entirety.

The case can therefore be made that the Irish Republican Brotherhood, whose agents succeeded in radicalising so much of Irish political and cultural life, sparked a war which was so bitter that its protagonists could not initially extricate themselves from it despite a number of reasonable offers being placed before them. Firstly during the Irish Convention, before the Anglo-Irish War broke out, and then again when David Lloyd George brought in the Government of Ireland Act 1920. The IRB may well have actually retarded the cause of Irish unity and further embittered relations between the different religious groups on the island; a conflict which is still with us today.

The not unexpected decision of the Parliament of Northern Ireland to use the terms of the Anglo-Irish Treaty to withdraw from the Irish Free State was a matter of great and continuing controversy as it led to the division that still lasts to this day. What is more, the partition of Ireland along county boundaries was a crude device. Due to the varied nature of Irish society such a division left many on what some would argue was the wrong side of the border. To resolve this and deal with changes in the make-up of the population it was envisaged that there would be a Boundary Commission to review and potentially redraw the partition line. However, its leaked proposals for changes sparked protests from all sides and it was decided to abandon the notion of changing the border in any meaningful way and the demarcation was finally confirmed in 1925.

Minor provisions in the treaty were that British military forces would withdraw from the Irish Free State but a presence would be retained in three Irish ports where the Royal Navy kept possession of some bases. These were eventually handed over to the Irish government in 1938 and as such the British military were denied their use when trying to defend the Atlantic Convoys from attack during the Second World War.

The Sinn Féin dominated alternative Republican Parliament, the *Dáil*, narrowly accepted the partition peace agreement in a vote on 7th January 1922. Furthermore, the partition settlement was supported by most of the population in Ireland's southern 26 counties, In the Irish General Election of June 1922 over three quarters of the electorate voted into office candidates that supported the peace treaty. Despite many Loyalists wishing for the whole of Ireland to remain within the UK the agreement did secure the position of the strongly Unionist north-east in the United Kingdom and therefore was an acceptable compromise to those who lived in British Ulster.

This agreement officially led to peace between the Republicans and the British government. However, this peace agreement, like so many political compromises, did not bring about anything like an immediate end to the violence and it was deeply unpopular with many in the IRA. The transition from war to peace was a difficult one and attacks by Republican guerrilla bands, who were often a law unto themselves, on British soldiers continued until as late as June 1922.

During the latter stages of the conflict before the Irish Free State's authority could be imposed in the lawless South-West Monty wrote to his father, Bishop Henry Montgomery, in March 1922 that;

'The situation is really impossible; we have had two officers murdered in the last fortnight; ambulances and lorries are held up almost daily by armed men and the vehicles stolen.'

The *Dáil* and its Provisional Government were in the process of building a viable Irish state out of the wreckage of the war and managing the transition of power from the Crown institutions to those of the Irish Free State. It also set about creating an Irish national army out of the limited number of IRA units that supported the peace treaty. However, as most members of the IRA were opposed to the Treaty they rebelled against their Sinn Féin political leadership in the Provisional Government. These rebels felt that they had been betrayed by the pro-Treaty Dublin based Provisional Government of the Irish Free State which accepted a partitioned Ireland.

They therefore believed that they owed no loyalty to this body, despite it consisting of some of their former comrades-in-arms, which were looking to establish home rule in just 26 of Ireland's 32 counties. In March 1922 the IRA took the step of denouncing the Provisional Government and fought for its overthrow.

Within the power vacuum that was created following the standing down of the forces of the Crown from offensive operations to restore British control Montgomery had to walk a difficult military and political tightrope. He had to balance the contradictory and seeming impossible tasks of maintaining the security of his men, helping to establish the authority of the Provisional Government which was backed by both the pro-Treaty Sinn Féin MPs and the British government whilst at the same time seeking not to respond to the provocation of the IRA guerrillas. As the British Army was preparing to withdraw from the south there was the very real fear that the anti-Treaty forces would mount a *coup d'état*. The IRA also hoped that by continuing the fight against the British army they would ignite a new war where Irish Republicans would unite and resume hostilities against the British in a war where nothing short of full Irish independence would be acceptable. Montgomery was determined not to rise to the bait. In his letter to his father he stated that;

'Our policy is that we do not care what anyone does, or what happens, so long as the troops are left alone and are not interfered with…'

However, Montgomery would not let any aggression towards his men go unpunished, he added that;

'… any civilian, or Republican soldier or policeman, who interferes with any officer or soldier is shot at once… Three armed civilians held up one of our closed cars the other day; they thought it was empty except for the chauffer, and that they would be able to steal it. Unluckily for them there were three British officers inside it; they opened fire at once through the windows with revolvers; two of the civilians were killed, but the third escaped. It was a good lesson for them.'

The continuing attacks even after the peace agreement had been signed took its toll on Montgomery. In his letter he referred in particular to the IRA's taxing of the local population which amounted to little more than a protection racket and by which the 'volunteers' drew their pay. He wrote; 'I shall be heartily glad to see the last of the people and the place.'[42]

According to Monty's younger brother, Brian Montgomery, in his book *A Field Marshal in the Family*, Bernard Law Montgomery thought that the continued presence of British troops in Southern Ireland was a difficult and demoralising task. Monty wrote that,

'It really is most degrading for us soldiers to stay on here…
It is very difficult to find out how long they intend to keep us
here in the south of Ireland… We have to be very careful as a
false step would be a match that would set the whole country
ablaze again… '

Montgomery was careful that he did not ignite a new fire. During a particularly tense time following the IRA's seizing on 29th March 1922 of a significant cache of British arms and ammunition which were due to be transported back to Britain an event occurred which may have led to even more bloodshed. There was a fear that the troops of the Royal Warwickshire Regiment would retaliate after a number of their fellow soldiers including one of Monty's intelligence officers, the well-liked Lieutenant H D Hendy, were taken captive and murdered by the IRA in April 1922. Therefore, Montgomery did not initially inform the Royal Warwickshires of this outrage which happened many months after the war was meant to be over. In May, after painstaking negotiations and near clashes between the IRA and an army search party the bodies of the murdered men were eventually recovered by Montgomery.[43]

Following the British withdrawal from the 26 counties the ethnic cleansing of some of those that were from Ireland's minority tradition, Protestantism, continued. Before the fighting started Protestants constituted 10% of the population of what became the Irish Free State. However, following home rule this number shrank rapidly to as little as 3%. Likewise, the area in the north run by the Belfast Parliament based at Stormont became perceived to be enforcing sectarian divisions against the Roman Catholics.

The pro-Treaty leaders in the south felt that any questioning of the authority of the Irish Free State was an act of rebellion by their former comrades which would have to be put down by force of arms. A bloody civil war followed in which it has been estimated that more people were killed than died in the previous years fighting against the forces of the British Crown.

Once the Irish Civil War had ended in favour of the Irish Free State's government peace finally came to the south and in time it officially became independent of the British Empire when it adopted its own statehood and new constitution in 1937. The last vestiges of Crown Authority being removed in 1949 when the Republic of Ireland was formed and so, bar the six counties of the North, the Irish Free State evolved into a new nation that was completely independent of the United Kingdom. The Irish polity adopted a politically liberal-democratic constitution but this was not without some controversial social aspects which some can argue were not appropriate in a modern society. The Republic was certainly a state that in terms of family law was less liberal than that of the remaining United Kingdom.

Montgomery's conduct during the campaign

Montgomery reflected on the campaign, writing about the effectiveness of the men under his command. He wrote;

"In many ways this war was far worse than the Great War which had ended in 1918. It developed into a murder campaign in which, in the end, the soldiers became very skilful and more than held their own."

However, he did not view this conflict positively as he recognised the physiological impact such fighting had;

"… Such a war is thoroughly bad for officers and men; it tends to lower their standards of decency and chivalry, and I was glad when it was over."[44]

A prime example of this murderous struggle occurred on 20th February 1921 in County Cork. After a series of attacks on the forces of the Crown, including a bomb which targeted a marching military band, IRA activists were cornered in a farmhouse in the hamlet of Clonmult. When the twenty IRA men realised that they had been trapped fighting broke out between the besieging Hampshire Regiment of the British Army, supported by members of the Royal Irish Constabulary and the Black and Tan auxiliaries, and the rebels. In the initial exchanges the two guerillas who noticed the advance of the Crown forces and opened fire were shot and killed. Four of the IRA men attempted to break out, three of whom were killed, with one making good his escape.

The fog of war and political propaganda means that there is a dispute as to what happened next. Two of the Black and Tans were killed, allegedly when they tried to take the surrender of the Republicans. The standoff was brought to an end when the thatched roof of the cottage in which the IRA men were holding out was set alight and this forced the surrender of those inside. . Seven of the prisoners were then summarily executed by the Black and Tans. Further killings by the Black and Tans were stopped by Lieutenant A. Koe, the commanding officer of the British soldiers involved in the operation. What is certain is that of the 20 original members of the cottage only eight survived, four of whom were wounded, but two of these prisoners were later tried by a military court and were sentenced to death and executed. This action led to the near complete elimination of the East Cork flying column of active IRA insurgents.

However, it is worth noting in any evaluation of Montgomery's role in Ireland that the killing of the IRA militants who had surrendered was carried out by members of the Black and Tans and the Royal Irish Constabulary. The killers may have been as Irish as the rebels, as they would have seen them. Also Irish were the six civilians who were alleged by the IRA to be British spies and were blamed by them for the uncovering of the rebel safe house. These scapegoats for the massacre were killed by the IRA in the week following the Clonmult ambush.

Montgomery had his own personal stake in this contest over the future of Ireland, yet the evidence suggests that unlike many of his contemporaries he fought an honourable war. This is remarkable when it is considered that Monty's cousin, Hugh Montgomery, was assassinated by the IRA. And it is especially extraordinary when his Protestant Irish Unionist heritage, anathema to the Republicans, was taken into account. The bloodiest aspect of the Anglo-Irish War was the internecine nature of the conflict between fellow Irishmen, those who favoured a separation from the United Kingdom and those who remained Loyal. Furthermore, Montgomery's family had much to lose if an independent Irish Republic was formed but still Montgomery remained professional. He was opposed to reprisals against the civilian population and carried out his duties in an 'objective, dispassionate and efficient way.'[45]

The view that he was a hard but fair opponent is supported even by some in the IRA. Tom Barry, one of the outstanding IRA guerrilla leaders of the war and a key opponent of Montgomery in Cork, said that Monty "behaved with great correctness".[46]

Chapter 7

AFTERMATH IN IRELAND

Although the casualties from the Anglo-Irish War were not as severe as those which occurred in the Irish Civil War which followed the peace Treaty, but they were still significant.

Out of the 66,000 soldiers and policemen based in Ireland 555 had lost their lives and 1,027 were wounded as a result of the fighting. The vast majority of those killed came from the police service and numbered 513. The IRA, whose active guerrilla force consisted of several thousand volunteers, suffered around 650 deaths in the war. Many thousands of insurgents were also imprisoned and interred. Assessments of the number of civilians killed in Ireland during the conflict vary from 300 to as many as 1,000. 198 of these deaths took place in County Cork where 189 also suffered wounds as a result of the conflict. Of the 198 deaths, 122 were assassinated by the IRA on the grounds that they were spies for the British. Far more were killed than actually informed for the police. The majority of the victims were innocent civilians. Evidence suggests that just 38 of those killed were involved in supplying information to the forces of the Crown. Groups which often fell victim to the IRA and were disproportionally targeted included travellers, tramps and of course Protestants.

From 1920 to the 'truce' in July 1921 there were six people

killed and 19 wounded by the IRA on the British mainland.[47] The assassination of Sir Henry Wilson occurred in London in June 1922 after the UK had agreed to the creation of the Irish Free State and had already withdrawn many troops from the south.

Lessons to be learned

Montgomery recognised that achieving victory in Ireland would have involved one of two main alternatives. The first was to escalate the conflict to a level not yet seen and crush the rebellion. The second alternative was to find a political solution. Politics was outside of Montgomery's remit, so he understandably concentrated on the military option.

Successful guerrilla campaigns rely upon close cooperation between the fighters and their civilian base of support, which the guerrillas rely on for shelter, supplies of food, arms and ammunition. The insurgents were often indistinguishable from the general population; therefore to stop their attacks and weed out the rebels and separate them from their civilian base of support which they relied upon would have involved severe measures to lock down the Irish countryside as well as its cities. This would have inevitably involved the introduction of even harsher repressive measures against the general population. Despite the fact that many civilians were aiding and abetting the Republican insurgency, this would have caused outrage in Britain, let alone in Ireland, and even more resentment amongst many on that island which would have smouldered and no doubt erupted again at some point in the future.

Montgomery wrote about the conflict in a letter to Arthur Percival who was a British Army Major and would later surrender Singapore to the Japanese in 1942. Percival had served as an intelligence officer and aggressive counter-insurgency commander during the fighting in County Cork. Monty wrote;

'My own view is that to win a war of that sort you must be ruthless; Oliver Cromwell, or the Germans, would have settled it in a very short time. Now-a-days public opinion precludes such methods; the nation would never allow it, and the politicians would lose their jobs if they sanctioned it.[48]

When Montgomery wrote of the role of Oliver Cromwell in Ireland he was referring to his actions commanding the New Model Army, the magnificent force that had won the English Civil War for Parliament against King Charles I. This army along with its Irish Protestant allies managed, between 1649 and 1653, to engage and crush the Irish Roman Catholic and English Royalist resistance to the Puritan dominated Commonwealth (republic) which had recently been established.

This conflict did involve some conventional warfare which proved disastrous for the Royalist and Roman Catholic Irish forces, but it soon descended into a bloody guerrilla war. Large bands of native Irish forces, known as Tories from the Irish word *tóraidhe* which means outlaw or pursued man, roamed the Irish countryside. The New Model Army's response to these insurgents was one of severe repression. Ireland was divided up into different zones. Some were protected areas and were safe from the repressive actions of the army. But others suffered a scorched earth policy. In these 'Tory' areas all civilians would be treated as enemy combatants and many were killed or sold into slavery. To prevent the guerrillas living off the land cattle and peasants, whom the insurgents would have relied upon, were driven out. The fighting eventually petered out in favour of the Cromwellian forces.

What Montgomery was most likely unaware of was the little known fact that the repressive measures of the English Protestant forces actually led to many Irish Roman Catholics joining the ranks of the New Model Army as a matter of necessity. These volunteers would thus be fed and receive a living.

Notwithstanding that largely unknown fact, the legacy of that bitter conflict endured and was whipped up against the Crown during Montgomery's time. This was the case even though Cromwell was a republican fighting against the Royalist forces that supported the Stuart dynasty which many Irish recognised as their lawful rulers. Nevertheless, in that day and age history and its resentments and perceived injustices were alive and ever present. Furthermore, despite Republican propaganda, Cromwell had banned his forces from plundering. He ordered his troops to purchase their food from the local inhabitants. What is more, many of the most famous incidents of the murder and systematic slaughter of civilians –like those that followed the storming of the Royalist fortress of Drogheda – have been greatly exaggerated or entirely invented by cynical political propagandists.

Montgomery had thought about the war's bigger political picture and after reflecting at great length on the issue of Ireland he came to the conclusion that there was a definite need for a political solution. Nevertheless, there were those in the British Army who thought that the forces of the crown were on the verge of achieving a military victory where they would crush the IRA. It was certainly the case that the Republican guerrillas never came anywhere near to accomplishing the end game scenario of guerrilla warfare; that of confining the army to its bases and urban centres whilst the irregular forces would rule in the countryside. This would have allowed the IRA to gradually whittle down the conventional army until it lost parity with the rebels in terms of military strength. In reality throughout most of Ireland the IRA and its leadership realised that it was the Republican forces, and not the British, which were being worn down and forced on to the back foot. It is worth considering if a supreme effort by the British Army and its supporting police units would have delivered a lasting peace?

Arthur Percival, for one, believed a British military victory was at hand and he was not alone in holding that view. Lieutenant General Sir Peter Strickland, the commander of 6th Division and military governor of the martial law area of Ireland, was also of the opinion that the British Army was winning the war in Ireland and they were on the verge of defeating the IRA. In military terms such men thought that the 'truce' and peace talks effectively allowed the British authorities to snatch defeat out of the jaws of victory. Perhaps the ceasefire had allowed the Republican forces to escape being routed; but Montgomery could see the bigger picture. In a letter between Montgomery and Arthur Percival, where Monty discussed his experiences in Ireland he also presented his thoughts on the necessity as he saw it of reaching a peace deal with his enemies;

'… I consider that Lloyd George was really right in what he did; if we had gone on we could probably have squashed the rebellion as a temporary measure, but it would have broken out again like an ulcer the moment we had removed the troops; I think the rebels would probably have refused battles, and hidden their arms, etc. until we had gone. The only way therefore was to give them some form of self-government, and let them squash the rebellion themselves… [49]

Montgomery was not alone in drawing the conclusion that reaching a political settlement was the right course of action. Winston Churchill recognised the murderous nature of the conflict and saw that in 1921 there was a need for negotiations to end the conflict. Churchill wrote;

What was the alternative? It was to plunge one small corner of the empire into an iron repression, which could not be carried out without an admixture of murder and counter-murder…. Only national self-preservation could have excused such a policy, and no reasonable man could allege that self-preservation was involved. [50]

Perhaps this is a case of great minds thinking alike.

Key to Montgomery's conclusions was his unique understanding of the nature of the rebellion against the presence of the British state in Ireland. Montgomery understood that this was a nationalist uprising against British rule. And that this rebellion was by the 1920s supported by the overwhelming Roman Catholic population of the area that Montgomery was trying to pacify. What is more, the IRA knew that this base of support made a British victory highly improbable. It may seem surprising that the much smaller and less well equipped IRA were not wiped out by the militarily superior British army and supporting units. However, despite the fact that the IRA was greatly outnumbered the answer to the enigma of why a full British victory was never achieved was summed up by the West Cork guerrilla commander Tom Barry. He wrote that,

'... in the last analysis the struggle was never one between the British Army and a small force of Flying Columns and Active Service Units. Had this been so, the few Flying Columns operating would not have existed for a month, no matter how bravely and skilfully they fought.'

Barry further explained that,

This was a war between the British Army and the Irish people, and the problem before the British from mid-1920 was not how to smash the Flying Columns, but how to destroy the resistance of a people, for, as sure as day follows night, if a Flying Column were wiped out in any area, another would arise to continue the attacks on, and the resistance to the alien rulers. The Irish people had many weapons which the British lacked: their belief in the righteousness of their cause, their determination to be free... and a strong body of militant youth, who, though as yet unarmed, were a potential army of great possibilities. [51]

However, what was politically acceptable, i.e. the British army evacuating the mostly southern 26 counties of Ireland and the partition of that island, was not immediately practical. It did ultimately bring a peace of a kind; but only after more ethnic cleansing, a bloody civil war and a continuing on/off armed conflict against the British Army and the authorities of the largely pro-British Parliament based at Stormont in Belfast which administered the North-eastern and mostly Protestant and Unionist six counties.

The Irish Civil War was a vicious conflict. It lasted from June 1922 until May 1923. It was a direct consequence of the disagreements over the Anglo-Irish Treaty which ended British rule in most of Ireland and brought about the creation of the Irish Free State. The military forces of the fledgling Irish Free State were aided in their fight against the anti-treaty faction by the UK who supplied the Irish provisional government with arms and ammunition. It was almost a proxy war between the forces of the Crown and the militants in the IRA. In that conflict the hard-line Republicans in the IRA were finally defeated by the forces of their fellow Irishmen serving the newly formed Government of the Irish Free State. Montgomery in his discussions with Arthur Percival insightfully wrote about this internecine conflict. In the Irish Civil War, and the Irish Free State's struggle against the most radical of the nationalist forces, Montgomery thought that the Irish are;

'... the only people who could really stamp it out, and they are still trying to do so and as far as one can tell they seem to be having a fair amount of success. I am not however in close touch with the situation over there; but it seems to me that they have had more success than we had'. [52]

Tom Barry, who had evaded the best efforts of the Crown

forces to capture him since the Anglo-Irish War began, was seized by the army of the Irish Free State on 29th June 1922 as he attempted to link up with the anti-Treaty forces of the IRA who were opposed to the peace agreement with Britain. It is ironic that during his time in prison the troops guarding him had served with Irish Regiments in the British Army which had been dissolved when the peace deal was finally agreed upon. These former soldiers in the British Army had then sought employment with the new government of Ireland's 26 southern counties.

Montgomery's military insights were correct. Law and order was finally restored but this could not be achieved by an army that had come to be perceived by many of the local inhabitants as an occupying force from a foreign land. The Anglo-Irish War was, as Montgomery correctly concluded, primarily a nationalist revolt and any attempt to enforce peace upon that troubled island by anyone other than fellow Irishmen would be bound to just add to the bitterness and was destined to eventually fail unless of course the most oppressive measures were undertaken.

Montgomery, with his reputation greatly enhanced, left Ireland in May 1922 to become the Brigade-Major of the 8th Infantry Brigade, based on the British mainland in Plymouth. This new appointment saw him join part of the Army's 3rd Division the force which he would lead into combat against Germany in less than two decades later.

Chapter 8

MONTGOMERY AFTER IRELAND

'Monty taught the students how to win battles.' [53]
General Sir Dudley Ward on Montgomery's military tuition

Montgomery had a multitude of different roles after he and his troops had left southern Ireland. Following Monty's time with the 8th Infantry Brigade; the different positions that he held included an appointment which he took up in 1923 that effectively made him the Chief of Staff of a Territorial Army Division. He was also posted back to his original regiment, the Royal Warwickshire Regiment, in 1925 and in 1926 he became an instructor at his old Staff College based in Camberley where he had once been a student. The role of a Military Instructor was to suit him and he performed well at this task in a later appointment. He certainly had a lot to teach.

In 1930 Montgomery's knowledge was recognised by the War Office who commissioned him to re-write the British Army's *Infantry Training Manual*. Monty turned this into what he described as, 'a comprehensive treatise on war for the infantry officer.' Montgomery was not afraid to make sure that the manual reflected his vision. He wrote in his memoirs that;

'All my work had to be approved by a committee in the War

*Office and some heated arguments took place; I could not
accept many of their amendments to my doctrine of infantry
war. We went through the manual, chapter by chapter. I then
recommended that the committee should disband and that I
complete the book in my own time; this was agreed. I produced
the final draft, omitting all the amendments the committee
had put forward. The book when published was considered
excellent, especially by its author.'* [54]

One of the key aspects which emerged in Montgomery's
theory of warfare was his emphasis on meticulous planning and
preparation and the building up of an overwhelming force that
could be concentrated against a relatively narrow part of the
enemies lines where it would achieve a decisive breakthrough.
Monty believed that these military operations should follow the
commander's master plan and all other tactics used on the
battlefield should be subordinated to fulfilling the overall
strategic objectives of his plans. Montgomery also advocated
that offensive plans should be flexible, what he described as
having balance, with reserves that could meet the changing
demands on the battlefield as the fighting develops. Mobile
warfare was part of this theory but his concept on the conduct
of war did not encourage the use of random uncoordinated
attacks in the hope of achieving a breakthrough which could
then hopefully be exploited. Montgomery's way was a very
deliberate approach to combat which he championed and he
was not without his critics.

The *Infantry Training Manual* was not the only work on
military theory and battle tactics that he would write during the
earlier part of his career. Throughout the 1920s and the 1930s
Montgomery was a prolific author of articles on the successful
execution of his profession – warfare.

In the mid-1920s Montgomery had a number of articles
published in the military journal of the Royal Warwickshire

Regiment known as *The Antelope*; which was named after the mascot of that regiment. His publications on military theory included articles on 'The Growth of Modern Infantry Tactics' and another on 'Some Problems of Mechanization'.

Monty did not confine his writing to the Royal Warwickshire Regiment's journal. In the Army Quarterly he also wrote about issues relating to training in the Territorial Army in an article which the editors of that publication titled 'Letter of Advice to a Newly Appointed Adjutant in the TA'. Through his writing he also gave advice on how a battle should be conducted when opposing armies collide and meet each other in battle without being able to organise their offence or defence in advance. In 1938, as the storm clouds began to grow over Europe, Montgomery wrote an article titled 'The Major Tactics of the Encounter Battle'. This was published in *The Army Quarterly*. *The Royal Engineers Journal* also published his theories when his work titled 'The Problem of the Encounter Battle as Affected by Modern British War Establishment' was reproduced.

It would not be long until he could put his concepts to the test. Before that Monty's career continued to flourish, in 1931 he was promoted to full Lieutenant Colonel and given command of the 1st Battalion of the Royal Warwickshire Regiment. Early that same year Montgomery and his battalion were posted to Palestine.

Palestine 1931

After the Irish campaign the next posting that added to Montgomery's counter-insurgency experience, and would most certainly give him a superb grounding in tackling the 1936 - 39 Arab Revolt, was his first role in the Holy Land.

In 1931 Montgomery was dispatched to Palestine where he commanded all British troops there, including his own Royal Warwickshire Regiment and a battalion of the King's Own as well as Arab cavalry stationed in the valley area of the River Jordon. Montgomery also had the role of liaising with the French forces based in Syria and the Lebanon and the forces stationed in Transjordan (now the Kingdom of Jordan).

He was the overall commander of the British Army in Palestine and as Montgomery was the senior officer there he was effectively the military governor of the mandated territory. As the military commander of Palestine on his arrival he travelled all over the country, understanding the military situation, the topography of the land and characteristically of Montgomery he got to know the many troops stationed there and just as importantly allowed them to get to know him.

During this first tour in Palestine Montgomery had to use the forces under his control as part of a continual policing operation in order to keep a lid on the tinderbox environment of increasing tensions between Jewish settlers, the Arab population and the British army. The task of keeping order was not one that could be taken lightly. British forces were virtually on a permanent state of readiness in case the tensions, which were always brewing just under the surface, erupted into open violence and ultimately rebellion. Despite the various religious groups provoking each other Montgomery's policing of Palestine successfully kept the peace allbeit an uneasy one. A measure of Montgomery's success is that rebellion did not break out until several years after he had departed Palestine. And his return to the Mandate in 1938 was the key to quashing the serious conflict that was the 1936 – 1939 Arab Revolt.

After Montgomery's first tour of duty in Palestine his next posting was to a strategically significant part of the Middle East, Egypt. Unlike many of his contemporaries he did not care for excessive spit and polish nor for endless drill. In Monty's outlook pomp and ceremony were not the essential pre-requisites to success in warfare. Montgomery concentrated on training his soldiers in useful battlefield skills which included taking the troops out on manoeuvres that would in some instances last for several days. All the tactics that an infantry man would need were practiced; these ranged from taking part in operations where the object was to defend a location from attack to others aimed at successfully prosecuting an assault. Many of these simulated operations were carried out at night. Not only did the soldiers benefit from these exercises, but just as importantly Montgomery's leadership skills were sharpened by these manoeuvres. This was to have important consequences when the British army under his control was to face their German counterparts in 1940.

When Montgomery was a Divisional commander of part of the British Expeditionary Force sent to the continent to fight the forces of Nazi Germany, his professionalism enabled him to recognise the parlous state that the Allied forces were in. He knew that the Allies were ill-prepared to face the German Blitzkrieg on France and the Low Countries in 1940. Montgomery, however, was able to use his leadership skills to extricate his men from the tactical mess the ineffective higher leadership had placed them in. Montgomery's repeated practicing of night time operations gave him the skills to move his division after dark. He managed to successfully bring them out of danger allowing the British line to be reinforced until they were evacuated from Dunkirk along with hundreds of thousands of other allied servicemen.

Montgomery did not just care for the welfare of the men by making sure that they were properly prepared to face an enemy in combat. Part of the problem for British soldiers in rural isolated Ireland had been the lack of entertainment and opportunities for relaxation where the troops could escape the stresses and strains of soldiering. A decade after the war with the IRA Montgomery made sure that this was not a scenario faced by his men in Egypt. During his time in the land of the pyramids in the early 1930s he showed concern for the health and happiness of his men in a very unique way. Montgomery established a brothel for the soldiers of his battalion. As his ability to train soldiers were obvious for all to see his superiors turned a blind eye to this nonconformist behaviour.

Back to the Frontier

Before the brewing conflict in Palestine could erupt into open warfare Montgomery was posted back to the area that gave him his first experience of soldiering, the North-West Frontier. After a brief time stationed in India Montgomery was given a task that suited him to the utmost. From 1934 to 1937 Montgomery trained the troops at a college that was close to the Afghan border and home to the forefathers of our present opponents in modern Afghanistan. He taught the British soldiers at the highly regarded Indian Army Staff College based at Quetta. Close to the Afghan border Quetta is a city typical of the North-West Frontier; it is in mountainous country with a lofty altitude of over 6,000 feet above sea level. It is an ironic that Quetta, now in Pakistan and once a seat of British power, is nowadays the homeland of the Pakistani Taleban and a training ground for Britain's modern opponents in Afghanistan and a centre of organisation against the West's continued presence in that troubled country.

As the Staff College was held in high-esteem it was an honour for Montgomery to be posted there especially as the then Colonel Montgomery was the Chief Instructor with all the instructors operating under his leadership. Here he trained the future leaders of the British Army whilst facing Afghan tribesman across the border. There had been a third Anglo-Afghan War in 1919 and this left a legacy of tension amongst the population on both sides of the border.

Montgomery not only taught but, as was the nature of the man, also learnt at the Staff College. He became an early advocate of the use of air power in conjunction with ground forces and the integration of the different branches of the armed services, combining them in operations. He also noted that a Commander-in-Chief needs to be visible. Montgomery's appreciation of this important part of leadership became a key trait of his generalship not only in his future battles against insurgents but also in the campaigns for which he is now most celebrated, his victories at El-Alamein and at D-Day and the resulting Normandy campaign. In these key and decisive battles he became renowned for his prior preparation and his meeting with the troops and making sure they knew the role they had to play. Importantly for the coming conflict in Palestine he taught all aspects of warfare including internal security, a skill that was needed in that region then as it is now in the modern era. This would have sharpened his mind towards counter-insurgency operations.

Montgomery won many plaudits for his superb teaching and was considered a successful instructor. One former student that rose to become a general in the Second World War, Sir Dudley Ward, said of his tuition 'Monty taught the students how to win battles.'[55] He was not alone in his assessment of Montgomery. Michael Carver, who like Monty himself later became a Field Marshal and Chief of the Defence Staff, wrote in the book *Churchill's Generals* that Monty 'excelled as an instructor, analysing the problem with remorseless logic, simplifying and explaining it with terse clarity and mastery of detail.' [56]

Montgomery not only taught, he also used his organisation skills to their utmost when he ran a refugee camp following an earthquake in 1935 which blighted the frontier region and killed 30,000 people. His tackling of the devastation following the disaster against a backdrop of terrible conditions with disease threatening to break out was widely considered a success. His achievement was all the greater as the even wrose humanitarian twin disasters of there being both a typhoid and cholera epidemic were avoided. This region to this day remains one that is regularly blighted by natural disasters from earthquakes to floods.

In 1937 Montgomery received promotion to the rank of Brigadier and was given command of the 9th Infantry Brigade. This brigade was part of the 3rd (Iron) Division, now known as the 3rd Mechanised Division. The next year Montgomery was to be sent back to Palestine to end the Arab Revolt and restore law and order.

Part III

Palestine

Chapter 9

MONTGOMERY AND THE ARAB REVOLT IN PALESTINE 1936–39

'... hunt down and destroy the rebel armed gangs. They must be hunted relentlessly; when engaged in battle we must shoot to kill... This is the surest way to end the war.'
Montgomery on tackling Palestine's Arab Revolt [57]

This campaign was Montgomery's *tour de force* when combatting guerrilla forces. His entry into this conflict began in late 1938 and he described it as 'a task greatly to my liking'.[58] He estimated in January 1939 that he would take six months to crush the Arab Rebellion. By July of that same year Montgomery reported 'This rebellion is now definitely and finally smashed.' [59]

Background to the conflict

Britain took over Palestine during the First World War after driving out the forces of the Turkish Ottoman Empire. Although British rule had been sanctioned by the League of Nations, the forerunner of the United Nations, which Mandated the territory to the UK the reality was that Palestine was a colony of the British Empire. At this time many different peoples around the world desired self-determination, so the Arab people were not unique in this. They had started a rebellion against the Ottomans which they hoped would achieve independence and self-rule but seen this snatched away by both the British and the French. The French took control of the Lebanon and Syria as their mandated territories, and they themselves had to face rebellion from Syria's Arab population.

However, a new dimension into the mix of occupiers and occupied had been added which made a bloody rebellion even more likely. In the 19th Century the idea of the Jewish people being given a homeland, a concept known as Zionism, began to take hold. By the early 20th Century, a time when Arab nationalism was also developing, many Jews were settling in Palestine an area that roughly corresponds to the ancient biblical lands of Israel.

Although Jewish settlement in Palestine pre-dated the First World War, the policy of the British Government had then became one of actively supporting the immigration of Jews into the Holy Land. In 1917 the British Government issued what is known as the Balfour Declaration. This read,

'His Majesty's Government view with favour the establishment in Palestine of a national home for the Jewish people and will use their best endeavours to facilitate the achievement of that object...

Interestingly it goes on to state,

'... it being understood that nothing shall be done which may

prejudice the Civil and Religious rights of existing non-Jewish communities in Palestine or the rights and political status enjoyed by the Jews in any other country.'

This declaration was later included in the League of Nations Mandate, which formally approved British control over Palestine, and was endorsed by the other members of the League.

However, the term 'national home' was never clearly defined. The British had suggested that it only meant land on which they can establish homes and farms. Yet many Zionists did not disguise their intentions of creating a majority Jewish sovereign state. Indeed, the hard-line Jewish Revisionist Party actually advocated the forceful conquest of both Palestine and Trans-Jordan to create a Jewish state on both sides of the River Jordan.

Much of the problem was caused by confusion over the conflicting international legal obligations and their interpretation. The British authorities were fulfilling those laid down to them by the Balfour Declaration and the League of Nations Mandate, however, the Arab population had no reason to accept this and counter claimed that the 1915 Damascus Protocol, made to King Hussein of the Hedjaz, promised that the area of Palestine was part of the Arab lands that would be made independent after the Ottoman Turks were driven out.

When the rebellion began the majority of the population were Arabs. Of a total population of 1,336,000, 942,000 were Arabic of which 843,000 were Muslim and 87,000 Christian and 12,000 belonging to other faiths, such as the Druze who are a unique religious sect that evolved out of Islam but is seen as heretical by many Muslim leaders and as such has suffered persecution throughout much of their history. There was also an assortment of other ethnicities in Palestine with 24,000 coming from a number of varied backgrounds but there was already a significant and growing Jewish population of 370,000. In the two years preceding the rebellion over 100,000 Jewish immigrants arrived in Palestine, many fleeing anti-semitic persecution in Europe. Significant land purchases by Jews resulted in many Arabs having to leave their land.

The conflict between Arab and Israeli has been viewed as a battle between two distinct communities of different ethnic and linguistic backgrounds. However, the ethnicity of the combatants was not the only factor in determining how a resident of Palestine viewed British rule. The leaders of the Arab Revolt were mostly Muslim as were the bulk of the Arab guerrilla bands. Palestine's Arab Christian and Druze population displayed a markedly different attitude to the British authorities. During the Arab Revolt, the Christians and Druze population of Palestine, although ethnically and linguistically as Arab as their Muslim neighbours, were less opposed to the colonial authorities and often welcomed the British army.[60]

There had been limited outbreaks of violence and attempts by Palestinian Arab nationalists to foment rebellion against British rule in Palestine twice in the early 1920s and in 1929, again in 1933 and in 1935. These were quickly suppressed by the British Imperial forces and the uprisings failed to spark a general Arab rebellion, but this was not far away.

The tensions and violence between the Jewish settlers, their Arab neighbours and the British occupying forces resulted in the Arab General Strike which began on 19th April 1936. This strike included an Arab boycott of Jewish and British businesses. Violent rioting and civil disobedience quickly followed; and from there the situation rapidly spiralled out of control to a full rebellion against the British presence in Palestine and Jewish immigration. By 7th September 1936 the government described the events in Palestine as; "A direct challenge to the authority of the British Government in Palestine."[61] As 1937 got under way British control of large parts of Palestine had effectively ceased, and law and order had broken down with much of the Mandate erupting in conflict.

The influx of immigrants was not however the only factor. It did of course mean the writing was on the wall for the viability, or lack of, a continued Arab presence in much of Palestine; yet there were other issues that drove the revolt. There was of course the economic hardships caused by a drop in the number of tourists, and there was the feeling that with Iraq gaining independence from the British the time had come for an independent Arab state in Palestine. However, key to the tensions boiling over into revolt was the British loss of prestige during the 1935 Mediterranean Crisis which came along after the failure to prevent Fascist Italy from seizing Abyssinia; this made the British Empire appear to be vulnerable and reaching a nadir.

Chapter 10

THE OPPOSING FORCES IN PALESTINE

The Arab Leaders

Much of the violence had sprung up organically amongst the Arab people often driven by wild and unfounded rumours of massacres by Jews. Following the breakdown in law and order prominent Arabs then used the unstable conditions as an opportunity to create the full-scale rebellion of which they had long dreamed.

At the head was the Grand Mufti of Jerusalem, the Cleric who had authority over Islam's Holy Places in Jerusalem. His full name and title was Haj Mohammad Effendi Amin al Husseini. He was also President of the Supreme Muslim Council. This organisation was in charge of the affairs of Palestine's Muslim community. Its purpose was to advise the British High Commissioner for Palestine but gradually gained more authority over the religious activities of the local Islamic inhabitants.

The Mufti was the most ardent opponent of British rule, ironically the position of Mufti had increased in political authority and influence throughout Palestine as a result of changes made by the British authorities. What is more, Haj Mohammad Effendi Amin al Husseini, a known Arab nationalist, was actually appointed to the role by the British High Commissioner of Palestine, Sir, later Viscount, Herbert Samuel.

The Grand Mufti's hand was strengthened when the moderate President of the Defence Party, Ragheb Bey Nashashibi, joined with him to oppose the continued British presence in Palestine. When these forces combined, on 25th April 1936, the insurgency began its bloody escalation. They formed what was called the Arab Higher Committee. This led the Palestinian fight for home rule, an end to Jewish immigration and to keep the remaining land in Arab hands. The rebel leadership used the cause of Arab nationalism, the threat posed by Jewish immigration and even Islamic propaganda to fuel the revolt.

A key military leader was Fawzi el Qawukji. He was a Syrian who had developed his martial skills during the First World War and later in the 1925 Arab Revolt against French rule in Syria. He also brought to bear on the British forces in Palestine his experience from his service with the Iraqi army.

The Mufti was the political leader of the revolt and he had most of his influence in northern Palestine. Other important military leaders were Abdullah el Asbar, whose forces operated in the north particularly around Galilee. The leadership of the guerrilla bands in the centre of Palestine was taken by Sheikh Attieh. Many of the Arab bands remained a law unto themselves and did not operate in unison with each other along centralised lines of command and control.

The British Leaders

The Prime Minister at the start of the conflict was the Conservative politician Stanley Baldwin. He and his government had begun a process of rearmament; at the time this was politically controversial and was attacked by the Opposition

Labour Party. Despite later accusations that the programme of improving Britain's military capability was not enough it was an important beginning that would help improve Britain's defences in the coming conflict with the Nazis. In May 1937 Baldwin was succeeded by Neville Chamberlain, he also supported rearmament in particular a strengthening of Britain's airpower. Chamberlain will ever be associated with the policy of appeasement towards Hitler and German expansionism; yet his government, despite his leaning towards the Arab side was to prosecute a ruthless war in Palestine in defence of Britain's imperial interests.

During the Arab Revolt in Palestine there were three Whitehall based professional heads of the British Army, known as The Chief of the Imperial General Staff (CIGS). These were firstly Field Marshall Archibald Montgomery-Massingberd, he was a Montgomery from Ulster in Ireland; Massingberd was the surname he adopted from his aristocratic wife. Montgomery-Massingberd retired soon after the conflict had started. He was succeeded by Field Marshall Sir Cyril John Deverell who stayed in post until 1937 when the Viscount Gort assumed the role of CIGS. Gort was later to command the retreat to Dunkirk in 1940, serve as Governor of Malta 1942-44 and became the High Commissioner for Palestine in 1944.

The key military figures based in Palestine included General Sir Arthur Grenfell Wauchope who served from the beginning of the conflict until March 1938 as the High Commissioner for Palestine and Trans-Jordan. He was also the Commander-in-Chief of British military forces in the Mandate territory. During his spell as the head of Britain's administration in Palestine the handling of the revolt was lacklustre and he failed to deal with the conflict successfully. Upon General Grenfell Wauchope's retirement in 1938 Sir Harold MacMichael, a professional civil servant and experienced colonial administrator, took over the position of High Commissioner in 1938 and would remain in post throughout the remainder of the conflict and was succeeded by Viscount Gort.

From September 1936 British forces in Palestine were headed by General John Dill, who later become a Field Marshall and Chief of the Imperial General Staff and later served on the Combined Chiefs of Staff committee which was the supreme military command of the Western Allies in World War II. Dill commanded British forces in Palestine for nearly a year when in August 1937 General Archibald Percival Wavell became the General Officer Commanding-in-Chief of British forces in Palestine and Trans-Jordan. He held this position until 1938 when he departed for Britain to take over the command of troops in the south of the United Kingdom. He later rose to become both a Field Marshal and an Earl. He achieved some stunning victories over the Italians in North Africa during Second World War, but stripped of resources by Churchill who diverted much of his strength to Greece, he suffered defeat at the hands of Montgomery's later opponent in North Africa and Normandy, Erwin Rommel. He also became the penultimate Viceroy of India. Wavell was succeeded by Lieutenant-General Sir Robert Hadden Haining who then took over the command.

When Palestine was divided up into military districts in the autumn of 1938 Montgomery was made area commander for the key northern sector, with his 8th Division. The 7th Division under Major-General General Richard O'Connor had the responsibility of fighting the insurgents in the south of the country. Richard O'Connor, under Wavell, was to be a highly successful soldier in North Africa in the battle against the Italians. He was later captured by the German Africa Corps but escaped from captivity. O'Connor later served under Montgomery in the Normandy Campaign and throughout the fighting in France in 1944.

Britain's airpower in Palestine was initially led Roderic Maxwell Hill who served in Palestine until 1938. He later became an Air Chief Marshal and received a Knighthood. Interestingly Arthur Harris, who was to become known as Bomber Harris, took over as the Air Officer Commanding Palestine and Transjordan in 1938; a position he was to remain in until September 1939. As Head of Bomber Command during much of World War II he was responsible for implementing the policy known as area bombing which devastated German cities. This strategy designed to break both the enemy's ability and will to fight was first practiced by Harris in suppressing revolts in the Middle-East during the inter-war years where it was known as air policing and air-pin.

Arab insurgents

Some rebels possessed light machine guns but their main weapons ranged from the rifle to the bomb and even spikes to puncture car tyres so that they could disrupt road transport. When the Arab Revolt became a guerrilla war they operated in mobile armed groups at first numbering between 15 – 20 fighters. As the conflict developed the units became larger in size with often as many as 50 – 70 fighters. By 1938, when the conflict was at its most intense, the armed bands consisted of up to 150 men.

The Arab guerrillas may have been less well armed than their British rivals but they had the distinct advantage that they had superior local knowledge especially regarding the terrain and were, at least for the earlier stages of the conflict, much more mobile than the Imperial forces.

The insurgents can be divided into eight categories of violence against continued British rule in Palestine.

1. The leadership which planned operations and stirred up the revolt.

2. The intelligence organisation.

3. Those involved in the intimidation of Arab policeman, witnesses and not only anyone who may assist the military but also those who were part of Palestine's infrastructure.

4. Saboteurs who had the aim of destroying the infrastructure and all forms of communication.

5. Those whose tools of trade were the gun and the bomb and would attack by stealth any agents of the state.

6. The often uniformed armed bands of guerrillas who sought to destroy the British army and police through attrition. When not in action the Arab bands wore civilian clothes so that they could move more easily around the country. Their usual uniform was a rudimentary one consisting of a saffron colour high neck polo top with khaki trousers and riding boots.

7. Men operating a developed signalling organisation which enabled the rebels to seize the initiative.

8. And finally there were those taking part in passive resistance such as striking and writing graffiti slogans.[62]

Montgomery thought that the Arab guerrillas 'constitute an Army, with a definite though somewhat crude organisation. There are three "Army" commanders and they take their orders from Damascus; there is little cohesion in the rebel forces and the esprit-de-corps is a "gang" one.'[63] The rebel bands were controlled by commanders via sub-area commanders. They are based in the hills and mountainous areas and conduct their operations mainly in the countryside. They use threats of violence and destruction of property to force the local peasantry to assist them and even join their fight against the British forces and the police. The guerrilla forces also had agents in Palestine's towns through which they could instigate assassinations and acts of terrorism.

In the months before the outbreak of the Second World War it was suspected that the Arab insurgents were being subsidised by Nazi Germany who were supplying them with arms, ammunition and money. The rebels also benefited from support in terms of men and material from Arabs in neighbouring states. Many of those that came to assist the uprising from abroad brought with them their training and experience from earlier uprisings against the French in Syria.

The Arab guerrillas also had the advantage that their brethren constituted a majority in the country. Furthermore, Arab towns and villages were spread throughout Palestine giving the guerrillas the freedom to move about the land from one safe haven to another where they could receive support and supplies from sympathetic civilians; a prerequisite for success against conventional armed forces. The multitude of Arab population centres also gave the Palestinian insurgents the opportunity to completely sever government and military communications throughout the Mandate; this would make the territory completely ungovernable.

British forces

Towards the end of the conflict the British Army in Palestine totalled the considerable number of 25,000 soldiers divided between two infantry divisions, one was operating in the north of the country and the other having responsibility for suppressing the revolt in the south.

Yet at the start of the conflict the authorities in the Mandate had a limited number of armed personnel in that region. There was just two infantry battalions, two squadrons of aircraft, a company of armoured cars and the Trans-Jordan Frontier Force. There were just 1,863 infantry soldiers in Palestine; that number included 60 officers. The army's Headquarters was in Jerusalem with the troops dispersed around the country with bases in Haifa, Nablus, Sarafand and Jerusalem. This was simply not enough to restore order and reinforcements were quickly brought into Palestine from Egypt which brought the army's strength to 11 infantry battalions. This number would gradually increase until victory was achieved.

The Royal Air Force also had one Armoured Car section at its disposal. This was based at their Headquarters in Ramleh as was a bomber squadron. The Royal Air Force in Palestine also had another bomber squadron which, for reasons of accommodation, was based in Ismailia in Egypt.

The Palestine based Trans-Jordan Frontier Force consisted of four under strength cavalry squadrons spread throughout the towns of Samakh, Rosh Pinna, Jisr Al Mejami and Beisan. Although these forces were mounted they were under the control of the Commander of the RAF.

There was also a British military presence in the neighbouring territory of Trans-Jordan. Here the RAF also had a bomber squadron based in Amman and an Armoured Car Company in Ma'an. The Trans-Jordan Frontier Force also had significant numbers of personnel based across the border in Trans-Jordan. There was an additional cavalry squadron based in Zerka, which was their HQ, and there were two mechanised companies split between Zerka and Ma'an. The make-up of this force, totalling 874 operatives with a reserve of 167, included 21 British Officers, 7 British Warrant officers, 28 local Officers (three of whom were Jewish) and 818 other ranks (17 of them were Jewish). The Army did not have a presence in Trans-Jordan but the Arab Legion, a lightly armed mobile force which was essentially the army of Jordan but under British leadership, had 1,004 men and 7 British officers and 35 Arab officers totalling a force of 1,046. The Trans-Jordan Frontier Force and the Arab Legion had the responsibility of patrolling Palestine's frontier with Trans-Jordan. To protect the oil pipeline that ran through Palestine the Iraq Petroleum Company also employed 1 British Officer and 58 Trans-Jordanians to guard their facilities there.

The British Mediterranean Fleet guarded the coast and through a determined campaign of searching ships headed for Palestine successfully prevented weapons being brought in to aid the rebels' fight. The Royal Navy also contributed detachments of men to guard the ports and a further four squadrons of aircraft. The fleet was also used to bombard positions on shore.[64]

In the autumn of 1938 the number of troops in Palestine was increased. Reinforcements came from Britain, India and Egypt and by November the army had 18 battalions of infantry, 2 cavalry regiments and a regiment of armoured cars split into two divisions.

There was a mismatch in weaponry between the British and Arab guerrillas. The Arab's relied on rifles and bombs. The British had those weapons but also had many more machine guns as well as artillery and air power. The mortar, an infantry weapon that fired explosives to drop on adversaries from above, was also of particular use in eradicating rebels that were hiding behind rocks. The imbalance in weaponry was, however, partly redressed after the Arab's successfully 'captured' machine guns and ammunition from the Arab Police. At first the machine gun which the British relied on was the Lewis Automatic Machine gun which dated from the First World War. Later in the conflict the British forces were equipped with the Bren Gun; Montgomery found this to be a most effective weapon against the guerrillas who suffered under its reliability as well as its accurate and withering fire.[65]

Police
When the conflict opened there 2,883 police in Palestine; just over a quarter of this force were British. 13% were Jewish and the remainder, the majority, were Arabs. Most senior officers, however, were of British extraction.[66] Over the course of the

conflict police numbers steadily increased. The weaponry available to the police included hand guns, rifles and even the Lewis gun.

Jewish Militias

The heightened ethno-religious tensions led the British authorities to establish, equip, arm and train two distinct Jewish forces in 1936. These were firstly; the Jewish Supernumerary Police, also known as the Jewish Auxiliary Police, whose role was to defend Jewish civilian areas from attacks by Arab insurgents. And the second was the Jewish Settlement Police which used the tactic of aggressive patrolling to hunt down and eliminate the Arab guerrilla forces.

There armament was of a similar nature and capability as the regular police units in Palestine. Yet in time the creation of these auxiliary police forces were to have a decisive effect on the nature and the outcome of the forthcoming coming Arab-Israeli Wars. Although these units had the title of Police some aspects of their role moved far beyond the legitimate function of defending civilian settlements and routing out the Arab militias. In time they became a base for hard-line and militant Jewish paramilitary organisations whose members were later absorbed into the Israeli Army and gave the fledgling Israeli Defence Force an experienced backbone of soldiers whose skills and equipment proved decisive when war began in earnest between the Holy Land's two rival claimants when Britain departed in 1948.

The Haganah, which means in Hebrew "The Defence", was the main Jewish paramilitary organisation and it was this body of men whose numbers have been estimated at approximately 20,000 members which later evolved into the army of the Israeli State. Although this force was outside of the legitimate armed service of the Mandate's lawful government the Haganah closely co-operated with the British authorities in defending Jewish areas from Arab attack, and it also played an important role in offensive operations against the Arab guerrillas. Also of great importance to the British war effort in Palestine was the role that the Haganah played in supply intelligence on the movements of the Arab irregular military forces.

Many of the state of Israel's most accomplished military commanders were the graduates of training supplied by the Jewish Police to the Haganah militia. Amongst the alumni was Moshe Dayan who as Defence Minister oversaw the Israeli Defence Force victory over their Arab neighbours in the 1967 Six Day War.

Another notable Jewish paramilitary organisation was known as the Irgun, which was officially known as the National Military Organization in the Land of Israel. This force, also called the Etzel, emerged in 1931 when a group of Haganah activists who were growing increasingly unhappy about that militia's main defensive role split off to form a more aggressive paramilitary force. The Irgun was a much smaller force than the Haganah, during the Arab Revolt its numbers were no more than 4,000 operatives. Yet what it lacked in size it made up for through its lack of restraint. It sought to help psychologically defeat the Arabs by installing fear in their ranks through aggressive operations known as Active Defence. Furthermore, some of its members were not above carrying out reprisals on Arab civilians which were condemned and in some cases successfully punished by the British Authorities.

As the conflict between Arab and Jew intensified the Haganah benefited from its close co-operation with the British authorities and became a real force to be reckoned with especially as it adopted a far more aggressive and proactive approach in the fight to supress the Arab Revolt. The Haganah also took on the role of smuggling more Jewish immigrants into Palestine which had formerly been the preserve of the Irgun. As such the Haganah not only greatly increased in stature, but also effectively adopted the ideology of the Irgun and many members of the Irgun re-joined their original militia, the Haganah. The Irgun, however, still existed until 1948 when under pressure from the Israeli government it finally folded and its members were integrated into the Israeli Defence Force.

The Battlefield

The territory of Palestine was a strip of land totalling approximately 10,000 square miles. On its western side it was bordered by the Mediterranean Sea, which was firmly under the control of the Royal Navy. This seaboard developed into a green coastal plain. Most of the Jewish settlements were located here. This area had good rail links but the roads were poor. The south consisted of desert country, which is mostly hard and stony ground. As trees are scarce there is little cover and the Royal Air Force made particular use of this area. Initially it was also patrolled at length by the 8th King's Royal Irish Hussars in their pick-up trucks.

To the west is the river Jordan valley which is below sea level. Here the climate is hot, prone to malaria, and particularly difficult for British troops and as such they did not operate there at first, leaving it to the Trans-Jordan Frontier Force to police and patrol. This area is the border with what was then known as Trans-Jordan. Lake Hula, and its surrounding marshes, and the Sea of Galilee exist on the northern part of the Jordan Valley border region. In the centre is the Dead Sea and to the south is the Gulf of Aqaba.

Palestine is not without mountains. At their height these stretch to four thousand feet above sea level. These are to be found in the north of the country and dominate the northern border. The mountains descend as they reach the centre of

Palestine. Although the northern border was mountainous it did have a reasonable road network.

The guerrillas made the mountains their home and at first most of the fighting took place in this region. As the British authorities were about to discover these borders would be crisscrossed at will by Arab guerrillas who were evading the forces of the government and by Arab sympathisers joining the fight in Palestine. To fuel the flames of rebellion weapons were also smuggled across the frontier. These borders were in realities arbitrary lines drawn up by the western powers after the end of the First World War.

Chapter 11

THE FIGHTING BEGINS

As the revolt quickly got out of control, new stages of violence developed. Sniper and bomb attacks took place as the rebellion evolved into a campaign of intimidation and terrorism. Palestine's infrastructure, communications and transportation were also sabotaged as part of the rebellion. The rebellion then became a full blown guerrilla war with highly mobile Arab units carrying out attacks throughout the country on the army, the police and Jewish settlements.

The British response was at first slow. There were, of course, efforts to contain the violence but members of the Arab Higher Committee were left free to whip up opposition to British rule throughout the country. In early June the government did establish an internment camp and sent some rebel leaders there, however, the key leaders including the Mufti remained at large.

Defensive measures were taken and the violence was responded to with counter-attacks on the rebel forces. Mobile army units were formed to offer a rapid response to the Arab guerrilla bands.

An example of an early confrontation was the rebel capture of Jaffa's old town, which had become a rebel base. The civil government did not want to risk heavy casualties recapturing it so the army was limited in how it could respond to rebel sniping and bomb throwing. Typically attacks with machine guns and rifle grenades would be made after giving a warning.. Barricades were then removed from the old town by forced labour. The property of rebels was later demolished as a punishment. However the civil administration stated on 17th June that the demolitions had been part of a town planning scheme and compensation was paid, even to the rebels. The army thought that this ruse fooled no one and that it had simply alienated those in Jaffa who had remained loyal.

Although British reinforcements were brought to Palestine they were first used on defensive duties and as such had little effect on quashing the rebellion. Gradually, however, the British army took the offensive and the extra numbers started to make an impact on the conflict. This reversal for the Arabs, together with the establishment of the Peel Commission, which was founded to look into the causes of the violence and chart a way forward, led to the Arab Higher Committee to temporarily call off the rebellion on 12th October 1936. This was, however, just a brief interruption in the violence.[67]

In early 1937 Arabs began to be targeted by the Arab rebels. Those who had dealings with the Jews, especially the Arabs that were involved in selling them land, began to be assassinated. Jews were also attacked and their retaliatory attacks raised the tension still further; especially in July 1937 when the Peel Commission's recommendations failed to satisfy the Arab belligerents. The Commission's main proposals were to partition Palestine. It was proposed that there would be an Arab state and a small but separate Jewish state which would exist mainly in the north of Palestine and a strip of land along the north-eastern coast. It also included limiting the Mandate mainly to an area linking Jerusalem to the Mediterranean Sea. Incidentally the proposed Jewish area was one that would be much smaller than the territory later recommended by the

UN's 1947 partition proposals and that taken following the First Arab Israeli War of 1948.

From the autumn of 1937 rumours were circulating that the guerrilla warfare was to be resumed and armed bands were already crossing the border from Syria and taking up positions in the mountains. However, they were not engaged at first by the British army. By the winter of 1937 the fighting had resumed again in earnest. The renewal of the revolt was planned and orchestrated in advance and the Mufti and his followers were expending a considerable amount of money and distributing propaganda to ferment the rebellion.

The tactics used

The rebels sought to undermine the civil administration of the country by attacking the Mandate's civil servants, including fellow Arabs who were employed by the British authorities and those who were sympathetic to the administration's rule. However, most of their attacks involved attempts to kill members of the security services. When targeting the armed forces the Arab guerrillas mainly used rifle fire to attack motor vehicles on the roads as well as attacking police and army patrols. The rebels also targeted soldiers as they moved into positions which they were tasked with defending.

When attacking at night the Arab bands would primarily be ambushing anti-sabotage guards and attacking troops as they move out on, or come back from, patrols. To defend against such attacks the army took the decision to replace unarmoured vehicles with motor transports that offered better protection. Day attacks consisted of targeting cars, buses and workmen trying to repair damage caused by night time sabotage. Although, these may have been viewed as soft targets by the rebels it did mean they had to come out into the open and were exposed to British counter-attacks; subsequently the rebels lost most of their number when attacking during the day.

To threaten army convoys, Arab guerrillas also created road blocks. Here the British military would use artillery fire, even from naval guns, to clear the area of rebel forces which could then be combated with machine gun fire. To make the convoys more secure armoured cars backed up by lorries containing light artillery pieces and searchlights were used in formation.

The Arab guerrillas 'taxed' villages for supplies in particular money and food as well as gathering new recruits to the war. When the Arabs attacked they often engaged the British forces at a considerable distance and when counter-attacked with force the guerrillas would retreat under the defence of a rear guard and take refuge in villages, caves or ravines. Often through the rebel intelligence and signals network the guerrillas knew in advance of British troop movements.

Although the Arab rebel units referred to themselves as gangs they were officially controlled by the rebel leadership and presented with a full set of instruction as to how they should operate in the field. The rebel Field Service Regulations, as summarised below, called on the guerrillas to fight and die for Allah and set down the following instructions:

1. Strength of Gangs The units should be small in number and under the control of one leader.

2. Leaders and men A Leader of a band must be courageous, thoughtful, intelligent, of quick decision and a good administrator. He must be able to read a map, use a compass and know intimately the country in which he is operating.

The individual gangster must have the qualities of his leader and be obedient, resolute and patient.

3.The Aim of Guerrilla Fighting The aim of guerrilla fighting is to weaken the enemy by worrying him continually.

4. The armament of the Gang The arms of the gang should

be light so not to reduce mobility, and at the same time effective. They should include revolvers, rifles, modern light machine guns, hand grenades, daggers and explosives, and tools for sabotage of bridges, railways, roads, telephone wires, etc.

5. Relations with the Population The warrior fighting for God and his country must be merciful, just and lenient with the people. He must not injure them or rob them.

6. Care of Arms Arms and ammunition are usually scanty compared with those of the enemy. Special care must therefore be taken to use them with discretion and without waste, and to maintain them in good condition.

7. Use of Cover Cover is of two kinds:-

(a) Natural cover, e.g. hills, ditches, rocks, trees, etc.

(b) Artificial, e.g. walls, sand bags, etc.

The gangster must know how to use all types of cover. Gangs should operate whenever possible in mountainous country or forests, which provide natural cover and at the same time are obstacles to the enemy. They should only operate in plains and deserts in cases of necessity or at suitable times such as at night or in fog.

8. Protection from aircraft The Field Service Regulations also specified how best to evade aircraft by lying stationary and wearing camouflage and how best to deal with bombing attacks from planes.

9. Protection against tanks The guerrillas were advised not to confront tanks and instead hide and engage the troops which follow.

10. Protection against guns This referred to artillery and the advice to the gang member was that they should disperse so that there is a distance of 5 – 10 metres between them.

11. Protection against Infantry The rebel leadership perceived infantry to be the main enemy. They were initially advised not to take part in pitched battles. The gangs were told to use speed and surprise focussing their attacks on small units and attempting to take their arms and ammunition and prevent enemy movements so that the British could not concentrate their forces.

Finally the rebel instructions ordered that the insurgents 'should kill proven spies and traitors who betray the movements of the bands.'

Throughout the earlier phases of the conflict the problem of engaging the Arab gangs persisted. To solve this quandary ground and air forces were integrated. Convoys that were fitted with radio transmitters were dispatched to draw out the rebels. The British army decided that a 'bait' was needed to draw the enemy out into the open. And when contact had been achieved the insurgents, even the snipers, should be hit hard, pursued and not allowed to escape. The tactics to achieve this were that when the British troops were engaged the call went in to summon down air support to strike at the insurgents from above with their guns and bombs. When attacked from the air the rebels' superior mobility over ground forces counted for naught against this new type of warfare; and heavy casualties were inflicted upon the Arab bands. In the early part of the conflict one such unit suffered 50% casualties. Despite that fact it was recognised that air power alone could not win the war and that the armed groups could be eliminated only by ground forces.

To supplement the use of air power the cordon system was established. When contact with the rebels was established this strategy brought in troops by armoured cars to surround the area where the fighting was taking place and attempted to prevent the guerrillas from escaping. The troops would also converge on the fighting, often following the sound of gun fire or observing where the planes were striking.[68] This system proved to be a successful and the insurgents suffered heavy casualties.

In response by early 1938 the rebels formed into even larger units and sought to engage the forces of the British, taking the fight to the army. As the cordon system depended upon small swift units getting into place they were susceptible to attack from the larger rebel units and they suffered too many casualties. The army therefore decided to abandon the cordon system even though it was delivering results.

The new system which came into force in March 1938 used large well-armed mobile columns. They travelled in motor transports on Palestine's roads and had donkeys with them which allowed them to travel off the tracks and still retain their heavier weapons and supplies. These columns as they were known often totalled nearly 90 officers and men each with a defined role ranging from Commander to Lewis Gunner, from cooks, when required, to mortar operators and the donkey handlers. The mobile columns could also call in support from the air and from other columns and operated in essentially the same way as had the cordon system but as they were better equipped and organised they were ready for action when it came. Cooperation between brigades and command and control was also easier in the pre-established mobile columns than in the *ad hoc* units that were used in the cordon system.

Clashes led to the important battle near Yammun, in central Palestine, on 4th March 1938. At this confrontation the Arab force took significant casualties from the mobile columns and a major rebel leader, Sheikh Attieh, killed himself. Further blows followed and in mid-March another rebel commander, Abdullah el Asbar, was killed in Northern Galilee. The battle near Yammun, and the later confrontations, led to the rebels changing their tactics again. They now no longer attempted to take on the army in set piece confrontations and instead formed smaller units. The effect was that the larger mobile columns could no longer locate these new smaller Arab bands. The insurgents also shifted their focus to terrorising the countryside with the purpose of eliminating moderate Arabs and those who may be providing information to the British Army.

The response of the British military was to place static forces in towns and villages where Arab intimidation was high. These units were backed up by mobile columns that could strike out into the countryside in response to an attack. Roads were also built to aid the troop movements between the villages. The effect was to re-establish Government control in those villages that were occupied and reduce Arab activity in adjacent areas. However, it also pushed the guerrilla war out into other parts of the country. It now spread throughout Palestine including the South which had been relatively peaceful in comparison to the North. The revolt also encompassed even more attacks on Jewish settlements, more terrorist outrages in the towns and the rebels also steadily increased their efforts to punish Arab supporters of the government throughout the conflict.

Resulting from this strategic chaos the British Army re-instigated their offensive operations, and added a new air cordon system to its renewed offensive operations. This was developed so that the British army could reclaim the element of surprise which was being lost as a result of the rebels far-reaching signals and intelligence network which detected army movements and warned of their operations. The air cordon used the speed of the aircraft to overcome the rebel's sentries. It worked in conjunction with the mobile columns. At a pre-appointed time the planes converged on an area that was due to be searched and sealed off the area. Anyone attempting to leave this location received warning shots and were fully engaged if they did not halt. The perimeter was held until the arrival of the mobile columns that would then search the area and fight any rebels. This system allowed the British military to recapture the essential element of surprise.[69]

In addition to the powerful mobile columns there were other units being used which resemble what we now know as Special Forces Commandos. It is often thought that Special Forces and their tactics consisting of small groups operating in enemy territory were originally developed during the Second World War. However, in 1930s Palestine the British Army was already using special small highly mobile units of lightly armed and lightly clothed men travelling in fast motor transport whose aim was to hunt and ambush the rebels. These soldiers were even equipped with special rubber soled shoes to make them more nimble and to give them the ability to operate silently.

Of particular note were the Special Night Squads which were established in 1938. These special force units comprised handpicked personnel from both the British Army and Jewish recruits selected from the Jewish Settlement Police. They worked in close co-operation with Jewish paramilitaries from the Haganah. The Special Night Squads excelled in conducting counter-insurgency operations and they took the war to the Arab guerrilla bands.

The operations of the Special Night Squads were sanctioned by Montgomery in his area of command in Northern Palestine, in particular the region known as Galilee. They were the brain child of a British Protestant Zionist army Captain called Orde Wingate, who later reached the rank of Major-General during the Second World War. During that conflict he became the master of unconventional and asymmetric warfare leading operations behind enemy lines. He devised and led guerrilla style incursions into Ethiopia which played a key role in helping to liberate that country from Italian occupation. And in the fight against the Japanese in Burma he organised and led units, known as the Chindits, who penetrated deep into enemy held territory to harass the forces of the Empire of Japan.

The military lessons from Palestine were clear; when the

British forces took the offensive to both the guerrillas and the local inhabitants who supported the Arab rebels the army were successful in putting down the revolt. Whether the tactics used included closing with snipers and responding with heavy machine gun fire, or aggressive patrolling to defend lines of communication by denying parts of the country to the enemy; taking the fight to the Arab insurgents worked. However, the actions of the civil authorities undermined the fight to restore law and order.

How British control was lost

Opportunities were lost in the earlier part of the conflict to make sure that the rebellion would be ended permanently. By late May 1936 the armed forces and the police began to take preventative measures by hunting down the rebels in the villages from which they came. These were intended not only to capture the rebels and their weapons but also to punish rebel-supporting villagers. It was considered that these searches were a success. However, rebel propaganda falsely alleged that these punitive measures led to the desecration of Mosques and the Qur'an, which meant that the civil authorities no longer favoured such a stern, but successful, course of action.

On 30th May 1936 the High Commissioner, the Head of the Civilian Government in Palestine, gave the instruction that the severity of these raids was to be reduced and that they should no longer be punitive. This policy was called 'Reasonable Moderation'. This softer approach took away the initiative from the army and handed it back to the rebels. The British army thus lost the only means by which they could strike effectively in advance of rebel action coupled with the fact that the Emergency Defence Regulations which allowed the armed forces to punish rebel action were not enforced meant that little pro-active action was taken against the guerrillas. This led to a renewed upsurge of violence in June. The government had played into rebel hands and for much of the conflict the British administration had effectively ceded control of much of Palestine to the Arab guerrillas.

The new Arab tactics, adopted in the Spring of 1938, which used smaller units moving around the country at will gave them the upper hand and by the summer of 1938 the situation was looking increasingly dire. The rebels were freely moving around the country by night and by day. The lawless state of affairs deteriorated further when the number of rebels was swelled by the conscription of new members from the villages which the insurgent gangs entered.

A spirit of defeatism then began to pervade the civil administration's approach to dealing with the revolt. This led Lieutenant-General Robert Hadden Haining, General Officer Commanding the British forces in Palestine and Trans-Jordan, to comment that 'The defeatist spirit needs overcoming.' In June 1938 he officially complained about the civilian government of Palestine and how they failed to 'realize how weakness is regarded by the Arab and Mohammedan world.' He also stated that, 'I do feel that the fact so many of the Administration here have been in this one colony or mandated area for so many years has blinded their eyes to what is done elsewhere and what should be done here.'[70]

This crisis was made worse when many soldiers were withdrawn in August and September 1938 at the height of the crisis caused by Hitler's demands for the German speaking Czechoslovak Sudetenland to be ceded to the German Reich. This not only weakened Britain's military presence in Palestine but also led to the belief among the local population that Britain's power was waning. This led to increased efforts to stir the rebellion.[71]

In an almost identical situation to the earlier rebellion in

Ireland, which had its own shadow state emerge during the fighting, the power of the rebels was enhanced by the creation of their own court network throughout the country that was controlled by the senior rebel leadership. The courts were originally created to convict and take retribution against those working for the British Authorities. The often brutal judgments of the shadow courts were carried out by the rebel groups and this greatly enhanced the standing of the revolt amongst the local Arabs. In time their remit was extended beyond punishing suspected 'collaborators' to include many different areas.

The police especially suffered a number of severe setbacks. On midnight of 16th August 1938 Arab rebels seized the Nablus urban police station and stole rifles and a large quantity of ammunition. The telephone lines were also cut. This scenario was repeated on 19th August in Hebron, on 24th August the same situation occurred in Jenin and Lydda. The number of almost identical attacks accelerated throughout September; clearly the Police had become not fit for purpose.

Throughout the summer of 1938 the British forces primarily remained on the defensive. However, when the opposing forces met in their almost daily clashes the British came out on top and in September alone at least 311 guerrillas were killed.[72]

Yet the situation became so dire for the Mandate's administration that in October 1938 the Old City of Jerusalem, was lost to the rebels for the better part of a week. As law and order had broken down it became apparent that the enforcing of peace upon a rebellious population must take precedence over every other consideration. Hence on 18th October 1938 military control in Palestine came into force and from then on the army enjoyed wide ranging legal power over two main military districts, one in the north the other in the south. Each district was under the command of its own Major General.

Chapter 12

ENTER MONTGOMERY

On 11th October 1938 Montgomery was ordered to Palestine to take command of the British 8th Division. He was given the rank of Major General. General, later Field Marshal, Wavell; comments on this new arrival were that "he will do extremely well".[73] Montgomery was not to disappoint.

His arrival back in Palestine occurred at a time when the conflict was particularly fierce. In 1938 alone there were 2,357 attacks by the Arab guerrillas; 720 were against lines of communication, 986 were against British military and police personnel, killing 77. There were also 651 attacks on Palestine's Jewish population killing 255. These attacks came at the expense of approximately 1,000 Arab insurgent deaths. The British also detained 2,500 suspected rebels that year.[74]

The situation and the mood of defeatism that pervaded Palestine's civil authorities was set to change very soon. The administration's Chief Secretary in Jerusalem, William Battershill, wrote of the new arrival, 'A new star has burst in our firmament in the shape of Major-General Montgomery who goes to command the new 8th Division in the North.' William Battershill wrote about Montgomery again on 13th November 1938 that,

'He called on me last week and put me through a cross-examination which would have come rather amiss from the GOC himself… He is sharp featured and evidently has a brain. I fear this man will try to be a new broom and will successfully put the backs up of most people.' [75]

Battershill's judgment was not wrong and this ability to put noses out of joint to further his military objectives was to be an effect that Montgomery was to have on people throughout his later military career.

Monty and his 8th Division was responsible for Palestine's northern sector, which was a significant chunk of the country running from the border with Syria and the Lebanon down to a line running between Tel Aviv and the River Jordan. This was the most challenging area in the Mandate. In this part of the country the Mufti, the chief rebel agitator, had a powerful hold over the population. Northern Palestine was also a very difficult area for some very important reasons. These are that its terrain is mountainous and that Montgomery's forces also had to control the border and tackle the all too common attempts by neighbouring Arab tribes, who had much in common with the Palestinians, to penetrate the frontier and join their brethren in battle against the British. What is more, Montgomery found that the mountains of Northern Palestine were home to 'a hardy and martial type of Arab.'[76] His experience on India's North-West Frontier where he faced a similar situation would have been a significant help in this latest challenge to British imperial authority.

A British military victory in the northern sector of Palestine, the heartland of the rebellion and its principle route of supply for both men and material would allow for peace to be restored in the remainder of the country. Montgomery was to use newly established powers to fight the war his way.

Military Control: The strategy that secured victory

At the heart of Montgomery's strategy to restore order was the concept known as Military Control. This does not mean that Palestine became a military dictatorship but it recognised the need for swift and decisive action in military operations and against those who were suspected of taking part in and assisting the rebellion. In reality the term Military Control referred to a situation where the military was the senior partner in tackling the conflict with the civil authorities working in conjunction with the armed forces as the junior partner. In that sense the situation in Palestine can be best described as dual control.

Military Control was a concerted effort to crush the revolt. Its full effects came into force in the autumn of 1938 and coincided with the arrival of Montgomery and reinforcements. It drew upon early military regulations which allowed for retribution and collective punishment to be imposed on civilians and awarded the two military commanders a great deal of discretion as to when and how best to take action against the general population if they were aiding the revolt. This strategy also took advantage of rules which created Military Courts. It also gave the military effective command over the police.

It was felt necessary to introduce military control because the situation in Palestine had slipped out of control. The guerrilla warfare, terrorism, abduction and murder had not only spread to the south of the country but also into the towns. In September 1938 the rebels pulled off a number of coups including the capture of police stations and had destroyed much of the railway network. The situation further deteriorated as many of the Arab police were not only unable to resist the rebels but in many cases their loyalties were called into question and they had to be disarmed.

Imposing military control was the task set to the then Major General Montgomery. Military control, it should be noted does not mean officially sanctioned atrocities such as summary firing squads. What it does mean is that the ultimate authority for suppressing the revolt would rest with one man who was a soldier. However, unlike martial law there was still a role for the civilian government to play but this was mainly for political reasons. It was recognised in a report into the practical application of military control that a great deal of goodwill is required between the civil and military authorities who naturally approach the situation from a very different background and have an all too often opposing ethos to that of the army. Such a sharing of authority required the military to have the patience and diplomacy of statesmen, and the civil authorities to think like soldiers and to recognise the need for swift action to be taken against the civilian population. Yet security measures, which are often repressive in nature, directly impacted on the lives of the local population and were anathema to the civilian government.

Lieutenant General Robert Hadden Haining remarked that;
'The Civil authorities are loath to carry out measures which will antagonise the inhabitants even though they may agree that such measures ought to be taken.' [77]

As a result procrastination took place and action was delayed. It was estimated that the civil authorities would take as much as three weeks to enforce security measures whereas the military could impose them within 48 hours.

The other outcome of civil, as opposed to military, control is that it was recognised that civilian authority gave the initiative to the rebels. If the rebels were overly-belligerent, the arms of the state equipped to deal with peace time scenarios are overwhelmed. Conversely, however, if the rebels choose to go underground and bide their time the civil authorities will not have the opportunity to engage and defeat their enemy. With the armed forces as the senior partner action could be taken when and where the military saw fit and guerrilla forces can be hunted down. Furthermore, the commanding officer can stand firm against the calls for a political solution until the rebels have recognised that they have been defeated.

The concept of Military Control required the recognition that the defeat of the rebellion was the primary aim of British policy which in turn allowed for the focus of the forces of law and order to move away from obligations which committed the forces to be tied up guarding civilian installations across the country and gave them the freedom to be concentrated against the Arab guerrilla forces. The rebuilding of the country's infrastructure was left to wait until after the enemy had been engaged and eliminated.

The psychological effect of imposing military control on the local population was a key part of the strategy. The intention being to make sure that the villagers recognised and respected the supremacy of the Government rather than the power of the rebels.

The Defence Regulations which laid down the legal authority for the security measures also established Military Magistrates who dealt with minor contraventions of the peace and Military Courts which tried the more serious offences. The Courts had the power to impose the death penalty from which there was no appeal, however the decision had to be approved by the General Officer Commanding Palestine. Although the Courts were established to impose swift justice the accused were entitled to a lawyer of his choosing. However, as a result of the intimidation of witnesses by the rebel forces requirements for evidence were lessened.

Communications management was a key part of the Military Control strategy. The practical steps that were put in place included censorship of both the press and private telegrams. Although much of the local media was anti-government the necessary resources to enforce full censorship were not available to the government. As such both the carrot as well as the stick was used to manage the media. Journalists were regularly kept informed of developments and they knew that reports would be forthcoming so they would often stay in Jerusalem where they could be supervised. When the journalists did choose to observe the operations at first hand special press passes were issued which enabled them to move about the country freely. Conversely, this increased the military's influence over the journalists as the withdrawal of the pass entailed losing a substantial privilege. Generally, relations were good between the military, the media and the Public Information Bureau and the Press Bureau of Military News who advised the press as to what should and should not be published. Later in the conflict Montgomery would even take the step of removing journalists from his units so that his troops would not be distracted from their work.

The steps taken did enable a degree of news control to ensure that reports that were deemed to be favourable to the rebels were not published. However, the supply of information to the press did not stop some journalists from sending news out of the country from where it would be sent back to the Palestinian newspapers for publication. It was not considered that this caused any major problems and the punishment of journalists that undertook such methods would often be as light as being told that their methods were known.

Restrictions on travel and transportation on both the roads and railways were also introduced. The military took the power to stop and search, detain suspected rebels, conduct deportations – some rebel leaders were sent to the Seychelles – and demolish the property of rebels and rebel sympathisers. This policy radically changed the architecture of many old Palestinian towns and caused a great deal of suffering.

Suspects could be detained for up to one year without trial. Initially in the conflict these orders were sanctioned by civil District Commissioners, after the imposition of Military Control the power of detention was awarded to the Military Commanders and the subsequent use of such orders increased. It was considered that although the use of detention without trial was abhorrent to the British forces, let alone the Arabs, it was considered necessary because due to the insurgent campaign of intimidation obtaining witness evidence in open court was difficult.

Special village searches were introduced to catch the rebels who would be fighting one moment and then transform themselves into apparently peaceful inhabitants of their village the next. The military would surround a location, then separate the population on gender grounds and check the identity of the men. Meanwhile informers, who were often paid, pinpointed rebel suspects who were then arrested. In practice, although these powers did come to rest with the Military Commanders, they were generally only applied when the civil forces (the police) and the military were in agreement. This also applied to the release of inmates. Suspects were then taken to army run Examination Camps where they would be interrogated. Due to the large number of prisoners these camps later also took on the role of detaining those who had been punished with sentences of three months or less. There also existed Detention Camps which were run by the civil authorities and housed the more dangerous rebels.

Other measures introduced which enabled the military to impose order included; controls over the possession of firearms and travel permits and identity cards. The civil government would not make ID cards compulsory and would only countenance a voluntary scheme. However, the military responded by ordering that no travel pass would be issued without an identity card first being produced. After a brief Arab boycott the subsequent 'voluntary' take-up of the scheme became overwhelming. This meant that many Palestinians had their identities checked in person, they had to be vouched for by known residents, and the applicant's photograph was taken. Those who did not have travel permits were restricted from obtaining petrol.

Both mobile and static traffic check points were introduced to enforce the travel restrictions. On all roads outside of the towns a curfew was introduced which generally ran from 5pm in the evening to 6am in the morning. Special measures were taken on the borders of Palestine to make sure that movement across the frontier was properly policed.

One area where the military authorities would have liked even more power was the ability to prosecute and punish those that were inciting others to rebellion. Lieutenant-General Hadden Haining thought that power in this area would have allowed peace to be restored much sooner.

There were other benefits to Military Control than just allowing for better security measures to be imposed. Security roads were built to project the military's power into areas that were known, but inaccessible, rebel strong points. These new roads were also used to resupply remote garrisons. Prior to the establishment of Military Control the building of such roads also suffered from the bureaucratic divisions that existed in the government's Public Works Department and Civil Administration Roads. The military felt that this divided control was 'complicated, clumsy and in-elastic'. However, once Military Control was established with Area Commanders taking charge of the army, Montgomery and O'Connor, felt that these problems were rectified. The roads were constructed mainly by using voluntary paid labour; but forced labour, both paid and unpaid, was also used as was the use of prisoners.

Military cooperation with the Police

Military Control required the formation of special links with the police. The police consisted of Arab recruits and British colonial policemen operating in Palestine as part of the UK's imperial obligations. Incidentally many members of this force were veterans of the Anglo-Irish war where they had served as auxiliary police units and as Black and Tans; and again they were not without controversy. Weston Henry Stewart, the Anglican Archdeacon of Palestine, Syria and Trans-Jordan and later the Bishop of Jerusalem, wrote that, 'For a time I was seriously troubled at the "Black and Tan" methods of the police, of which I had overwhelming evidence'. [78]

There also existed a force of Temporary Additional Police. These were raised to perform the basic, but dangerous, function of guarding Palestine's infrastructure, villages and Jewish settlements from attack.

The effectiveness of the Police in the earlier phases on the conflict was hampered by the civil authorities retaining control over their operations. This lack of coordination with the military was eventually addressed when the army become the senior partner in Palestine's security. Following this the police began operating under military direction; however, instructions from the military were not considered compulsory.

Initially, the Police were quite simply not equipped to deal with the rebellion. They were often based in secluded stations that were vulnerable and could not be held if attacked in force. The eventual collapse of the Arab police was brought on following a determined campaign of intimidation against them and their families. Furthermore, inadequate facilities for recreation, bad housing and canteen amenities, poor leadership, a lack of discipline, poor pay and prospects left even the British police badly motivated. When the police were placed under Military Control they became a very different force, especially as the army sought to address those problems. Better opportunities for promotion were also introduced. Furthermore, the presence of British troops went some way to increasing their morale. Ineffective police commanders were removed and replaced by more able men.

Apart from in the Northern Frontier Division, which consisted of mixed British and Arab personnel, the Arab Police were disarmed. Some Arab police whose loyalties were questioned were dismissed, but others were kept available for unarmed duties. Communication and transportation was also taken out of the hands of Arab policemen. The Arab Temporary Additional Police units were disbanded and a Jewish force of Temporary Additional Police was created in their place to make up for the loss of their Arab colleagues. Mobile units of the Temporary Additional Police were also created with a small strike force that could rapidly relieve besieged settlements. These new initiatives worked in conjunction with the army's plans to increase the Jewish settlements' defences whose militias were also reorganised by the army to improve their military capability. Orde Wingate's Special Night Squads were now given a free hand to eradicate the Arab insurgents.

The outlying police stations were closed to prevent them and the weapons stored there falling into rebel hands which would cause much loss of life. The police then concentrated on holding the more defensible stations that remained. These were also made more secure and were better guarded. Excess arms and ammunition were taken to larger centres where they could be looked after more securely.

It was considered a waste of resources to use the army on tasks that should be the remit of the police. The army's role was to engage the enemy and bring them to battle. The army also undertook the mission to create security in the countryside. This still left a valuable role for the Palestinian Police Force which was law enforcement and basic internal security in the urban areas.

Despite different roles being defined for these different security services it was still required to make the Police a more robust force. This included equipping them with increased firepower including the Lewis machine gun and rifle grenades. Armoured cars were given to the police so that they would receive better protection when out on patrol. Basic military training began to be given to the police.

Tasks for the Palestinian Police even included guarding the porous border surrounding the mandated territory. Here the Frontier Division had to guard against arms and guerrilla fighters penetrating from the Lebanon, Jordan and Syria. In urban areas where security was critical soldiers and police worked in close cooperation guarding key points but when security was achieved the army was withdrawn and the task handed over to the police and security in those vicinities then became their sole preserve.

The leadership of the police greatly improved when a Sir Charles Tegart was appointed by the Colonial Office to assist with the re-organisation of the Palestinian Police. Tegart was not an uncontroversial man; accusations of overly robust measures have dogged how posterity regards him. However, it must be noted that he did not have executive authority in Palestine and only held the position of Adviser on Police matters. What is certain is that he helped transform the police and thus helped bring order back to Palestine until after World War II had concluded when more mass Jewish immigration sparked a fresh crisis.

Tegart is famous for what became known as Tegart's Wall. This was a barbed wire frontier fence, protected by occasional forts and pillboxes, which stretched across Palestine's northern frontier. Its purpose was to try to stop Arab rebels infiltrating the border. Due to the difficultly of patrolling the fence incursions still took place and it was not considered to be an overwhelming success, although it was recognised that it did act as deterrent.[79] Some of its fortifications are still used by the Holy Land's various modern belligerents to this day. Some of the barbed wire fence was however taken down and used to reinforce allied positions in North Africa during the Second World War, the theatre of operations that made Montgomery a household name.

Tegart also assisted with the re-organisation of the Criminal Investigation Department and the creation of a rural mounted police force. He also laid the plans for the expansion of British police numbers in Palestine; this plan involved recruiting ex-servicemen for the task. The extra police were necessary to make sure that isolated rural police stations could be re-opened with a compliment of not less that 50% British personnel. Rather than drip feeding the new recruits piecemeal across the whole country, areas were brought up to full operational strength one at a time. That way if there was to be the abrupt removal of troops from an area, perhaps if there were to be another crisis in Europe, then security in that region could be handled by the police.

Gradually, rural police stations were re-opened, and in the urban areas the police were able to fully take on the task of security. This allowed more soldiers to be relieved from policing duties freeing them up to take the fight to the rebels.

The expansion of police numbers increased significantly over the period of 31st March 1938 to 31st March 1939. The number of all classes of paid police increased from 4,924 to 9,180 in just one year. This included enlarging the British contingent to 2,837 from 1,100. Jewish personnel were also of a much greater number than before; swelling from 1,806 to 4,861. This is largely due to the push to expand the number of Temporary Additional

Police numbers with only a small boost in the numbers of regular Jewish police officers. However, the numbers of Arab Police officers decreased from a total of 2,018 in 31st March 1938 to 1,482 by 31st March 1939. This included a slight drop in the number of regular police and those used and employed by private institutions to defend their property. The abolition of the Arab Temporary Addition Police made up the most significant part of the reduction. The Jewish Settlement Defence Force, equipped by the British but not paid, increased from 3,853 to 13,650.[80]

In May 1939, with much of his advice now taken, Sir Charles Tegart left Palestine.

Montgomery's strategy

Upon his arrival Montgomery made a full assessment of the situation. Just as Montgomery did when he was first in Palestine in 1931, and as he would in his later commands. He toured his area of operations, visited every unit and even interviewed the police and civil servants. This was quite an undertaking but it allowed him to assess the reasons as to why the military situation had got so out of hand. Montgomery identified several major problems. There was the fact that the civil authorities had failed to keep control. The Government's writ ran only in the towns and then just to a small extent. Another problem was the disintegration of the Arab police. There was also the challenge from the intensity of the guerrilla war and an equal lack of willingness amongst the authorities to force closure upon the conflict.

Montgomery was not alone in his scathing criticisms of how the emergency had been handled to date. The Commander-in-Chief of French forces in neighbouring Syria confided in him during their liaison meetings that he had thought the previous British attempts to control the rebellion were woefully inadequate. The French were already preparing for the possibility of violence in Syria and had stationed 28,000 troops in that country and planned to crush any rebellion there as quickly as possible.

Montgomery's appraisal of the situation allowed him to develop a plan as to how he would take the campaign forward. This organised and thought through proactive approach, rather than responding to the whims of the enemy, was also to be a fundamental part of Montgomery's generalship in the Second World War. The strategy that Montgomery would develop depended upon the answer to what he saw was an important question which he sought to answer for himself. This was 'is the campaign that is being waged against us a National movement, or is it a campaign that is being carried on by gangs of professional bandits?'[81] The Jerusalem based Force HQ thought that the revolt was a national movement. Montgomery, however, during his tour to assess the situation came to a very different conclusion. His view of the revolt was that 'the campaign against us is being waged by gangs of professional bandits.'[82]

Following this revelation Montgomery set out the operational strategy that would take back control of Palestine from the rebel gangs. Montgomery made sure that his future policy was clearly set out in a formal statement so that the soldiers and other security services under his command knew what their duty was and would work towards the same goal.

Of prime importance was the need to act offensively with the aim of 'killing armed rebels in battle'.[83] The termination of the rebel leaders was also part of this plan. Montgomery's strategy, however, was more sophisticated than imposing his will on the guerrilla bands, not that this was going to be an easy undertaking. Montgomery also ordered that efforts should be made to get the towns people and peasantry on the side of the

British. The approach he demanded from his subordinates was a hard but fair one. He wanted the local population to know that the British army will always treat them fairly; 'but if they assist the rebels in any way they must expect to be treated as rebels; and anyone who takes up arms against us will certainly lose his life.'[84]

Montgomery also had one eye on the eventual exit of the British army. He ordered that his troops should train the police force to make sure that once the rebellion was crushed the newly arrived British policemen would be strong enough to keep law and order. During the transitional stage from the army having responsibility for the fight in the countryside to the police eventually taking over security outside of the towns, Montgomery arranged for members of the police force to be embedded with his military units on operations. Montgomery, just like he did throughout his years of military service, put a special emphasis on training. He arranged for the training of the police to be improved to create a mounted gendarmerie which would in time take charge of the countryside. He also ordered that the newly arriving police should learn Arabic.

Montgomery imposed strict curfews just as he had done in Cork, Ireland, during the Anglo-Irish War. One such example demonstrates that Montgomery took a particularly strict and stubborn approach to restricting the movements of civilians. Following serious conflict between the port of Haifa's Jewish and Arab communities Montgomery enforced a clamp-down on night-time movements upon large parts of the city. This operated without exception and even upon the workmen who were involved with the 24 hour building of an oil refinery. This had the effect of delaying the construction of this important piece of infrastructure. Montgomery relented upon this strict security measure only when the British Government in London complained.[85]

Montgomery, as he would in his later career, would often manage to stamp his own vision on how the war should be handled and lobby for the resources to carry out his plans. In Palestine he was no different. He felt that the campaign in the Jordan valley was not being handled properly, with little to no co-ordination with the British forces in surrounding areas. This section, he thought, had become a safe haven for the rebels he had chased out of his northern region. He therefore warned that the conflict would be lost unless the whole of the north was put under one operational command – his! Montgomery's lobbying was successful. The Jordan Valley area and the members of the Trans-Jordan Frontier Force, formerly under the command of the RAF, were placed under his command. He did not mind feelings being hurt to achieve this important end.

He also took from the 7th Division in the South of the country a cavalry regiment and combined it with his own and his recently acquired mounted squadrons of the Trans-Jordan Frontier Force to form a brigade, a significant force, and in early January 1939 moved it north to clean up the frontier zone. He combined the cavalry operations with mechanised infantry units. He thought this combination would be an interesting military experiment, and it was a success. Interestingly Montgomery kept historical parallels in mind when conducting operations. In a report to the Chief of the Imperial General Staff he noted that his cavalry drive took the same route north as General Allenby's British forces did when driving the Turks out of Palestine in World War One. In late January Montgomery swept these mobile units towards the south to eliminate the opposition there.

Montgomery, as became characteristic in his later campaigns in Italy and in north-western Europe, also expressed his views on areas that were beyond his immediate sphere of control. He recommended that the Inspector-General of the Palestinian

Police Force, Alan Saunders, was not up to the job and should be replaced with a man that was more resolute. Montgomery recommended Sir Charles Tegart to be appointed in his place. Otherwise, in Montgomery's opinion, the police would continue to be a failing organisation. In the meantime while improvements in the police were carried out Montgomery felt that it was vital that the army remain in Palestine.

Montgomery also wanted reforms to be carried out at the British military headquarters in Jerusalem. He successfully lobbied against the excessive centralisation and attempts by the HQ to micro-manage the conflict from afar, where those behind a desk sought to control the fight against mobile armed bands in the mountains of a lawless country. Furthermore, Montgomery felt that operational secrecy was threatened by the leadership of the army insisting that no action could be taken without prior approval, and that plans had to be submitted a week in advance. The delays this imposed and the risk of news leaking out meant that the rebels were often forewarned of operations. Montgomery thought that not allowing the enemy to learn of the plans was of crucial importance. Again, he won his point and central HQ backed down. Montgomery also sought an end to the excessive political interference in the fight to crush the rebellion and the bureaucratic administrative burden which he and his subordinate commanders had to deal with.

The establishment of Military Control, however, along with reinforcements allowed Montgomery to take the offensive and use his war fighting skills to their utmost. Montgomery wrote that from the very start 'intensive operations were undertaken in November, December and January... ' He further reported that, '...by 1st February, 1939, the military situation was well in hand.'[86]

The military results

Montgomery's approach delivered immediate and positive outcomes for the British army and eventually broke up the larger guerrilla gangs. On 28th November 1938 an Arab unit was surrounded and engaged in the Carmel mountain range. Knowing that no quarter was to be given Montgomery described how the guerrillas fought like 'wild beasts' and at one point there was hand-to-hand fighting between one of the Arabs and a Corporal of the Irish Fusiliers in which the Arab lost his life. In all 50 of the 60 rebels in this band were killed, Montgomery in his report made the point that they were all in uniform. During the course of this battle the rebel commander in the north, Abu Dorrah, was slain.

Montgomery noted that a good battle also proved to be very effective for the troops' morale. He recognised that the troops were magnificent when on the offensive but when they were placed on defensive duties they were open to assassination by the bullet and by the bomb. This had a disconcerting effect on the troops. However, after engaging the enemy in an open battle the soldiers spirits were improved and 'all the men are on their toes.'[87]

Montgomery understood that there was another significant benefit to the remorseless pursuit of the Arab gangs, and their leadership, beyond the destruction of the enemy's capacity to fight. He noted that this approach was damaging the status of the rebel leaders amongst the local population. 'They are ceasing to be public heroes and are becoming hunted outlaws.'[88] Montgomery's assessment was correct. The rural Arab population began to deny the guerrilla bands the resources which they demanded and the flow of new recruits, and even conscripts, to the ranks of the insurgents dried up. As the revolt began to enter its final phase the Muslim Palestinian Arabs began to cease describing the insurgents as *Mujahidin* meaning

Holy Warriors, but instead referred to them as *Thuwwar* which merely means rebels.[89]

Montgomery perceived that at the heart of this was the fact that the rebels were being humiliated by the British army. This took the lustre out of the revolt as did the threat that the British authorities would put in place ever more punitive measures, including higher taxes, on the Arabs who were suspected of supporting the rebellion. This drove a wedge between the guerrilla bands and the Palestinian Arabs. The local population became tired of the revolt and the hardships it was forcing upon them. Peace not idealistic dreams of statehood become their hope.

In January 1939 a rebel commander called Abd al-Halim al-Jaulani lamented at the actions of his fellow insurgents. He stated that; 'Our rebellion has become a rebellion against the villagers and not against the government or the Jews.' Abd al-Halim al-Jaulani was not alone in his criticisms of how the conflict had developed. Another Arab guerrilla commander by the name of Ahmad Mahmoud Hasan, known as Abu Bakr, in May 1939 reported on this state of affairs to the Arab Higher Committee. He wrote; 'we found that the spirit of the rebellion was waning... I found the villagers despondent... In the towns there is deep distrust... The spies are everywhere... ' He also went on to explain that the supporters of the revolt 'crawl into corners.' Ahmad Mahmoud Hasan also complained about the actions of his comrades; 'The behaviour of the fighters towards the villagers is extremely tyrannical and horrifying: brutal robbery, execution without prior investigation. Conflicts without any reason, disorder and complete inaction; and the villagers called upon God for help against such behaviour'.[90]

This terror, where the Arab fighters were being forced to extract more supplies and funds from the rural inhabitants, alienated the Arab population from the insurgents. According to Montgomery, the village headmen, known as Mukhtars, would actually ask that the army stay in their village to protect them from the Arab gangs.

As can be expected in a vicious war there were incidents of abuses and maltreatment of not just the Arab guerrilla fighters but also against civilians and their property. Dr Matthew Hughes has assessed the conduct of the British security services during the Arab Revolt in Palestine. He too cited the British destruction of the old town of Jaffa as an excessive act carried out by the British army. Many other excesses were to occur throughout the conflict. Such as in the village of Bayt Rima in central Palestine which was burnt by the soldiers of the West Yorkshire Regiment. A British police officer named John Briance commented that this was 'a disgrace to the British name.' Some villages that were particularly troublesome and noncompliant were completely demolished such as Mi'ar in Northern Palestine. On occasions, however, the destructive actions of the army were based upon the feeblest information. John Briance described the process of how the British security services responded to an insurgent attack; he wrote,

'It is very difficult to catch the culprits as there is absolutely no information to work on and you can receive no support from the population in the villages. You may follow the police dogs into one village and upon this vague clue you may smash the village and burn it down but the next night the wires are cut in another part of the road – and so it goes on'. [91]

A soldier who served under Montgomery in Upper Galilee with the 2nd Royal Ulster Rifles, Humphrey Edgar Nicholson 'Bala' Bredin, who later rose to the rank of Major-General, commented on the duties of the British army, he wrote their role was to,

'bash anybody on the head who broke the law, and if he didn't want to be bashed on the head then he had to be shot. It may

sound brutal but in fact it was a reasonably nice, simple objective and the soldiers understood it'.[92]

Bredin was awarded the Military Cross and Bar and was twice mentioned in dispatches for his service in suppressing the Arab Revolt in Palestine which included a number of clashes with the guerrilla forces which he was helping to track down.

A time when soldiers were at their most vulnerable was when the army was on patrol or carrying out a convoy. Here they would often face attacks from what we now call improvised explosive devices (IEDs) as well as from ambushes by gunmen. To stop these attacks some soldiers placed captured Arab insurgents on the front of military trains and vehicles. It was successful, but did on occasions lead to a much darker practice as one rank-and-file soldier named Arthur Lane of the Manchester Regiment recollected;

'… when you'd finished your duty you would come away nothing had happened no bombs or anything and the driver would switch his wheel back and to make the truck waver and the poor wog on the front would roll off into the deck. Well if he was lucky he'd get away with a broken leg but if he was unlucky the truck behind coming up behind would hit him. But nobody bothered to pick up the bits they were left.'

He went on to explain that;

'You know we were there we were the masters we were the bosses and whatever we did was right… Well you know you don't want him anymore. He's fulfilled his job. And that's when Bill Usher [the commanding officer] said that it had to stop because before long they'd be running out of bloody rebels to sit on the bonnet.'

Arthur Lane described similar actions that have been preserved for posterity by the Imperial war Museum. Following an engagement with the insurgents, which claimed several British lives, Lane described the treatment meted out to the prisoners which were taken during the battle;

'... they were in a state and they were really knocked about....
whoever had done it when they got them on the wagons to
bring them back to camp the lads had beat them up, set about
them.'

He goes on to describe how they were beaten with;

'Anything they could find. Rifle butts, bayonets, scabbard
bayonets, fists, boots, whatever.' [93]

There were many other examples. Punitive measures were also taken against the residents of a small mixed Christian and Muslim Arab village called al-Bassa. This punishment was designed to keep control of the northern frontier and seek revenge for the deaths of British soldiers who were killed by a land mine which their patrol had struck on the road. The headmen of the area had already been warned by a Lieutenant-Colonel Gerald Herbert Penn Whitfield that if there were any insurgent attacks on the security services then the village nearest to the scene of the incident would be punished. The nearest village to the attack which led to the British deaths was al-Bassa, which was duly sacked. Some of the male villagers were herded on to a bus and then forced to drive over a mine which had been placed in the ground by the British troops, soldiers of the Royal Ulster Rifles and the Royal Engineers. The dead, estimated to be 20, were then buried by the remaining residents of al-Bassa in a mass grave. According to a senior British police officer named Raymond Cafferata the effects of this punitive raid were that, 'Since that day not a single mine has been laid on that road.'[94]

Such actions by the security services, although militarily successful, were highly controversial and drew criticism from many quarters, even from the British establishment in Palestine. Montgomery was also caught-up in this controversy.

After the events at al-Bassa the Anglican Bishop of Jerusalem, the Rt Rev George Francis Graham Brown, complained to Montgomery about the actions of the British troops. Their discussion is reported by Edward Keith-Roach, a District Commissioner in the mandate's administration, in his book Pasha of Jerusalem. According to Keith-Roach the Bishop 'had a long interview with Montgomery and came back absolutely bewildered. To every question, he said, Monty had but one reply: "I shall shoot them." "The man is blood mad," the bishop moaned across my office table.' However, unbeknown to the Bishop before his confrontation with Montgomery; Monty had already asked the officer who commanded the punitive expedition, Lieutenant-Colonel Whitfield, to 'go a wee bit easier in the future.'[95]

The Anglican Church was not alone in criticising British attempts to quell the rebellion in Palestine. British strategy was also a matter of debate on the international stage. In April 1939 the army's methods received condemnation from Adolf Hitler who stated that Palestine, "is having its liberty restricted by the most brutal resort to force, is being robbed of its independence, and is suffering the cruellest maltreatment for the benefit of Jewish interlopers."[96]

Some British soldiers were reprimanded for excessive and inappropriate actions against civilians; however, only one incident led to the prosecution of British personnel. This followed the murder of an Arab prisoner by four British policemen. This incident occurred in Jerusalem in October 1938. The policemen received token sentences for their actions. Yet it is important to remember that these incidents, although carried out by British servicemen, were not officially sanctioned by the senior British authorities. They were acts of violence carried out by individual soldiers and policemen, but sometimes with their immediate officers giving their tacit approval or at least turning a blind eye to this cruelty. Much of it was caused by the need for some in the security services to take retaliation and let off steam when operating in a frustrating, vicious and dangerous war. And in those circumstances such abuses are perhaps the inevitable outcome when men are placed in a warzone where the insurgents and their civilian supporters who were often indistinguishable from each other.

Matthew Hughes, a historian who has investigated abuses by the British in Palestine, concluded in his research that 'the British were often brutal but they rarely committed atrocities.' He further argues that the British approach was 'relatively speaking, humane and restrained – the awfulness was less awful – when compared to the methods used by other colonial and neo-colonial powers operating in similar circumstances.'[97] He also commented on the process of military justice. His verdict on the military courts was that they dealt a swift and harsh judgement upon those placed before them. The system of justice used by the British army was, and remains, controversial but the hearings did follow a legal process when delivering punishments against the rebels. There were, however, undoubtedly cases of innocent people being convicted as rebels. It is important to consider that despite the Arab Revolt resembling to all intents and purposes a war; it was from the perspective of the British authorities an illegal insurgency against the lawful government and was not a formal war. As such the Geneva Convention did not apply to the Arab guerrillas who were not protected by its strictures; this made some of the harsh sentences imposed by the military courts legally acceptable.

Yet it was clearly the case that many abuses against non-combatants did take place as did legally permissible collective punishments against many Arabs which included; fines, forced labour and the confiscation and destruction of property. However, despite the mistreatment that some civilians suffered and the death sentences that were imposed upon 'Palestinian patriots', as some may perceive them to be, the overall effect was not as inflammatory as similar, yet less severe, actions had been in Ireland during the Anglo-Irish War.

British peace proposals

There was a last attempt at peace which came from the British. The report of the Woodhead Commission published in November 1938 essentially rejected partition and the creation of a Jewish state. Discussions were held in London in February 1939 but by March the discussions had ended in deadlock. Still the British Government published in May 1939 its proposals in a White Paper on the way forward for Palestine. These swung British policy firmly behind the Arab position. The main suggestions were;

a) There would be no separate Arab and Jewish state.

b) Within 10 years one independent Palestinian state would be established in which both the Jews and the Arabs would share in Government according to their numbers (Arabs were the majority). This new state would also guarantee the interests of both communities.

c) Jewish immigration into Palestine would be at the reduced rate of 10,000 a year for five years, with a one off allowance for an extra 25,000 who were fleeing persecution in Europe, and then cease. This would limit Jewish numbers to just 1/3 of the population.

d) The sale of Arab lands to Jews would also be prohibited.[98]

Naturally these proposals were rejected by Palestine's Jewish community who in response then started a campaign of violence against both Arabs and the British military. Tellingly, however, the proposals were also rejected by the Mufti and the Arab Higher Committee because the proposals did not immediately end Jewish immigration into Palestine. The transitional arrangements in creating an independent Palestinian state were also rejected. What had happened was that the Arabs Revolt had secured a favourable peace offer but had then thrown this away. Since the Arab leadership rejected what was in effect a political victory the Palestinian's were destined to lose out on every other 'peace' deal ever since bar the 2000 Israeli offer to end the occupation of the Gaza Strip and 95% of the West Bank. Which despite that being Israel's best offer it was also rejected by the then President of the Palestinian National Authority Yasser Arafat.

It was a tragedy for the general Arab population, who just wanted to live their lives in peace, that the hardliners did not accept a permanent solution which favoured the interests of Palestine's native population. For the non-belligerent residents the only hope of peace was for the extremist Arab leadership to realise that all hope of total victory had been lost. Then the hardliners may accept a reasonable settlement, but in the case of Palestine this small window was lost, apparently forever. An end to the Arab Revolt was finally achieved by military means and, unlike the Woodhead proposals, the peace that followed was hardly favourable to the Arab side.

The military victory

Peace was restored to Palestine by the overwhelming and sustained military pressure applied by the British army. The intense and relentless offensive action by the British army by both night and by day and the confrontations and casualties that came from these patrols, cordons and searches made people fearful of the army and broke the spirit of the rebels. The large number of searches also brought in many prisoners who were detained under the orders of the Military Commanders. The number of those interned reached more than 5,000. Many of the detainees were imprisoned on the grounds of merely being suspected of being rebels but the policy of interning did significantly reduce the number and severity of guerrilla attacks and played a key part in order being restored.

This does not amount to a policy which can be described as the 'winning of hearts and minds' but it was successful. The rebel organisation had been effectively destroyed and the leaders were either dead or had fled the country. Furthermore, the base of support for the insurgents amongst the general population had been smashed thus taking away from the insurgents the fundamental requirement for any guerrilla conflict to survive let alone succeed. By July 1939 the rebellion had all but finished.

However, the situation was still critical and there was still some fighting to be done against the last few rebel gangs which were now widely seen to be little more than small criminal bands. Montgomery warned the London based Chief of the Imperial General Staff, Lord Gort, that if there is a let up in the drive to defeat the rebels, or if prisoners were released from the detention camps, then the conflict was likely to be re-ignited. He also thought that any such return of the rebellion should be stamped out quickly and firmly. Unfortunately in July 1939 a significant number of rebels were released and, just as Montgomery had warned, this lead to a resurgence of rebel violence. This time quick and decisive action was taken, as Montgomery advised it must be, and soon approximately 200 guerrilla rifles were being captured or surrendered to the British authorities per week.[99]

The Arab Revolt was over.

Chapter 13

AFTERMATH IN PALESTINE

Montgomery in his assessment of how long the fighting would last demonstrates the accuracy of his military insights into how the Jewish/Arab conflict would develop. Although one half of the problem had been solved by force of arms, that is the Arab rebellion against British rule, the other half had not. This unresolved part of the conflict was the intractable problem emanating from the tensions between the Jews and the Arabs. This was set to scar the MiddleEast for many decades to come. Montgomery predicted this and he wrote in his report; 'The Jew murders the Arab, and the Arabs murder the Jew... And it will go on for the next 50 years in all probability.'[100] Again Montgomery was not wrong.

The Arab Revolt in Palestine of 1936 to 1939 was also to resonate in the Arab national psyche. It has since become known as the Great Arab Revolt and more tellingly it has also been described as an *Intifada* which is an Arabic term which is translated into English as "uprising". That word is used to describe the modern uprisings against the Israeli occupation of Arab lands captured in the 1967 Six-Day War. The use of the word Intifada frames the 1930s revolt in the same political context, one of a fight for national freedom, and adds a further historical dimension to the on-going conflict. However, romanticising the 1936 – 1939 Arab Revolt in that way ignores the violence carried out by the Arab guerrillas against their fellow Arabs and their wanton criminality against the very people that they claimed to be fighting for.

Montgomery felt that this racial and religious conflict was not anti-British in nature. He also felt that the majority of the population was opposed to the violence. Montgomery blamed what he described as 'young hot-heads' on both sides for the bloodletting. He was correct in his assessment. The conflict had been provoked and intensified by attacks on civilians and it was the clear aim of some members of groups like the Irgun to terrorise the general Arab population. And in line with the times some members of both Palestine's Arab and Jewish communities were influenced by the radicalisation of European politics which in the years before the outbreak of the revolt saw the emergence of evermore militaristic anti-democratic regimes that had no inhibitions about using violence as a political tool. Furthermore, as a result of the pressures of social change brought about through Palestine's move towards industrialisation the Arab community had become increasingly radicalised. This brought the 'young hot-heads', as Montgomery described them, to the fore and they could no longer be contained by political means.

The fighting meant that the Arab forces were fatally wakened, their leaders discredited and many members of the Arab guerrilla bands had been killed, wounded or interred. The number of Arabs that received death sentences for their part in the revolt was more than 100. This figure, however, contrasts sharply with the number of Jewish people executed during the revolt which is thought to number just four.[101] There was also some token disciplinary action taken against British servicemen for abuses of the civilian population.

The casualty figures also give a telling picture of the scale of the victory achieved by the British army and their Jewish allies. Whereas just several hundred British soldiers had been killed in the fighting with a similar number of deaths amongst the Jewish militias; estimates put the number of Arabs killed by the end of the Arab Revolt in the summer of 1939 in the thousands. Many of these would have been combatants but would also include some civilian deaths. Studies conducted by Benny Morris, a Professor of History in the Middle East Studies department of Ben-Gurion University, Beersheba in Israel, suggest that the number of Arabs killed in the fighting between 1936 and 1939 numbered from 3,000 to 6,000.[102] It is likely that the most accurate single estimation of Arab lives lost in in the revolt was around the 5,000 mark. The conflict also caused between 10,000 and as many as 15,000 wounded. Furthermore, at the close of the conflict in 1939 there were still more than 5,500 held in the British detention camps. A significant number of the Arab casualties in the latter stages of the Revolt came from fighting between different Arab guerrilla bands as they clashed over territory and the spoils of war which they were looting from their fellow Arabs.

While the intra-Arab fighting hastened the defeat of their cause; the disputes between British trained and equipped Jewish militias were reduced as many members of the extremist Irgun re-joined the Haganah. Those same groups would later commit atrocities against the British in post-war Palestine were strengthened. The loss of life and disunity amongst those fighting on the Arab side of the conflict was not the only way in which the Palestinians became decisively weakened. It has been estimated that in the decade following the outbreak of the revolt in 1936 the British authorities took away more than 13,200 guns as well as large quantities of ammunition from Palestine's Arabs. Yet only 531 firearms were confiscated from members of the Jewish community.[103] Furthermore, those figures do not take into consideration the disparity of firepower caused through the British arming and training the Jewish police units which mixed with the Haganah, later to become the backbone of the Israeli army known as the Israeli Defence Force. This shift in the balance of power would tell when hostilities reopened when the British withdrew from Palestine in 1948.

The Palestinian Arab economy had also been badly hurt not only by the conflict and the British imposed curfews but also the strike which preceded the fighting. This dislocation of daily life hampered seriously the Arab economy and their commercial activities. The collective fines and penalties imposed upon the inhabitants of rebellious communities and the destruction of their homes and farms did further lasting damage to the wealth of the local Arab communities.

Yet it was not only the British army's activities that hurt the general population. The 'taxation' placed upon many Palestinians by those who were claiming to be fighting for the freedom of those which they were extorting also had an effect. This would harm the economic viability of Arab areas leaving them further weakened, and this led to an increase in the sale of land to Jewish immigrants. The Arab revolt therefore unwittingly committed a serious own goal and undermined a major plank as to why the rebellion began in the first place. Furthermore, as a result of Jewish immigration, the deaths of Arabs and the exile and exodus of others the Arab population was reduced to being less than 70% of the population of Palestine in 1939 from over 82% three years earlier.

Conversely, the Jewish inhabitants of Palestine through their loyalty to the British authorities had increased their influence over militarily important areas of land and over large parts of Palestine's transportation system and the economy. This meant that the Arab population were less able to defeat their Jewish neighbours when the Arabs tried to snuff out the Jewish state at its inception in 1948.[104] The following war gave the Israelis a further opportunity to expunge more of the Arab population from that disputed land.

Another impact of the Revolt was that as law and order had for some time broken down and as the security services had to use their resources containing the rebellion there was ample opportunities for criminals to exploit the weakness of the government. Bandits were free to carry out abductions for ransom and murder their enemies in vendettas. Montgomery felt that a large part of the population was engaged in this criminality.

The defeat of the Arab Revolt also had the important result that the British Empire was not humbled and humiliated in what had in part became a proxy war between the UK and Germany on the eve of World War II. This was especially important because the rebel leadership had close political ties to the Germans and Arab lands were to be a key battleground in the war.

Montgomery advised that as the rebellion had been 'smashed' the number of battalions could be drawn down. He recommended that the cavalry contingent could be halved to just one regiment and that nine battalions, instead of the current twelve, would be sufficient to maintain law and order. This time, now that the job had been followed through to its conclusion, Montgomery wrote that, 'It is not possible for the rebellion to raise its head again on the scale we previously experienced.'[105]

He left Palestine in July 1939 on sick leave and prepared for the coming war with Germany. The war in Palestine greatly helped Montgomery develop his war fighting skills, which would be used to their full in the coming conflict with the Nazis. Tackling the Arab Revolt and its required use of night manoeuvres were amongst the important expertise that would have been honed and were used to their fullest when Germany launched its Blitzkrieg on France and the Low Countries in 1940.

Here Monty commanded a Division and he made sure that they were effective at night.

This skill was fundamental in bringing his troops out of the tactical mess the ineffective allied leadership of the French military and the British Expeditionary Force had forced upon his troops allowing him to help secure the perimeter around Dunkirk and thus help with the vital evacuation of hundreds of thousands of French, British and allied soldiers. He won many plaudits for this outstanding manoeuvre, especially from the man who became Chief of the Imperial General Staff, Field Marshal Alan Brooke, later Lord Alanbrooke. He nurtured Montgomery's career throughout the Second World War.

The campaign in Palestine would have also helped develop Montgomery's ability to coordinate air and ground forces. Montgomery noted in a letter reporting back on the situation in Palestine that, 'the war out here is the most magnificent training for the Army and the RAF, and we are producing seasoned fighting men second to none.'[106] The conflict in Palestine would have helped Montgomery become psychologically prepared for the fighting in the Second World War. His first description of the use of 'crumbling' operations, the strategy of wearing down and gradually eliminating an opponent, came from the fighting in Palestine. That approach to warfare added to Montgomery's experience in dealing with hard attritional warfare which Montgomery described as crumbling. This was fundamental in his victory over Rommel at El-Alamein and again in Northern France. Where, during the Battle of Normandy, small fields surrounded by high hedgerows, known as the *Bocage*, permitted only a slow grinding and murderous slog.

The Mufti, after failing to rekindle the rebellion at the start of the Second World War, fled to Iraq disguised as a woman whilst being under the surveillance of the French in the Lebanon. In Iraq he mixed with that country's pro-Nazi circles.[107] He later spent the rest of the war years in Nazi Germany where he supported their war efforts by encouraging Muslims from Bosnia and Herzegovina to join the Waffen SS. It is a matter of historical debate as to whether or not he knew of the Holocaust through his connections with Adolf Eichmann.

The British soldiers who took part in this conflict had their service recognised by the awarding of the General Service Medal. Montgomery played an important role in making sure that this was awarded to the troops.

Lessons to be learned

Posterity is fortunate that Bernard Law Montgomery and the military establishment set out their thoughts on tackling the Arab Revolt so that other generations in future conflicts could learn from their experience and apply the correct approach elsewhere from the start. However, as this conflict was on the eve of the biggest conventional war in human history it is not surprising that until now the lessons have been lost.

When the conflict was over it was recognised that the authorities in Palestine had clearly not learned the lessons from the earlier guerrilla war in Ireland. The Royal Irish Constabulary had not been adequately supported at the earliest opportunity, and so they had not been able to contain the rebellion in Ireland. They had been a dispersed force, under civilian control, which found itself overwhelmed as its isolated rural posts were destroyed, its officers killed and their families intimidated. The same had happened to the police in Palestine in the early stages of the troubles. The lessons were clear, dual control, let alone civilian control, did not offer security; it could not deliver peace. In such times of crisis the military should control the police with ultimate authority resting with the Military Commander who will then be able to ensure that both security services work as one.

In short, it was realised that the seven golden rules for better policing are;

(i) Speedy disarmament of unreliable police and the removal of arms to safety.

(ii) Giving up weak posts and concentrating forces in strengthened positions.

(iii) A general tightening up of discipline and improvement of amenities wherever possible.

(iv) Ensuring the safety and efficiency of signal communications and transport.

(v) Re-organizing and tightening control of auxiliaries.

(vi) Responsibilities of Army and Police clearly defined.

(vii) Subsequent steady expansion of Police working on a set plan.[108]

Giving the police better pay and conditions, especially improved accommodation, also enhances their ability to deal with the most testing of circumstances.

It was also recognised that it was important to show the population that the Government was in control. Examples of notable symbolic operations were the recapture of Jerusalem's Old City which took place from 18th to 22nd October 1938. The recapture of Haifa, Jaffa, Acre and Gaza, also in October, although playing little part in the overall victory did succeed in raising British prestige. Another notable case came on 31st December 1938 when the military forced the re-opening of the Jerusalem to Lydda railway. These operations were of little strategic value but they sent a message that the army was determined and would not give up the fight.[109]

Another key lesson is that throughout the conflict when troop numbers declined the rebel violence increased to a point where it seemed as if the revolt would succeed. Furthermore, when prisoners were released the violence intensified. Montgomery had learned from the events in Ireland that releasing prisoners from detention camps as a sign of good will whilst the conflict was still raging had succeeded only in making the British appear weak. In turn this had replenished the ranks of the rebel army thus fuelling the insurgency. Furthermore, the civil government in Palestine refused to build more detention camps and dealt with the problem of overcrowding by letting 300 rebel prisoners out. This meant that if Montgomery wanted to have for example 50 prisoners detained, 50 would first have to be released to make room for them. Montgomery wrote of the release of prisoners in Palestine;

'One must, I suppose, preserve a sense of humour. But this letting out of rebels to make room for other rebels may not be so funny in the end, and may be the cause of British soldiers losing their lives.' [110]

The positions amongst the different groups in Palestine became so entrenched and so deeply in opposition to one another that there could never be a meeting of minds between the Jewish settlers and the Palestinian Arabs. This stopped the British army from withdrawing and handing over the defence and administration of the area to its inhabitants. The lessons of peace discussions in Palestine were that they were counter-productive. The discussions which followed the establishment of the Peel Commission were that they only delayed the inevitable. What is more, the ceasing of military operations and the grace shown to the rebels allowed them to recuperate, reorganise and rearm just when they were being unbalanced by the army's offensive action. This just made the fighting far more threatening when it resumed.

Montgomery also had one eye on the future and the need to train the troops in the latest techniques for dealing with conventional warfare, skills which they would soon need. He recognised that the soldiers in Palestine excelled at dealing with 'a savage and mobile enemy'.[111] Yet, the British soldiers were not trained in other forms of warfare. Montgomery knew then that the purpose of the army should not be restricted to dealing with one type of conflict. The armed forces must be prepared to deal with whatever scenario may emerge in an unpredictable world. Perhaps that is an approach which should be kept in mind in the modern era.

Three clear mantras have emerged from the conflict in Palestine:

1. The lives and property of those that remain loyal must be defended. This should remain the priority of the police.

2. Communications must be protected. This task is one that requires police and troops to work together. As it was recognised that defending the whole communication infrastructure was impossible it was concluded that 'offence will provide the best defence.'

3. The rebel armed forces must be defeated. This should be the sole responsibility of the military and at the heart of this is the aggressive use of the army in combat and not wasting their finite numbers on tasks to which the police are more suited. [112]

The importance of offensive action in bringing the rebels to battle is of key importance. As a contemporary military report emphasised;

'The bandit leaders must not be allowed to call the tune to which the Forces dance. They must be brought to the defensive – it must be they who are wondering what next they will have to counter – they must not be able to sit down and devise plans for offence but should be kept wondering how to protect themselves against offence. As they begin to lose the initiative, so do their followers lose courage; and as the number of their adherents diminish and they become increasingly hunted – instead of hunting – the leaders themselves will finally be checkmated and disappear.' [113]

Authority for this hunting down of the rebels should be decentralised to the local commanders on the ground to act as they see fit without interference from the civil authorities and the politicians.

The lessons of failing to crush the rebellion from the start were summed up in another report from the time. This argued that the adoption of repressive action to restore law and order will in the long-term be the most humane way forward. A key conclusion read;

'The rebellion in Palestine provides perhaps more than anything else an example of the consequences of delaying the application of force to meet force. The failure of a policy of conciliation led in the end to the despatch of a Field Force from England and the adoption of more severe repression than might perhaps have been needed had it been applied from the beginning.

The report continues;

'The years which followed the rebellion show the results of a failure to carry repression to its logical conclusion by leaving the armed forces of the enemy intact in the field. In rebellion as in war, peace can seldom be restored in full so long as the latter remain undefeated; to defeat them, therefore, should be the first and foremost object of the Fighting Forces.' [114]

Furthermore, Lieutenant-General Wavell, who had served as the General Officer Commanding-in-Chief of British forces in Palestine had commented to a fellow British officer, Brigadier Evetts, that, "if the Germans were in occupation in Haifa we'd not have any bloody trouble from the Arabs". [115]

Would the British military and their political masters learn the lessons of this conflict? Montgomery wrote of a trait unique to the peoples of the United Kingdom that;

'There is no doubt that we British are an amazing people. We never seem to learn from past mistakes... However, we seem to

win our wars in the end.' [116]

Montgomery, his health shattered from Palestine's climate and the excessive demands of his work, left the Mandate in July 1939. Before Montgomery left he wrote to the War Office's head of personnel management known as the Military Secretary, Lieutenant-Gnereral Sir Wellesley Douglas Studholme, that,

> *'... you can go from one end of Palestine to the other looking for a fight and you can't get one; it is very difficult to find Arabs to kill; they have had the stuffing knocked right out of them... I shall be sorry to leave Palestine in many ways as I have enjoyed the 'war' out here.'* [117]

Montgomery, with his reputation greatly enhanced, came back to the UK to take over the training of the 3rd, also known as the 'Iron', Division in southern England. He was to command this division as part of the British Expeditionary Force in France and Belgium.

Part IV

Lessons to be Learned

Chapter 14

ASSESSING MONTGOMERY IN ACTION

'I have always admired you for definitely outstanding characteristics that were of the most tremendous value in whipping the Germans.'

General Dwight D Eisenhower, who was the Supreme Commander of Allied forces in Europe during World War Two, praising the fighting qualities of Montgomery in a personal letter sent to him in February 1946

Some have analysed Montgomery's actions during the Second World War and used the simple yet clichéd argument that Monty was a mere infantry officer who approached his battles in an overly methodical fashion. And unfavourably compare him with commanders who had a background in the cavalry which apparently explains their more audacious battle tactics. Such an analysis is as indolent as it is incorrect. Not only did Montgomery conceive some bold operations throughout his time as a military leader but he also commanded cavalry in the earlier part of his career. In both Ireland and Palestine he used mounted units as well as soldiers using highly mobile armoured cars in fast sweeps throughout the battlespace. And during the so-called One Hundred Days Offensive at the close of the First World War, which Montgomery had a role in planning; cavalry was a part of the operations that reintroduced mobile warfare to the Western Front.

Monty's strategy and tactics in World War II are still a subject of heated debate amongst military historians. Perhaps the on-going controversy surrounding his later career is a mark that he truly was an influential character. Whereas his performance in the Second World War is a matter for historians, his experience gained from the fighting in two counter-insurgencies and the conclusions that he drew from these guerrilla wars are still relevant to military planners in the modern era. They will no doubt remain so into the future. But how did he perform as a military commander in the conflicts in Ireland and Palestine?

Montgomery can be assessed against a number of core military tenets. These are benchmarks known as the Principles of War. These should be adhered to by military commanders. They were first advocated by the soldier and renowned military theorist Carl von Clausewitz. They have since been enhanced and built-upon by other strategists and have been adapted to suit the needs of each era and nation. Most militarily significant states now have their own Principles of War and the British military is not alone in having its own unique advice which it supplies to its commanders. The United Kingdom's modern guidance is contained within a Ministry of Defence publication known as the *British Defence Doctrine* (BDD). According to NATO, defence doctrine is a reference point to the 'fundamental principles by which military forces guide their actions in support of objectives.'

The British Defence Doctrine has 10 Principles of War which should be referred to by military commanders to give them a foundation in the art of warfare and guide their operations to ensure success on the battlefield. The ten British Principles of War are; Selection and Maintenance of the Aim, Maintenance of Morale, Offensive Action, Security, Surprise, Concentration of Force, Economy of Effort, Flexibility, Cooperation and Sustainability. But how did Montgomery's actions in Ireland and Palestine compare to the yardsticks of the modern British Army which are summarised below? It is important to apply the BDD because the resolution to an insurgency will not come through an attempt to broker a political compromise with an undefeated enemy instead it will ultimately flow from military success.

- **Selection and Maintenance of the Aim** A single, unambiguous aim is the keystone of successful military operations. Selection and maintenance of the aim is regarded as the master principle of war. It is fundamentally important that this single aim pervades subordinate operations, all of which should contribute coherently to achieving this end-state, and that resources are allocated accordingly. Therefore, plans should be continually checked against the related objectives of the campaign to ensure they remain valid. In practice, uncertainty, political reality and insufficient initial understanding of a situation frequently conspire against achieving an unambiguous aim from the outset. This ambiguity is exacerbated in multinational operations by differing national ambitions and perspectives. Military operations may, therefore, begin on the basis of an aim which at the time seems sensible but may need to be reconsidered as circumstances change.

When it came to the setting of clear aims and objectives Montgomery was unambiguous. He instructions were that the role of the army was to take the fight to the enemy and eliminate the insurgents through aggressive action. Throughout Montgomery's career he also stressed the need to have a master plan to which all other plans must be subordinated.

However, as can be shown in Ireland when the political situation changed so did Montgomery's military strategy. Instead of pursing an aggressive approach towards the IRA, he sought to aid the establishment of the Irish Free State as well as maintain the security of his soldiers whilst seeking not to inflame the political situation.

• **Maintenance of Morale** Morale is a positive state of mind derived from inspired political and military leadership, a shared sense of purpose and values, well-being, perceptions of worth and group cohesion.

Morale was always at the heart to Montgomery's approach as a commanding officer. Monty also recognised the benefit of offensive action as a morale booster, particularly when engagements with the enemy were successful.

• **Offensive Action** Offensive action is the practical way in which a commander seeks to gain advantage, sustain momentum and seize the initiative. Offensive action delivers the benefits inferred by action rather than reaction, and the freedom to force a decision. At its heart is the notion of an offensive spirit, which imbues forces with confidence, encourages enterprise and determination not to cede the initiative, as well as promoting a culture of success and achievement.

Montgomery' clearly took the offensive in Palestine as is shown by the advice he gave to the Chief of the Imperial General Staff to; '... hunt down and destroy the rebel armed gangs. They must be hunted relentlessly; when engaged in battle we must shoot to kill... This is the surest way to end the war.' In Ireland, however, the demands placed upon British soldiers were at times too great.

• **Security** Security is the provision and maintenance of an operating environment that affords the necessary freedom of action, when and where required, to achieve objectives. It demands prudent risk management and the protection of high value assets, including personnel, material, information and infrastructure, as well as those military activities vital to operational success.

Security was at the heart of his operations. Montgomery believed that the most important asset in an army was the individual soldier. In both guerilla wars he paid close attention to making sure his troops were protected from attack particularly enemy ambushes. In the battle with the Arab insurgents in Palestine Montgomery considered that the protection of infrastructure from acts of sabotage was one that should be undertaken by the police. Guard duty, Montgomery felt, was not only bad for the soldier's morale but also failed to utilize their main strength which was offensive action.

- **Surprise** Surprise is the consequence of shock and confusion induced by the deliberate or incidental introduction of the unexpected. It involves, to varying degrees, secrecy, concealment, deception, originality, audacity and tempo, and confuses, paralyses or disrupts effective decision-making and undermines an opponent's cohesion and morale.

In the war in Ireland it was difficult to surprise the IRA who would avoid contact with the British army and thus become difficult to locate. Montgomery took the step of advocating foot patrols which could approach a town without being heard. The opportunities for surprise were, however, limited due to poor air cover. The introduction of wireless communications to coordinate attacks to take advantage of intelligence allowed the mobile columns to have a greater opportunity so surprise the guerrillas. Due to more effective airpower and radio communications these tactics worked with much greater success in the fighting in Palestine. Outwitting the opponents would later become a hallmark of Montgomery's tactics in the Second World War.

- **Concentration of Force** Concentration of force involves the decisive, synchronized application of superior fighting power (conceptual, physical, and moral) to realize intended effects, when and where required. Concentration does not necessarily require the physical massing of forces, but their agile disposition such that they can engage and prevail through the aggregation and coordination of appropriate elements of fighting power at critical points and times.

This is a proactive policy rather than reacting to attacks from an enemy force. Such a course of action was at the centre of Montgomery's military tactics in Palestine and in Ireland where he pursued the guerrillas with the intention of overwhelming them in battle.

- **Economy of Effort** Economy of effort is the judicious exploitation of manpower, materiel and time in relation to the achievement of objectives. Economy of effort is best summarized as the right tool, in the right place, at the right time, leading to the right result.

The sizeable sweeps of the Irish countryside cannot be considered as an economic use of force. As a result of their large and cumbersome nature they were too easy for the IRA to detect and avoid. In Palestine the much smaller and more nimble special force operations had greater success in locating the Arab bands. More powerful forces could then be called in to engage the guerrillas.

- **Flexibility** Flexibility – the ability to change readily to meet new circumstances – comprises agility, responsiveness, resilience, acuity and adaptability. Agility is the physical and structural ability that allows forces to adjust rapidly and decisively, especially when operating in complex situations or in the face of new or unforeseen circumstances. Responsiveness is a measure of not only speed of action and reaction, but also how quickly a commander seizes (or regains) the initiative.

Montgomery throughout his military career was always seeking to take the initiative, His effective planning mostly led to the opposing forces having to react to his tactics. In the fighting in Palestine, and even in the struggle in Ireland Montgomery held the initiative. Republican military leaders testified that Monty was effective and even in the battle with the highly organised IRA Montgomery's tactics 'seriously menaced the survival of the I.R.A. units.'

• **Cooperation** Cooperation entails the incorporation of teamwork and a sharing of dangers, burdens, risks and opportunities in every aspect of warfare. Within alliances or coalitions, potentially disparate goals and interests need to be harmonized, and political and military cohesion promoted and protected, to ensure solidarity in the face of difficulties or dangers, and to preserve overall unity of effort.

In the north of Ireland the use of the loyalist militia as Special Constables reinforced the ability of the Crown forces to fight the IRA. However, it also led to British forces becoming too closely associated with one particular side in Ireland's vicious internal sectarian conflict which further alienated the Roman Catholic population and encouraged them to revolt against the institutions of the British state. This is one charge, however, that cannot be levelled at Montgomery who failed to utilise, let alone adequately defend, loyalists in County Cork; a matter which he regretted. Nevertheless he would have worked closely with the Auxiliary Division of the Royal Irish Constabulary and their supporting units known as the Black and Tans. In Palestine allied Jewish militias were exploited to their full potential. They not only assisted by taking the offensive alongside army units but also supplied valuable intelligence on the Arab forces. In the fight against the Arab insurgents Montgomery's cooperation with the police was very much one where he was the senior partner and he became in effect the de facto commander of the civilian security services.

• **Sustainability** To sustain a force is to generate the means by which its fighting power and freedom of action are maintained. A rigorous assessment of logistic realities is essential to operational planning; indeed, it may be the deciding factor in assessing the feasibility of a particular campaign.

The martial law area of southern Ireland had an enormous concentration of British soldiers. Given the international demands placed upon the UK and the workload of the troops in Ireland this was barely sustainable and still the rebellion endured. Montgomery was a master of organising both men and material yet the sustainability of keeping operations underway in Ireland was questionable at best.

Other nations have additional notions of how to achieve victory in their Principles of War. The Russian military has long advocated the concept of annihilation. This emphasises that commanders should use combined arms, such as ground and airpower, not only to defeat but also to destroy the opposing forces. The Russian Principle also stresses the need to achieve a deep penetration of an opponent's line from where the rear area of an enemy force can be disrupted and subsequently the main body of the opposing army can be encircled and then annihilated. Montgomery had exactly that same aim in Ireland and especially so in Palestine where his sweeps were intended to surround and then destroy the insurgents. In the Mandate territory Montgomery also successfully employed combined arms tactics to fight the Arab guerrillas.

The armed forces of the United States of America also differ from the British Principles of War by adding the notion of simplicity. The Americans emphasise that simple and straightforward tactics are more likely to deliver success on the battlefield. The tactics used by Montgomery throughout his career can be considered multifaceted at best and at worst excessively complex. This made some operations subject to too many variables. Perhaps it was the case that his knowledge of military affairs outweighed the need for economy and frugality. However, in Ireland his highly organised sweeps of the countryside converging on a given location did nearly succeed in eliminating the IRA in parts of County Cork. In Palestine Monty's combined operations involving aeroplanes, armoured cars and cavalry did win the war for the British Army. The US concept of simplicity also emphasises the importance of issuing clear and concise instructions. In this regard Montgomery truly excelled. He ensured that every soldier new what his role was and how he fitted into the wider strategic aims of the operation.

The modern British army's advice on how to deal with a guerrilla war stresses the need for commanders to counter the advantages of irregular opponents by employing, 'the selective application of appropriate elements of fighting power to counter and exceed their particular attributes.' The advantages that the Arab bands utilised in Palestine were speed and ease of movement. Montgomery's effective use of even more mobile units combined with airpower surpassed the main strengths which the Arab guerrillas possessed at the start of the fighting.

Victory over a guerrilla force is by no means guaranteed even if their strong points are neutralised. The *British Defence Doctrine*, however, warns an army commander that, 'high morale and a strong resolve, or will to fight, may enable an apparently inferior opponent to absorb punishment yet sustain the determination and capacity to re-engage.' In Palestine Montgomery through his aggressive hunting of the rebel bands broke both their will and ability to continue waging war upon the British authorities.

American military advice warns that the commanders of conventional larger units can become extremely vulnerable to attacks from asymmetric forces which will often seek to strike at them using acts of terror and hit and run guerrilla style tactics. Military thinkers in the United States of America recognise that attacks by insurgents can be at times little more than a nuisance to the overall tactical aims of a mission; with their greatest impact being only to temporarily disrupt a unit from reaching its objective. However, it is accepted that an unconventional attack from irregular forces can also have far wider strategic consequences. In 1983 US peacekeeping forces based in Beirut in the Lebanon were attacked by a massive truck bomb leading to much loss of life. This led to the political decision to withdraw from the Lebanon; an act which was to convince Osama Bin Laden that America lacked resolve. In fact following the assassination of Osama Bin Laden's documents were captured which showed that the terror chief's aims were to make the price that America and her allies pay for their involvement in the Islamic world too high. Bin Laden hoped this would force the withdrawal of western influence from Muslim territory. In the US asymmetric warfare is given as an example of where conventional forces can be strategically defeated by unconventional and unethical means. The modern military commander must be on guard against such occurrences especially as the danger of such attacks of terror grows if insurgents use even more deadly weapons, such as those which have a biological or nuclear component.

Montgomery recognised one important way in which the guerrilla war in Ireland could strategically defeat the forces of the United Kingdom. Montgomery in his *Summary of Important Instructions to the 17th Infantry Brigade* outlawed the troops from taking reprisals against civilians who were not part of the IRA's network. However, a number of atrocities carried out by those Temporary Constables of the Royal Irish Constabulary who were not directly under the command of the British Army were causing a great deal of alarm back in mainland Britain. And many British politicians wanted to disengage the forces of the Crown from what was becoming an increasingly sordid conflict. This was defeat being delivered by way of bad public relations.

In the past the US armed forces have not had the concept of flexibility as one of its Principles of War, they have instead incorporated it in other areas of their military doctrine such as in advice on the manoeuvring of an enemy into a vulnerable position. The need for flexibility is now receiving a special emphasis from American strategists. As their forces increasingly have to face irregular forces in the guerrilla wars that they are being drawn into the need for flexibility is becoming ever more prominent. Montgomery was also a firm believer in flexibility. And British Defence Doctrine also establishes the principle of what is known as 'Mission Command'. If flexibility is to be more than just a phrase then a commander must have the freedom to make decisions without having to refer to distant superiors who will delay his or her decision making. According to the UK's defence establishment this system of managing military affairs known as Mission Command allows a commander in the field to, '… carry out missions with the maximum freedom of action and appropriate resources. It is predicated upon delegation of authority and agility in execution.'

At the core of mission command is flexibility of decision making where, 'Subordinates decide for themselves how best to achieve their superior's intentions and objectives.' Montgomery not only lived by that principle in Palestine he actually went beyond it and actually lobbied for the removal of staff at headquarters that he considered to be ineffectual. This was a pattern that he was to repeat throughout his career.

Mission Command and flexibility of decision making needs to be at the core of any conventional army's response to a meeting a challenge if they are to be successful. This is especially the case when dealing with an asymmetric danger, be that an act of terrorism or a guerrilla attack or the threat posed by an improvised explosive device. Commanders need to be able to choose their best defence and the appropriate level of offensive response to either deter an attack or to eliminate the opposing forces and thus ensure future security. This should not only mean that a commander must concentrate on improving the physical security of the troops and keeping critical information out of enemy hands. It will also mean that even the rules of engagement need to be altered by a military commander so that they can deal with the situation as they see fit.

Montgomery recognised the need for mission command in Palestine and he acted without the civil authorities in the Mandate undermining his efforts and as such peace was resorted through his taking the fighting to the insurgents. Monty's abilities and actions in Palestine are also in harmony with British military theory. The philosophy of Her Majesty's armed forces promotes an attacking ethos; and states that, 'An offensive spirit and a desire to get to grips with an opponent or problem are persistent features of British military operations.' The British Defence Doctrine also asserts that, 'The British Way implies a can do approach and demands that, no matter how difficult the circumstances or remote the immediate chances of success, the urge to succeed should predominate over the need to avoid failure.'

Nevertheless, this does not mean that the British Army is being allowed to fulfil its full martial potential in the modern war on terror that the UK has been drawn into.

The main lessons from Ireland and Palestine
The lessons that Montgomery would have drawn from his two guerrilla wars were manifold. Amongst them is that troop numbers is always of prime importance. This is the case in most

conflicts but of equal importance is how they are used and the training they have received to complete their task. Montgomery was to make sure that his troops were more than adequately prepared and in Palestine his units found the answer to beating an insurgency. In the Middle-East the aggressive use of highly-mobile detachments was to prove successful in securing victory for the government's forces.

The key military lesson is that to defeat an insurgency fast and flexible mobile forces must be used to take away the advantages that guerrillas have. They will be able to achieve tactical surprise and reverse the usual scenario of guerrilla war where the irregular forces ambush those of a conventional army. The guerrillas must be effectively hunted and located; other forces can then be brought in to isolate them, cut off any means of escape and apply overwhelming firepower to complete the defeat of the rebels.

Montgomery was by nature a man that had an innate need to get his own way. This character flaw, as some may perceive it, was an essential element in suppressing the insurgency in Palestine. In the British Mandate the principle of Military Control was established and this gave Montgomery the authority to take the action that he deemed necessary. What is more he had the drive and determination to push these measures through. Military Control, although a step short of full Martial Law, gave the military the ability to respond quickly to events and apply military solutions to what were military problems, namely security and attacks from rebel gangs. Furthermore, the military became in a position to subordinate the often indecisive and ineffectual civilian authorities, upon whose watch law and order had broken down, to the task of re-imposing British control over the Holy Land. This entailed effective measures being taken that ranged from effective use of the police to the building of new roads. Large parts of

Palestine in the 1930s were underdeveloped by modern standards and the improved all-weather road network which Montgomery had pushed for gave the army the ability to extend its reach and take the war to the guerrillas with greater ease and efficiency.

Another lesson was that the effectiveness of the police had to be improved to make them a much more robust force. In Ireland the virtual elimination of the Royal Irish Constabulary as a viable security service in many parts of Ireland gave the IRA a free hand to undermine British control. In Palestine the increase in police numbers helped restore order. Having a strong and effective police also freed the army from static defensive duties allowing it to take the offensive against the insurgents in greater numbers.

Victory is as much psychological as it is physical. If the rebels are afraid of the security services then they will be far from willing to engage them in combat and commit acts of terror. At first even the highly-organised Irish Republican Army was reluctant to take on the officers of the Auxiliary Division of the Royal Irish Constabulary. And the guerrilla forces in both Ireland and Palestine were averse to taking on the superior firepower of Montgomery's British army units. In Palestine the repressive measures of the soldiers succeeded in cowing the insurgent gangs into submission.

It is often the case that guerrilla armies are not the forces of legally established and recognised nation-states following the orders of a central and internationally recognised government. They are often popular uprisings from one section of the community; where the insurgents are motivated by political or religious radicalism, sometimes these are one and the same. The conflicts in both Ireland and Palestine show that what some may consider to be a reasonable compromise and political settlement was only achieved when the leadership of the guerrilla forces realised that their military objectives would not be met and that they were on the verge of defeat. Even in such circumstances the most hard-line will be unwilling to face the realities of the military situation in which they have placed themselves.

There are other intangible factors which Montgomery understood, most notably the issue of morale and in particular the danger posed to the soldiers' sense of purpose by criticisms of their actions at home in the media and in some political quarters. Monty made sure that his troops were properly motivated and believed in their work and were insulated from critical comments. Montgomery also understood that the motivations of the rebel forces were also important.

If the revolt is a nationalist uprising and the general population of the county which has become embroiled in conflict are motivated by a desire for national freedom then the insurgency would be very hard to suppress in anything but the short-term. In such a case it will often take troops who are of the same nationality as the rebels to root them out and re-impose law and order. That being the case it is also important to remember that the public will often back the side which has the upper hand. Both moral and practical support for the IRA and their cause grew amongst the civilian population when they saw that the insurgents were in some cases fighting the forces of the British crown to a stalemate. And in other instances the guerrillas had managed to eliminate the police force from certain areas. In Palestine, where much more repressive measures were taken, Montgomery observed how even the Muslim Arab population turned against his foe when the British forces successfully hunted them.

Montgomery recognised that many civilians will support the side that is winning. And as long as the civilian population receive fair treatment from the army when they complied with the military's control and did not support rebel activity then they would cease aiding the rebels and in some cases even switch allegiance to the British cause. In Palestine the response of many of the villagers to the repressive measures that were taken to restrict rebel activity also had the effect of turning the local Palestinian population against the insurgents. They blamed them and their continuation of the war for making their lives difficult. Their greatest desire was for peace and law and order; which only the army could deliver. As the rebels became evermore desperate for victory they began to push the civilians too hard for both new recruits and funds. The local population then withdrew their support for what had become little more than criminal gangs. In short, the hearts and minds of the local population followed the army's serious efforts to defeat the rebels and were not the cause of the military winning the conflict.

Montgomery also came to the conclusion that any anti-government violence must be stamped-out quickly and not allowed to fester otherwise it will continue to endanger peace and grow in intensity. Furthermore, the release of prisoners whilst the conflict is still underway will only lead to an upsurge in rebel activity.

There are modern conflicts that are reminiscent of the ones tackled by Montgomery. However, the British military leadership has not always learned the lessons of the past; particularly in the fields of planning and preparation.

Chapter 15

NORTHERN IRELAND, IRAQ AND AFGHANISTAN IN THE MODERN ERA

Three modern conflicts have been closely tied to each other. The British army ceased active service operations in Northern Ireland confident in the belief that it knew how to handle an insurgency. After another successful mission in Sierra Leone it took this confidence, or perhaps complacency, to its next major deployment in Iraq where it had the task of upholding the principle of law and order to aid the reconstruction of that land. The army's illusions were soon to be shattered by this conflict yet as an insurgency spiralled out of control the UK's military became heavily committed to a war on another front in Afghanistan. This began in earnest when in 2006 they were sent to the south-western part of Afghanistan known as Helmand Province; here the British military soon got caught-up in a guerrilla war waged by the Taleban. These two conflicts against Islamic inspired militias split the UK's resources; however, the Ministry of Defence made the task much more difficult for itself by failing to follow properly their own Principles of War. The military leadership also failed to apply the strategic lessons learned by Montgomery in those earlier guerrilla wars in Ireland and Palestine.

Northern Ireland

'Insurgent actions are similar in character to all others fought by second-rate troops: they start out full of vigour and enthusiasm, but there is little level-headedness and tenacity in the long run.'
Carl Von Clausewitz on The People in Arms in his renowned book
On War

The modern troubles and their resolution

The War in the 26 southern counties ended, but the sectarian conflict spread quickly to the six counties of Northern Ireland that remained part of Britain. There were periods known as the Border Wars which occurred soon after the Anglo-Irish War ended and flared up again in the 1950s. The period known as The Troubles began in the late 1960s and is presumed to have ended in 1998 with the approval of what is known as the Belfast Agreement, which some call the Good Friday Agreement. This peace deal was the result of many years of firstly unofficial and then official negotiations between the Republicans and the British authorities and Unionist and Loyalist politicians. And preceding those talks there was a process of informal discussions between moderate Irish Nationalist politicians and their more hard-line Republican counterparts.

Nevertheless, the legacy of the Anglo-Irish war is still with us today in Northern Ireland where there is still mistrust and sectarian violence between the Province's two communities. The modern pattern of violence in Northern Ireland was very different to the guerrilla war that was waged by the original Irish Republican Army in the years following the First World War. Ulster's troubles were often little more than uncoordinated acts of bombings, intimidation and the killing of those whose religion differed from the terrorists' own. In contrast, the actions of the original IRA in the Anglo-Irish War were just part of a wider political strategy. This was the creation of a shadow state and new Republican institutions which would in time replace those of the British administration in Ireland. This included the creation of a new police force and legal system. The terrorists in Northern Ireland did seek to regulate life in their respective territories; which they 'taxed' and 'policed' and imposed punishments where they saw fit. This, however, was little more than the terrorising of the people they claimed to be representing.

In recent years, however, despite there being occasional acts of rioting and a limited number of rudimentary bomb attacks the tit-for-tat murders between the different communities have markedly reduced in number. As have the attacks on the security services. There is still the occasional murder and inter-communal flashpoint but these are minor compared to the troubles at their height just a few decades ago. Much of this reduction in violence is in part down to war weariness amongst Ulster's population. Violence is now far less acceptable and there are fewer recruits coming through to join the ranks of the paramilitaries. The collapse of communism would also have played its part in lessoning the violence. During the 1970s and the 1980 there was an international network of revolutionary socialist groups which worked together supplying weapons, financial support and training. Members of Republican paramilitary groups were known to train alongside Palestinian militants. In time this nexus of terror, and the mutual assistance that it brought, became greatly diminished as large parts of the globe moved away from militant socialism.

Another factor was the fact that the IRA began to realise that they had consistently failed to make a military breakthrough against the British forces in Northern Ireland. The IRA and other Republican paramilitaries did achieve some successes, most notably ethnically cleansing large parts of the Protestant community from the counties which border the Republic of Ireland, particularly from south Armagh. They had also provoked many propaganda successes. Yet they had also been highly penetrated by the intelligence services and were effectively being outfought by the British Army. And by the security services of the Republic of Ireland, a state which the IRA did not recognise, which managed to curtail some of the IRA's activities in the 26 southern counties of Ireland.

Nonetheless, the most important individual factor in reducing the violence was the peace process and the agreement between most of the hitherto warring parties. This is a far from perfect peace and it would not have occurred had it not been for the previously mentioned military conditions, but it did deliver tangible results. Montgomery would have recognised the need for this second agreement to end the fighting in Northern Ireland just as he had seen the need for a settlement to end the war on that troubled island in the 1920s.

Peace Offers
The agreement which has the support of many terrorists groups and their political representatives, most notably Sinn Féin which is the political-wing of the Provisional IRA, established some all-Ireland institutions and most importantly brought in power sharing to Northern Ireland via a devolved

assembly. It is worth remembering that the principle that Northern Ireland could be incorporated into the Republic of Ireland - if that is what the majority wanted - was established long before the Belfast Agreement. It was officially recognised by the British Government in 1985 when the Anglo-Irish Agreement was signed by Prime Minister Margaret Thatcher; and reaffirmed by John Major during his Premiership in 1993.

The 1998 Belfast Agreement has had its difficulties but it has proved to be the basis for the removing of militarism from political discourse. It has also served as a stepping stone towards later agreements such as the St Andrew's Agreement of 2006. There were previous attempts to strike a peace accord. In the early 1970s the British Government, in conjunction with moderate Unionists and Nationalists and the Government of the Republic of Ireland, brokered a power sharing agreement. This also had a role for the institutions of the Irish Republic who would have input into Northern Irish affairs via a Council of Ireland. This Council may have evolved overtime to become an institution that would have begun a process of unifying the two political systems on the island of Ireland. This 'deal', however, did not receive support from Republicans, who withheld their co-operation from the settlement, and intensified their campaign of terror. The agreement also alarmed many Unionists and there was a corresponding upsurge in Loyalist violence. The agreement and the power sharing institutions quickly collapsed. In the mid-1980s the Prime Ministers of the United Kingdom and the Republic of Ireland agreed that the Republic would have a say in Northern Irish affairs. They also decided that the constitutional status of the Province was a matter for the majority of the population to decide. This was known as the Anglo-Irish Agreement; it also inflamed Unionist opinion and nearly sparked a major crisis. Like the Irish Convention and the Government of Ireland Act decades before, none of the attempts at a settlement in the 1970s and 80s secured peace. They were unilateral; but for a genuine settlement all sides must come to terms.

A significant factor that brought most of Northern Ireland's belligerents to the negotiating table and to commit to the cause of peace was the condition that convicted paramilitaries would be released from prison. Within criminal organisations it is often the case that a considerable amount of power rests with those in prison; the inmates being able to take retribution on their confederates if instructions are not followed and the wayward gang members are unfortunate enough to join them behind bars. However, the most important single catalyst for peace was the successful co-option of the terrorists and their political representatives, often one and the same, into the governing class of Northern Irish politics. Many former insurgents have now been given the responsibility of administering the UK's devolved governance in the six British counties of Ulster.

The peace process which involves some unscrupulous people receiving the benefits of office may seem distasteful to some. Furthermore, the various agreements also institutionalise sectarianism into the constitutional structure of Northern Ireland yet like the Anglo-Irish Treaty of 1921 the results of the Belfast Agreement have been to politically isolate the more militant members of Irish society. Former terrorists, just like the Government of the Irish Free State, now use their influence and links into their own community to quarantine and even root-out those who do not wish to accept the new order of a peaceful Northern Ireland. This was a task which the security services of the British state were never able do to, neither in Southern Ireland in the 1920s nor in the North from the 1960s onwards. The Republicans in Northern Ireland's government have little incentive to abolish their Statelet and their position of authority which they would surely loose if Northern Ireland was incorporated into the unitary state of the Republic of Ireland where there is little political support for Sinn Féin.

The Northern Ireland Assembly receives its legal authority from an Act of Parliament which received the Royal Assent when it was signed by the hand of Queen Elizabeth II the same hand that Martin McGuinness shook on 27th June 2012. The sectarians have prospered both politically and financially in the devolved assembly. And, in the case of the Sinn Féin MPs, some also reap the rewards on offer from membership of the UK Parliament in Westminster which they attend apart from entering the chamber. This is the most significant factor behind the continuing success of the peace process. Sinn Féin now eats from the King's table and has lost its political independence.

The senior echelons of Sinn Féin and the IRA may be in a state of denial about their co-option into the power structures of the United Kingdom and the personal benefits the illusion of power brings when in reality much political work is the rubbing stamping of proposals from bureaucrats based in Belfast, Westminster and Brussels. Martin McGuinness, when he was Northern Ireland's Minister for Education, did successfully deliver on the Sinn Féin policy to abolish Grammar Schools and the 11+ but this issue transcends constitutional arrangements. As the continuing efforts of the British government have shown since the Victorian era many politicians on the mainland do not actually want to directly run Northern Ireland and have only done so when the native population proved incapable of doing it properly for themselves. The terrorists in Northern Ireland have thankfully abandoned many of their former principles but were only willing to do so when the failure of their violence became apparent. Perhaps, however, this realisation would have come sooner if a number of security mistakes had not been made.

Peace through adequate security

In the 1970s a concession was made to the Nationalist and Republican leaders when the Ulster Special Constabulary (USC) was abolished. The USC, also known as the B-Special were the reserve units of the police and were tasked with combatting insurgents and their guerrilla operations. This was a task that they successfully carried out when combating the IRA's Border Campaign in 1922 and again in the 1950s. Like all police units in Northern Ireland its membership was mostly from the Protestant tradition, nevertheless it did at times defend Roman Catholics and their property from attacks by Protestants.

The abolition of the B-Specials only succeeded in increasing the violence. Not only were they effective at combating the IRA but their disbandment alarmed many Unionists. This fear led to a further upsurge in loyalist violence, which in turn begat more Republican violence. The Ulster Special Constabulary's abolition was also perceived to be a sign of weakness and that further terror could deliver even more results. This descent into anarchy meant there was an even greater need for the British Army. The army during Operation Motorman did manage to successfully eliminate the so-called no-go areas, most notably the IRA stronghold known as 'Free Derry'. And at first the soldiers were well received by many in Northern Ireland's Roman Catholic population but events were soon to change this. The army soon handed the Provisional IRA a number of propaganda victories which increased the violence. These resulted from a number of outrages which the troops committed and those actions were far worse than anything ever committed by members of the B-Specials.

When the Special Air Service (SAS) were first deployed to Northern Ireland in 1976 their operational freedom was restricted. The SAS were issued with the restrictive 'Yellow Card' rules of engagement, so named because they were written on a yellow card. This limited their fighting abilities because it stipulated that guns may only be fired as a last option and only if life is immediately under threat. And even then warnings had to be given. These rules also applied to the other British Army units at work in the Province.

However, when the SAS took action that was not in the spirit of restrictive rules of engagement it was to have results that in the long run aided the cause of peace. An example of this occurred in 1987 when the SAS succeeded in eliminating one of the most active IRA units in Northern Ireland; the East Tyrone Brigade. This IRA cell was in the process of attacking a police station in the village of Loughgall when it was ambushed by 26 soldiers, and all 8 IRA men were killed. It was alleged by Republicans at the time that the actions of the SAS in that counter-insurgency operation amounted to a shoot to kill operation. However, the defeat that they suffered did bring home to many members of the IRA the very real dangers they faced and that victories could be scored against them. As such minds began to become focused on finding a settlement to the conflict.

A similar situation occurred in Gibraltar in 1988 when the SAS as part of Operation Flavius killed the IRA operatives who were planning to launch a bomb attack against the British Army based on that self-governing British Overseas Territory. A similar SAS operation was launched in June 1991. This preemptive strike killed all three members of the IRA who were on their way to commit a sectarian attack on Coagh, a town in County Tyrone. It has been alleged that the SAS delayed their attack until the terrorists had armed themselves and could therefore be shot dead by the SAS without the restrictive rules of engagement being breached.

The creative interpretation of those rules came when the conflict had been underway for many years. Perhaps minds would have been focused earlier with the first steps towards peace undertaken much sooner if the Security Services' hands had not been tied by the initial strict interpretation of the 'Yellow Card' instructions. Nevertheless, in time the insurgency in parts of Northern Ireland had been suppressed to a point where it became manageable. Yet it was the political solution which delivered the final victory that allowed law and order to be restored, but IRA/Sinn Féin only accepted the path of peace because they realised that terror would not deliver victory. Yet just as many senior figures in the military, including Montgomery, supported peace negotiations in 1920 the *British Defence Doctrine* (BDD) also supports such an approach. The BDD states that, 'attempts to solve major security issues by military means alone seldom succeed in the long run (even if initially enjoying apparent success).' Yet it also recognises that in some conflicts;

'An irrational opponent, for example, may be unable to appreciate the potential repercussions of his actions; a fatalistic opponent, or martyr, may not care. Some opponents may not be susceptible to deterrence or coercion, and crisis resolution may depend, ultimately upon the application of force.'

This brings us on to more recent conflicts where the forces opposing the British Army showed an uncompromising attitude to the presence of the British security service in their country.

Iraq

'We must admit defeat here [Iraq] and move on for Afghanistan.' [118]

Colonel Tim Collins OBE, veteran of Northern Ireland's troubles and the Gulf War, commenting on the British failure in Iraq

British troops entered Iraq in March 2003. On the close of combat operations against what was left of Saddam Hussein's Ba'athist (secular Arab-nationalist) Regime they undertook a UN sanctioned occupation of southern Iraq which began in May of that year. Incidentally this land, like Palestine, was officially awarded to Britain by a League of Nations Mandate after the First World with the defeat of the Turkish Ottoman Empire. The boundaries of Iraq were also established by the United Kingdom. In 2003 the British area of occupation was the Shia dominated south of the country; this part of Iraq was quickly destabilised by a paramilitary group known as the Mahdi Army which is thought to have been supported by their co-religionists in the Islamic Republic of Iran. The principle city of this area is the key port of Basra on the Shatt al-Arab waterway; along the confluence of Iraq's two great rivers, the Euphrates and the Tigris.

Alarm bells should have rung

After Montgomery had secured victory in Palestine he wrote that, 'There is no doubt that we British are an amazing people. We never seem to learn from past mistakes... However, we seem to win our wars in the end.' [119] However, contrary to what he thought it is possible for Britain to lose conflicts and the 2003 to 2009 UK involvement in Iraq exemplifies this.

As the fighting got under way, and despite the fact that the Invasion of Iraq was an operation planned in advance, the British troops were not equipped adequately for combat. The armed forces even had to go to war without adequate body armour. This was admitted by the former Secretary of State for Defence, Geoff Hoon, at the Chilcot Inquiry, which was investigating the circumstances around the Iraq war. This failure to prepare our forces for combat not only led to a loss of British military prestige, British soldiers become known to their American counterparts as 'the borrowers' for their repeated requests for equipment, but the lack of protection also led to British soldiers being killed in action.

This sorry story is illustrated by a defence analyst named Dr Richard North in his book *Ministry of Defeat*. Here he paints a picture of how the UK's military establishment failed in their occupation of southern Iraq. Dr North particularly focuses on the procurement of equipment and its shortcomings which placed lives at risk. Poor procurement of vehicles and incorrect tactical choices of transport also left soldiers vulnerable to attacks from the numerous enemy militias. This was especially the case when troops had to travel in the now infamous Snatch Land Rover which had little armour to counter a blast from an Improvised Explosive Device (IED) or from a rocket propelled grenade or mortar attack. There was also a distinct lack of helicopters.

Despite repeated valiant efforts by British soldiers to root out the insurgents they were unable to contain the growing violence in Basra and effectively strike at the militants. There were also too few soldiers tasked with doing too much and operating without acceptable protection. Ultimately the UK forces effectively became confined to their base in Basra. Responsibility for security was handed back to the Iraqi authorities towards the end of 2007 and the troops that remained were limited to assisting with the training of the Iraqi army. The British military presence in Iraq finally came to an end when they withdrew in September 2009. The UK military presence not only failed to quell the violence but according to over half of the population of Basra it actually increased militia violence. Furthermore, despite the fact that the population of southern Iraq were marginalised during Saddam Hussein's regime the British army failed to win hearts and minds. 85% of Basra residents when polled in 2007 by Opinion Research

Business thought that the British presence had a detrimental impact on Iraq's southern provinces.[120]

Law and order was finally restored by the overwhelming force of the Iraqi army and police; who, in a series of unrelenting raids, took the fight to the militia groups. Ultimately following on from the so-called Battle of Basra in 2008 where the application of massive force was able to safely eliminate the insurgent strongholds, end the no-go-areas, and destroy the terrorist weapons factories.

The American experience in Iraq was quite different and their operations were eventually successful in securing law and order. They adapted quickly and brought in better protected vehicles and increased troop numbers so that the offensive could be taken; this was the so-called 'surge' where an extra 21,000 US troops were deployed to Iraq. The eventual American victory was also helped by them bringing on-board some of the various militias in the US zone of occupation. The American military formed an alliance with those groups who then took the fight to Al-Qaeda. This worked and the successful alliance with former insurgents who came from Iraq's Sunni tribes led to the tribal forces driving-out the terrorists from within their community. Furthermore, the American Commander of the Joint Special Operations Command, the controversial General McChrystal, successfully used an offensive strategy of raiding suspected Al-Qaeda operatives in Iraq. The raids, which often took place at night, helped break the back of the insurgency. General Stanley McChrystal later become the Commander of US Forces in Afghanistan (USFOR-A) and Commander of the International Security Assistance Force (ISAF) in that country - but was dismissed after it was reported that disparaging comments had been made by him and his staff about members of the American government.

The presence of British troops in Iraq is now over and that

fight has come to a close; but that was not the end to British military involvement overseas. The UK became even more heavily embroiled in the on-going guerrilla war in Afghanistan. Tackling the insurgency in Iraq was made even more difficult by the fact that the British armed forces were having to deal with another guerrilla war, a second front in Afghanistan. This split resources between the two conflicts but the lessons from the growing debacle in Iraq should have steered the UK in the right direction to avoid the same mistakes being made in Afghanistan. But did the British military establishment learn the lessons from the British occupation of Iraq as well as Montgomery's earlier conflicts in Ireland and Palestine?

Afghanistan

'We view it as unacceptable that UK Forces were deployed in Helmand for three years, as a result of a failure of military and political co-ordination, without the necessary personnel and equipment to succeed in their Mission.'
House of Commons Defence Committee

The war in Afghanistan has so far cost the British taxpayer approximately £14 billion. It is also the UK's most deadly conflict since the early 1950s. Here the UK is involved in trying to suppress the insurgency against the government of Afghanistan and prevent the Islamic fundamentalist and Al-Qaeda allied Taleban from returning to power. The fight against the guerrilla forces has claimed hundreds of British lives. Ministry of Defence figures show that from when the UK deployed to Helmand in 2006 to 31st August 2012, 420 British service personnel lost their lives in Afghanistan. Five British lives were lost in Afghanistan from when the initial involvement began on 7th October 2001 to 2005. During this time 2,005 servicemen have been admitted to hospital as a result of being wounded in action. Many of these casualties could have been avoided if the military leadership had prepared adequately for the conflict and followed their own Principles of War.

In the operations in Afghanistan there was on occasions scant regard paid to many of the British army's key tenets which should have been followed. The security of soldiers was risked due to a poor choice of vehicles and the deployment to isolated and untenable bases also endangered lives. The element of surprise was also at times willing abandoned. Furthermore, the Ministry of Defence and the army leadership also failed to concentrate sufficient amounts of force against the Taleban to enable British commanders to take adequate offensive action. This meant that they were at times unable to seize the initiate and were often merely reacting to events not shaping them. The principle of 'Flexibility' has also not been followed as the army was woefully slow in adapting to new challenges as the war developed. The aims and objectives of the British involvement have also been unclear and at times contradictory.

Below is a short précis of the strategic situation with some examples of where the lessons have not been learnt and where strategic mistakes have been made. So much so that the House of Commons Defence Committee report into Operations in Afghanistan considers that due to intelligence failures the effect has been to 'stir up a hornets' nest'.

The Combatants
The main opponents facing the UK and NATO forces in Afghanistan are known as the Taleban. They are thought to number in excess of 30,000 active fighters. They are conducting a guerrilla campaign against the government of Afghanistan and the NATO-led International Security Assistance Force that

is supporting the lawful regime and trying to restore order, reconstruct the country and eliminate Afghanistan's trade in illegal narcotics. Amongst the Taleban's military allies are Al-Qaeda inspired foreign Jihadists who have come to fight with their religious brethren. They are also bolstered by their tribal kin from across the border in Pakistan and by native drug lords. These organised criminal gangs are in alliance with the Islamic Fundamentalists who protect and safeguard their production of opium and the heroin trade from which the Taleban receive funding to fight their holy war. There is also a nationalist element to the Taleban's insurgency as they are taking advantage of the southern people's resentment of foreign intervention in their land and even of the Kabul based Afghan government. Some are even motivated by the money they receive from the Taleban leadership which the rebels have in turn received through their taxation of the drug trade and from foreign donations.

Their weapons are often light and rudimentary. In some conflicts a force can be defeated by the destruction of its ability to produce arms and ammunition which weakens its ability to strike back. This, however, does not apply to the Taleban. They are opposing British forces with weapons that can be made by cottage industries, such as the easy to produce and maintain AK-47 – one exists for every sixty people on the planet. And the Improvised Explosive Device which can be made from chemicals that are available to civilians and from ordnance left over from Afghanistan's many previous wars. Other equipment used includes the use of the RPG-7 a shoulder-launched rocket propelled grenade weapon. The Taleban possess superior knowledge of the terrain which is a combination of; desert, mountains and valleys where isolated rural communities exist. In many cases the Taleban benefit from the support of the residents of those settlements. This gives the insurgents the ability to strike and melt back into the local Pashtun civilian population with impunity.

The UN sanctioned International Security Force (ISAF) consists of troops from NATO members such as the United States, Britain, Tonga and Turkey to name but a few. Many other nations have also deployed to Afghanistan, including; Malaysia, Macedonia, Australia, the United Arab Emirates and South Korea. Britain's mission in Helmand has been supported by the armed forces of Georgia, Denmark, Estonia and the USA. As of 16th August 2011 these international forces consisted of just over 130,000 service personnel. At that time 90,000 soldiers came from the United States and 9,500 from the UK. These NATO-led forces possess the overwhelming advantage both in terms of training and firepower and can deploy airpower and artillery to attack the Taleban. The British and NATO forces are supported by Afghanistan's security services that are in turn trained by ISAF and British service personnel.

The Afghan National Security Forces consist of an army known as the Afghan National Army (ANA) and a police force called the Afghan National Police (ANP). Afghanistan's army consists of over 170,000 soldiers; however, it still needs a great deal more training and equipment; this has led to doubts being raised in regards to its viability. British forces have been involved in training the Afghan security forces. The instruction of the ANA and the police is considered by British commanders as 'Afghan good enough' but no benchmark has been set as to what this is and there is little coherence to the training program. In some instances different instructors have not been informed as to what has already been taught to the Afghans. And when questions have been raised about the quality of the instruction there have been instances when concerns have been dismissed as the tuition is 'Afghan good enough'. Furthermore, Afghanistan's police force remains a cause of a great amount of anxiety. The police force numbers approximately 130,000. Both these security services have the word National in their title but they are not full representative of Afghanistan's diverse society. Whereas the members of the Taleban are predominantly from the Pashtun tribes of Southern Afghanistan the ANA and ANP do not fully represent this important ethnic group.[121]

The fighting begins

When British soldiers were first deployed to Helmand Province they patrolled on foot in order to win over the local population to their presence. They would wear soft-hats and seek to engage with the public whom they would meet and greet with the aim of identifying reconstruction or infrastructure tasks which the aid agencies can help with.

In 2006 there were little more than 3,100 British soldiers in Helmand whose primary mission was meant to be reconstruction but they were just about to become embroiled in a conflict for which they were thoroughly unprepared. Only 600 of those troops were prepared for combat – those from the Parachute Regiment – the rest were there to assist with logistics and the rebuilding of Afghanistan. The fighting started in the undulating hills of northern Helmand where the valleys were dominated by opium production. The humanitarian mission soon became subject to what is known as mission creep, and a force initially sent to rebuild a broken land was asked to help with security and supressing the Taleban's shadow government and assist the powers based in Kabul to extend their writ into the lawless areas of Afghanistan.

As a result of intelligence failures the army were not prepared for the intensity of the Taleban assault. They were under resourced and quickly found themselves overstretched and outnumbered by the insurgents. The mission and the different scenarios had not been adequately thought through and the British military was surprised at how the fighting developed. The army leadership quickly fell into a pattern of muddling through; reacting from one crisis to the next and often waiting to be attacked by the Taleban instead of seeking to shape events by taking the fight to the guerrillas. The army was spread too thinly and repeatedly attacked in their bases by the guerrillas; in short they were trying to hold an area the size of Wales with too few troops. At the same time they were being faced with confusing and contradictory competing missions; on one hand they had to help the reconstruction on the other they had to battle against an insurgency. The uncoordinated and incoherent approach to taking war to the Taleban was to last for years.

British Aims and Objectives

Any campaign must have clearly defined aims and objectives. A goal has to be set and success defined. However, there is confusion at the heart of the UK's strategy in Afghanistan and this stems right from the very top. On 22nd May 2010 the confusion over Britain's strategy was made clear. Liam Fox MP the then Secretary of State for Defence said, whilst visiting Afghanistan that he wanted troops out, "as soon as possible". He also stated that British soldiers were not there, "for the sake of the education policy in a broken 13th- century country". However, during the same visit the International Development Secretary, Andrew Mitchell MP said that, "We need to ensure that we help the Afghan people to build a functioning state. That's about providing basic education and healthcare facilities, but it's also about ensuring there are opportunities for promoting livelihoods so that people have jobs."

The failure by the British political leadership to identify the aim of why British soldiers are in Afghanistan was restricting the war fighting abilities of the British Army and undermining the UK's efforts. The former Commander of British troops in Afghanistan, Colonel Richard Kemp, said that the Government needed to provide a coherent strategy saying, "It needs to be a unified message, which unfortunately it is not at present."

In contrast, the campaign in Palestine from 1938 onwards had clear military objectives set, namely the establishment of military control; which is a clear aim that was to bring about an end to the violence. In Afghanistan in the modern era the British Army was faced with an enemy that had simple and straight forward objectives. The Taleban strategy is to kill NATO soldiers and convince the West's governments that the price of remaining in Afghanistan is too high. They were also destabilising the Afghan government. The Taleban were attacking its security services and via suicide bombings and by targeted assassination killing those who are involved with the lawful governance of Afghanistan be they civil servants, police and even teachers. As of summer 2010 there are 3 suicide bombings per week. This was also accompanied by a 45% increase in assassinations. The aggressive military tactics of the Taleban also include them gradually seeking to re-extend their influence over large parts of the country isolating the Kabul based government.

The aims and objectives of the British and NATO forces are much more complex and therefore harder to achieve. On one level the British Army is involved in a fight with the guerrillas in a counter-insurgency role. On another level its aims are to enhance and extend the Afghan government's influence over the lives of its citizens; this includes protecting and even helping to develop the nation's infrastructure and social services. This is the so-called 'hearts and minds' strategy, but it has a number of problems at its core. It relies on too many political variables, such as the efficiency of the Afghan Government, matters that are out of the control of the armed forces and is thus difficult to achieve.

Hearts and Minds – A Mistaken Concept

The term 'hearts and minds' is thought to have delivered victory against the Mao Zedong inspired communist guerrillas in the Malayan Races Liberation Army (MRLA). They were conducting an insurgency against the British in a conflict known as the Malayan Emergency. Whereas it is true that some British units delivered food and humanitarian supplies to some ethnic groups, the conflict was also not without controversial actions such as the Batang Kali massacre. In the Malayan Emergency the key to victory was the tactic of aggressive patrolling and the bombing of rebel held positions and bases. Another major factor in the British success was the forced internment of hundreds of thousands of ethnically Chinese villagers into new settlements which were little more than prison camps. A similar strategy was employed at the turn of the last century to secure a British victory in the Second Boer War. It was this forced relocation which separated the guerrillas from their civilian base of support. The lesson, however, that was handed down to posterity was the positive aspects of the military operations. Yet it was the harsher measures that did most to secure victory and not the army's limited hearts and minds public relations strategy.

One of the key British and NATO indicator of success is the number of children in education. This is difficult to achieve considering that in this deeply conservative society where a child in education will in some instances be a worker lost from the family's small holding. The introduction of female education is also a matter that is unlikely to win over the Islamic radicals. This is a matter for the Afghan government and not the concern of the British military. Furthermore, the 'hearts and minds' strategy was evolving into a Whitehall box ticking exercise and like other initiatives devised by those who had become bureaucrats also developed a language of its own. It is now being referred to as the 'population centric strategy'. It is intended that this new approach will influence the behaviour of the insurgents with less reliance on 'hard kinetic engagement'. This is a triumph of hope, but perhaps not of reason and certainly not of plain English.

It was hoped that these operations could be conducted whilst at the same time risking as few casualties as possible. However, the complex series of goals contained within the governments so-called 'hearts and minds' strategy actually risked the lives of British service personnel. However, the blame does not solely rest with bureaucrats in the Ministry of Defence (MoD). Senior members of the British Army are also culpable.

Tactical Incompetence

The British political leadership was not alone in making mistakes in Afghanistan. The army leadership have also been known to make serious blunders which actually breach the armed forces own Principles of War. In some operations the key military principle of achieving tactical surprise has been deliberately abandoned by the army; allowing the Taleban not only to escape and live to fight another day but also to frustrate the campaign. Brigadier James Cowan the British Task Force Commander in Helmand Province in Afghanistan admitted that it was the policy of the British Army to announce attacks in advance. [122]

This not only gave the Taleban the opportunity to withdraw but it also handed them the tactical initiative. Before many withdrew in advance of the attacks they used the time before the operation got underway to plant Improvised Explosive Devices (IEDs) safe in the knowledge that soon they would be able to kill British soldiers. This policy of appeasing village elders by forewarning them of attacks in advance has also been a cause of tension with the UK's NATO allies. American forces in Operation Moshtarak, also operating in Helmand Province, reported on

15th February 2010 that progress was being slowed by IEDs. These deadly threats would not have been such a severe problem if the Taleban had not been informed by the British military leadership of the attacks in advance of them taking place. It is all reminiscent of the failures of the civil administration in Palestine before Montgomery arrived.

The indirect pre-warning of the Taleban just prolonged the war and allowed the Taleban to pick their time to mount sniper attacks and plant bombs. Yet when the Taleban are caught in a fire fight by British troops the soldiers' superior training, tactics and equipment tells. When confronted, either as a result of a Taleban attack or through a British patrol locating the guerrillas the action usually results in a decisive British tactical victory.

There have been times when British activity in Afghanistan was managed in a truly farcical fashion. In 2006 the British Army along with some NATO allies were under attack from the Taleban in the town of Musa Qala in Helmand Province. The British army commanders struck a deal with the Taleban where it was agreed that the soldiers could withdraw without coming under fire and that the town would be administered by village elders. The Taleban let the troops leave but contrary to the agreement they then took control of Musa Qala and imposed their will and strict brand of justice. The British and NATO forces then had to retake the town by force with several casualties.

Montgomery as a master of deception would have been appalled at the telegraphing of the UK's military intentions in some operations. Furthermore, if there were sufficient troops every effort could have been made to surprise the Taleban and trap them and not just temporarily drive them out from their positions. Sun Tze in his book *The Art of War* advised that a retreating enemy should be allowed to withdraw. He wrote, 'Do not interfere with an army that is returning home. When you surround an army, leave an outlet free. Do not press a desperate foe too hard.' In Afghanistan that advice is gravely mistaken. Nothing was gained by having too few troops and the subsequent inability to surround and trap the Taleban. It just allows the guerrillas to escape and return later; and then at a time and place of the Taleban's choosing and plant more IEDs.

There was not only been a failure to commit to a coherent overall strategic aim but also when the fight was taken to the Taleban the tactics on the ground kept on fluctuating. This prevented a consistent approach to the war being taken. This was not so much an application of flexibility but simply a change of approach from individual commanders who just happened to have a different tactical doctrine.

When the fighting began the British Army adopted an approach known as the 'Platoon Houses Strategy'. This basically consisted of the army staying in unsustainable and isolated bases which were subject to attack from the Taleban. According to General Sir Robert Alan Fry the use of this strategy meant that British soldiers were, "fighting for their lives... in a series of Alamos in the north of the province."[123] The use of airpower and artillery was an effective tool in defending British bases from attack by the Taleban. However, this often resulted in the deaths of civilians and at times this looked less like reconstruction and more like destruction. These blunt tools were also unable to root out the guerrillas at a time other than when they choose to show themselves. A more targeted surgical approach was needed.

Late in 2006, when the Royal Marines became active in Helmand, they developed a strategy of taking the fight to the Taleban and using small mobile groups to flush out the insurgents. They would penetrate into rebel held areas, thus inviting an attack from where superior British training and weapons would prevail. This tactic was known as 'advance into ambush'. These aggressive counter-insurgency operations raised the morale of the British armed forces and ended the overreliance on trying to hold ground where troops would be repeatedly attacked at a time of the Taleban's choosing but at the end of their six monthly tour personnel and commanders and tactics were changed again. As a result of their being not enough troops to cover the massive expanse of Helmand province in the summer of 2007 it was felt that larger sweeps into the insurgent's heartland would destroy the rebels at source. This tactic presented the Taleban with opportunities to snipe at the soldiers. However, when the offensive was taken the Taleban routinely lost the fire fights with the British service personnel. The guerrillas then began to concentrate on targeting the soldiers with terror attacks using IEDs. Whilst they were still at large they would be able to do this with impunity. The response of the Ministry of Defence to this new challenge was slow and scandalous.

Soldiers being placed at risk

Amongst its many tasks, the British Army was also following a deployment strategy where soldiers were sent to live and work in the community. This exposed the troops to danger, especially sniper attacks, and led to more casualties than would otherwise be necessary. There is also a severe vulnerability to Improvised Explosive Devises partly caused through the strategy to win public support. Colonel Chris Claydon, whilst serving as Head of Counter IED, described the key to winning a counter-insurgency is to win hearts and minds and to do this the army has to get out there and be accessible rather than being in heavily armoured vehicles. [124] Yet this places British personnel at risk of bomb attacks and has led to the dreadful losses at the hands of the Taleban terror tactics. Protection of British lives should rank higher in the army's lists of priorities than accessibility. In Ireland Montgomery recognised the need to make sure his soldiers were adequately protected, unfortunately the British Army in the modern era does not share the same concern. The Army can be best used on war fighting, rather than peace support operations which in a country without peace place lives at risk and does not bring an end to the fighting. In such circumstances soldiers should not be employed as social workers carrying guns on some vaguely defined outreach project.

A Failure of Preparation and Procurement
The lack of preparation for the war in Afghanistan went to the very top. When British soldiers were sent to Helmand Province in 2006 the task before them was greatly under estimated. On 21st April 2006 John Reid, who was the Secretary of State for Defence, spoke of the soldiers role as being to "protect the reconstruction". He thought that the troops may even come home without firing a single shot.

Furthermore, General Wall who was the Deputy Chief of Joint Operations at the time of the deployment acknowledged that there were intelligence failures. Whilst being questioned by the House of Commons Defence Committee he also stated that;

"I absolutely accept that what we found when we had forces on the ground was starkly different from what we had anticipated and hoped for… We were ready for an adverse reaction, but to be fair we did not expect it to be as vehement as it turned out to be."

Forward thinking was also lacking. Afghanistan is underdeveloped with an insufficient road network. This makes it difficult for the armed forces to project adequate ground forces against the insurgents. The road building program to extend British military influence was woefully insufficient. There was also a failure to give the armed forces equipment suitable to the tasks they faced. Like in Iraq, the British army was hamstrung by too few helicopters being made available. This shortage made it difficult to evacuate wounded soldiers. It has also meant that the army has had to rely on vulnerable convoys of vehicles travelling over Afghanistan's dubious road network to supply their far-flung outposts.

The ability of the army to conduct a war of manoeuvre was also held back by the fact that there was a 45% shortfall in the number of vehicles which the army had available.[125] Just as there was a poor choice of vehicles used in Iraq this was also replicated in Afghanistan. There was also many serious shortcomings in the equipment given to the British soldiers. An example of this is the FV107 Scimitar. This is an armoured reconnaissance vehicle whose design goes back over four decades. Its flat bottomed hull is extremely susceptible to attack by Improvised Explosive Devises (IEDs).

British soldiers also became especially exposed to IEDs as a result of the army's stubborn reliance on what has been described as a "Mobile Coffin". These are officially called the Snatch Land Rovers, and their up-graded but still insufficiently armoured successors known as Snatch Vixens. The Vixen range has a more robust chassis which allows it to generate more power so that it can better handle the weight of the still inadequate armour. The army's Wolf Land Rovers also provided unworthy protection for the soldiers. The Ministry of Defence accepted the need to replace these dangerous vehicles with new and much more robust transports but the decision came too late for many service personnel. This failure to provide the army with the correct tools gave hope to the Taleban and a way of hitting back at the British army.

The IEDs have been a major cause of British casualties. Yet this is a threat the British Army was not only initially unwilling to meet but also thoroughly unprepared for. This actually caused some consternation in the army. Colonel Bob Seddon, who held the post of Principal Ammunition Technical Officer, resigned because he was concerned with the problems created by a shortage of soldiers trained to defuse IEDs. Yet, the MoD have been slow to react. The situation was so bad that the House of Commons Defence Committee concluded that it was, 'unacceptable that UK Forces were deployed in Helmand for three years, as a result of a failure of military and political co-ordination, without the necessary personnel and equipment to succeed in their Mission.'

The Taleban realised that Improvised Explosive Devises are an effective way at striking at British service personnel. The British military leadership was slow to react even in the earlier stages of the conflict when soldiers were three times more likely to be killed by an IED than by gunfire. The situation steadily got worse. The use of IEDs rose by 400% in 2008 and a further 400% in 2009 with a total of 80 soldiers killed in such attacks. In the first four months of 2010 there was a 94% increase in the number of road side IED bombings. However, because of a cost cutting decision taken in 2002 the recruitment of bomb disposal experts was suspended for 18 months. This decision was taken at a time when Britain had already become involved in the war on terror in Afghanistan and when the Ministry of Defence were planning for a new foray into Iraq. It meant that the bomb disposal units were 40% under strength, meaning that the work load was just too great for the bomb disposal officers to cope with.

Despite the shortcomings in equipment and preparation the British military still enjoys a technical superiority over the Taleban. In this modern war on terror the armed forces possess equipment which ranges from advanced airpower and artillery at the largest end of the scale to in some cases superior body armour and helmets that can include night visioning technology. These are capabilities and kit which the insurgents do not have at their disposal.

Securing a peace

There have been some creative ideas to try and bring about an end to the Taleban insurgency. These schemes range from finding a political solution to even paying the members of the Taleban not to fight against the NATO forces and the lawful government of Afghanistan; and not to attack British aid convoys. The paying of the Taleban not only represents a lack of commitment to achieving a military victory; but it has also led to accusations that the West is indirectly sponsoring the guerrilla war that is being waged against them. In the face of this controversy it is unlikely that adequate financial resources will be made available to keep paying off the Taleban.

What is more, it may also be politically difficult for the West to match the support which comes from both Pakistan and some dissident radical elements in Saudi Arabia and the Gulf States who have traditionally directed funding to extremist Sunni groups around the globe. It can also be argued that paying-off the Taleban will only encourage more recruits to their ranks in the hope of a pay day. Furthermore, even if payments work in the short term it is unlikely that they will deliver a lasting peace. As the Taleban are religiously and politically motivated it is likely that they will resume their insurgency when NATO forces have been drawn down. The only difference is that they will be better resourced. The word "danegeld" springs to mind.

The proposal to find a political settlement to the fighting in Afghanistan is also fraught with danger. The hope that the Taleban can be brought to the negotiation table and a political solution reached is made that much harder to achieve because it also fails to appreciate the nature of the Taleban's internal organisation and the political structure of the revolt. It is wrong to presume that the Taleban is a cohesive group with a central command and control unit that can be politically bought off.

Taleban insurgents operate in a cellular structure often in localised uprisings against central Afghan control. That makes it less likely that the senior Taleban leaders, known as the Quetta Shura, based in Pakistan, can instruct the fighters to lay down their arms. The Quetta Shura provide ideological and intellectual leadership rather than direct military command and control. There are also other groups which have influence over the guerrillas in Afghanistan such as the Haqqani network which is based in the lawless autonomous regions of Pakistan, they too will have to be brought on side if there is to be a political compromise. However they are equally extreme as the Taleban, if not more so, and are also closely tied with Al-Qaeda.

Yet, what would be the political price of a deal with the Taleban and their allied groups? Even if a political compromise can be reached the political costs of allowing such people into government would make a farce of the UK's *raison d'être* for being involved in Afghanistan. The Western powers sought to justify the war on the grounds that NATO is fighting against the restoration of an extremely illiberal regime. Power sharing with Islamic radicals may well bring-in policies that the West finds distasteful and will lead to very real human rights abuses. What is more, a political solution is even harder to achieve in the religiously, ethnically and linguistically divided Afghanistan.

Such ideas, however, fail to recognise the motivations of many of the insurgents. Afghanistan's guerrillas fit into the category of being fatalistic and ideologically driven. As such the Taleban are unlikely to respond to what the NATO leadership considers a reasoned and reasonable offer. Furthermore, Zabiullah Mujahid, the acknowledged spokesman for the leadership of Afghani Taliban said in response to questions about the possibility of negotiations that;

"We do not want to talk to anyone - not to Karzai, nor to any foreigners - till the foreign forces withdraw from Afghanistan.

We are certain that we are winning. Why should we talk if we have the upper hand, and the foreign troops are considering withdrawal, and there are differences in the ranks of our enemies?"

No doubt this belligerence and optimism has been buoyed by the introduction of a timetable for the US and Britain to begin drawing down the NATO presence in Afghanistan.

Withdrawal – hope for the Taleban

The hope of restoring peace was hampered by the announcement that forces in Afghanistan will be withdrawn over a period of a matter of years; in fact the drawdown of troop numbers is already underway. It has been shown that there is a direct correlation between troop numbers and law and order. Yet, the deadline for withdrawal will mean that by 2014 there will be few NATO troops in Afghanistan and the UK is planning to end combat operations in that year. In short, the decision to set that date as the deadline was an arbitrary one which has military risks. On this subject the Defence Committee concluded that;

'A more significant drawdown, however, would have to involve a complete battle group. Weakening any battle group to withdraw numbers would be a dangerous move.'

Furthermore, the deadline is set according to domestic political timescales and not to the security needs of the Afghan people. In the eyes of the Taleban it merely represents a lack of resolve to see the operations through to their close. It made them believe that all they have to do is wait and victory will be theirs. Mullah Mohammed Omar, the Leader of the Taleban said of NATO that, "They may have the watches, but we have the time."

Therefore, anything less than the achievement of military control over large parts of Afghanistan, including the destruction of the Taleban as a fighting force, runs the risk of leaving the guerrillas intact and ready to reignite the war as soon the West has departed. Even half defeating them will just create a wounded tiger waiting to take revenge on the Afghan government. What is more, if Afghanistan if destabilised this is sure to affect the Pakistani autonomous regions which border that country. A conflict cannot be won by announcing withdrawal before security has been established. This will not only embolden the militants but it will also lead the beleaguered citizens of Afghanistan to believe that the NATO forces will abandon them; leaving them with little option but to support the Taleban. Evidence actually suggests that a major reason why the Taleban are receiving support is that the Western forces will indeed leave the population to their fate. Many Afghans, even those who are opposed to the Taliban, share this pessimistic, but perhaps realistic, outlook.

What is more, letting the enemy know that the NATO forces are leaving inevitably leads to more violence; and more attacks on British forces. That may be counter-intuitive but there is historical precedence for that scenario. A prime example of this occurred in the episode known as the Aden Emergency and as Retreat from Aden. This was a port and its surrounding territory on the south coast of Arabia which the United Kingdom had occupied for more than a century but it had ceased to be strategically important to British trade and imperial interests. In the face of guerrilla attacks from Arab nationalists, the British Government announced that the UK would be vacating the territory in 1967. In the face of these insurgent attacks Richard Turnbull, the penultimate Governor of the British Protectorate of Aden said in the 1960s that, "if the British Empire were to sink into the sea tomorrow, its greatest legacies to mankind would be Association Football and the phrase F**k Off." Of course that is ignoring the spreading of both Christianity and cricket. That aside; when the withdrawal date was announced the increasingly confident guerrillas reacted by intensifying their attacks. The various insurgent groups were hoping to score propaganda successes by making successful strikes against the British forces. Furthermore, in advance of the change in power the local police turned on the British authorities. This led to a complete breakdown in law and order which was only restored by the repressive measures of Lieutenant-Colonel Colin Campbell Mitchell. He led the Argyll and Sutherland Highlanders, then a regiment – but now a battalion – in the British Army in a controversial but successful operation to restore British control. It is worth mentioning the fate of Aden after Britain had left. This territory once had a bustling port at its heart, but after it was left in the hands of militant pan-Arab socialists and then militant Islamists its economic life has been seriously retarded.

It is also worth noting that there are a number of anti-NATO rebel forces operating against the ISAF and government forces in Afghanistan; most notably the Haqqani network and the Taleban. During the drawdown of western troops and their eventual withdrawal it is therefore likely that these likeminded but competing groups will step-up their attacks. The aim of this will be to increase both their prestige amongst the local population and their political significance in the post-NATO Afghanistan.

Therefore, that makes a military solution the answer to ending the conflict in Afghanistan; but is the UK's political and military leadership trying to achieve that aim? And to achieve that even more aggressive military action needs to be undertaken. However, the leadership of the British Army retreated into a strategy of placing the wagons in a circle. This approach was known as 'security by concentrating force'. This has been credited with limiting casualties, at least in the short term, but it also means that the UK forces will not be able to hunt the Taleban and wither away their strength. Such an approach is therefore making a military victory over the Taleban less likely.

Despite the use of helicopters increasing by over 140% from 2006 and British troop numbers being increased to around 10,000 by 2010, more than double the size of the original force sent to Helmand, the army were still unable to quash the Taleban revolt. The desire not to risk further casualties even led the British Government to remove troops from areas where the Taleban presence is strong. In July 2010 the now former Defence Secretary, Liam Fox, serving in the new coalition government with the anti-war Liberal Democrats, announced the withdrawal of British troops from the Sangin district of Helmand to safer areas in the province. They would now manage a much smaller area around the town of Nad Ali. The British soldiers were replaced by those from the United States of America whose leaders were more willing to supply the resources necessary for a major offensive to be taken against the Taleban. Whereas the approach of the modern British army is thought to have achieved little; the US experience has been quite different. They committed an extra 20,000 additional troops to Helmand province alone. The surge, as some call it, and the resulting American offensive has been far more successful. Throughout Afghanistan NATO also increased troop numbers by a total of 40,000 - 30,000 from the USA and a further 10,000 from other members, bringing the total number of UN supported international troops to 150,000.

**British Counter-Insurgency Strategy
and Operational Guidelines**

A lack of soldiers in theatre, the dearth of helicopters and inadequate defensive equipment supplied to the soldiers in both Iraq and Afghanistan and the top brass' generally poor procurement policies are not the only reasons why the British armed forces have failed to defeat the modern jihadi insurgencies. At the heart of the armed forces failure is the official advice that it teaches it's commanders in the field on how to suppress an insurgency.

The *Army Field Manual Combined Arms Operations* establishes strategic and operational guidelines in its chapter on how to conduct British Counter Insurgency Operations. These instructions would be anathema to Montgomery. This contrast with Monty's approach is not surprising as the guidelines do not properly deal with evaluating Montgomery's experience of the war in Palestine in the 1930s. Furthermore, it only briefly mentions the conflict in Ireland in the earlier part of the last century. These are major omissions on the part of the UK's military strategists as those insurgencies are two definitive guerrilla wars.

The guidance contained within this manual is flawed and militarily inadequate making the army's strategy in both Iraq and especially Afghanistan defective and unable to adequately meet the challenge of the Taleban and their allied insurgents. It was originally hoped that the Army's mission in Helmand Province and the application of the principles set out in the British military's counter-insurgency guidelines would win over the Afghanis to the British cause, yet the reality has proved to be very different and the commanders were psychologically unprepared for the bitter conflict which faced them.

The UK's armed forces have been following their six guiding principles to tackle insurgencies. These are more akin to political, as opposed to military, solutions and therefore they fail to recognise that success on the political front will follow victory in combat. The principles in the modern British guidelines advise commanders in theatre to concentrate on six main areas which they should follow. These are;

a. Political Primacy and Political Aim.

b. Coordinated Government Machinery.

c. Intelligence and Information.

d. Separating the Insurgent from his Support.

e. Neutralising the Insurgent.

f. Longer Term Post-Insurgency Planning.

Much of the guidance is concerned with the bureaucratic relationship between the armed forces and the civilian administration and it openly admits that the British military have not developed a general remedy designed to tackle an insurgency. Some is even concerned with database management and record keeping. It also mandates that the provision of social services and their improvement is an aim for the army as part of their counter-insurgency operations. This is an armed service whose strategy shies away from recognising that the solution to the military crisis in Afghanistan is a military victory. In fact the strategy rules out the use of a gloves-off military approach; instead it advocates 'soft' measures and the use of minimum force. In contrast to the experience of British service personnel in both the inter-war conflicts in Ireland and Palestine the current strategic guidelines advocate that too much emphasis can be placed on offensive operations. However, the lesson from the earlier conflicts was that soldiers are unsuited for defensive policing operations. Montgomery was clear from his experience that defensive operations during an insurgency do not take advantage of a soldier's skills and are bad for morale. Whereas victory in the field of combat resulting from a robustly prosecuted attack will lift morale. When Monty did use defensive tactics, such as in a picket or guarding a piece of infrastructure, it was intended to be a trap that would draw insurgents out into the open where they could be annihilated.

The effect of the guidelines is that its strictures effectively nullify the army's principle of Mission Command. Yet military commanders are not only being hamstrung by rules which restrict a commander's freedom of action; but the military are also being subordinated to the civilian authorities and legal advisors. The current guidelines recognise that a politician or civil servant will have overall command of the campaign, a recipe for delay and even inaction. Furthermore, the guidelines establish that commanders can be prosecuted for breaches of health and safety rules and recognises the relevance of the Health & Safety at Work Act 1974. The counter insurgency guidelines even accepts the jurisdiction of the European Court of Human Rights over their actions warning military personnel that they may be answerable to the ECHR which is based in Strasbourg, France.

Montgomery would not be risking his soldier's lives in a situation where he could not prosecute the war as he wished because the army had become the junior partner to a failing civilian administration which had already lost control of much of its territory. His leadership would have initiated the necessary policy of Military Control which would restore law and order. The establishment of the principle of Military Control also overcomes the obstacle that the British and allied military forces must follow the peacetime principle of the rule of law even when the insurgents are clearly not.

In contrast the modern British Army's guidance rules out what it describes as a 'gloves off approach'. It advises commanders that they should seek to damage the morale of an enemy rather than seek their opponent's wholesale destruction. The strategic guidelines advocate the use of so-called 'soft' measures such as arrest as an alternative to killing. Yet, in Afghanistan the limitations placed on British servicemen even make detention of a terrorist suspect difficult.

The guidelines rule out the use of punitive measures being taken against the supporters of an insurgency. However, it should be the case that the ultimate responsibility for any hardships which fall upon a rebellions supporters result from the criminal activities of those who have taken up arms against the lawful and internationally recognised government. In Palestine collective punishments often coming in the form of additional taxation separated the peasant population from the insurgents who came to be regarded as prolonging a losing and economically damaging conflict. The fault lies with the guerrillas and their supporters not allied serviceman and women.

Whereas there is a clear need for repressive measures to deal adequately with an opposing guerrilla force the British military guidelines expressly warn about the adoption of repression in the fear that it will provoke a backlash. Yet the failings of the UK's approach in Southern Iraq and Afghanistan has not been the use of repressive measures but the lack of them and the inability to back up the British presence with enough military force.

Ultimately, the local population will back the side that offers stability and a return to a normal life. It is the rational choice which is also supported by emotional factors such as public perception of the military prestige, or the lack of esteem, of the belligerents. Contrary to the modern British guidance it is necessary to demonstrate clearly who is in charge. The continued support at home for the war and its continued prosecution to the utmost will also largely depend upon the public's perception as to whether the armed forces are being successful in their theatre of operations. Montgomery would have understood that in a conflict like Afghanistan the answer to resolving the problem of banditry and lawlessness is the successful application of military force, that is what must come before all else and that was Montgomery's doctrine.

The American Strategy

President Barrack Obama followed a hawkish strategy in Afghanistan. Following the clear success of what is known as the Surge strategy in Iraq, the Obama administration increased troop numbers in Afghanistan. The American military leadership recognised that before the reconstruction of Afghanistan's economy and infrastructure can begin the defeat of the insurgency has to be achieved; and this depends on troop numbers. The so-called winning of hearts and minds must therefore take a back foot to clearing the area of the Taleban. Then sufficient troops need to be made available to hold the region and then, and only then, can the rebuilding of Afghanistan's truly broken society take place. However, the task of clearing the guerrillas from a district takes the application of overwhelming strength. At times this has even meant that the US has demolished selected areas where the Taleban have weapons-making facilities. Incidentally, this was a British tactic during the Arab Revolt in Palestine in the 1930s. Information from opinion polls does suggest that people who live in Afghanistan's most lawless regions place security amongst their highest priorities. There is also concern that the NATO-led forces may desert them.[126]

The American military also has a different deployment strategy to the British army. The UK forces serve a shorter tour of duty than their American counterparts who stay for a year. The British change battalions and their commanders every six months; this leaves too little time for the senior officers to appraise themselves with the situation and devise a consistent strategy. According to the Defence Committee the moving of important officers, 'would 'increase risks in the administration of the Armed Forces at any time but, in 2006 at such a crucial stage in both operations in Afghanistan and Iraq, it gave rise to unacceptable risks.'

The American approach in Afghanistan has been quite different from that followed by the UK's military leadership. Richard Holbrooke, during his time as the US Special Representative for Afghanistan and Pakistan, recognised that the Taleban need to be fought until they shrink in size to a position where they can be managed. The British strategy is quite the opposite. The UK's military leadership hoped to starve the Taleban of support by securing a moral victory over the insurgents. And finally end the guerrilla war by reaching a political settlement. However, the reality is that the reverse scenario is the most likely strategy to bring law and order. The lesson of history is that a political solution will follow once a military victory has been achieved. Montgomery would understand this.

President Obama has also been a consistent advocate of taking the war on terror directly to the extremists regardless of what state they may be in. He advocated as long ago as 2008 that US troops should cross the border in Pakistan to capture Osama Bin Laden if the Pakistani authorities were unwilling to prosecute an operation to capture him. Barack Obama delivered on this policy in 2011 when US Special Forces killed Osama Bin Laden at his compound in the Pakistani city of Abbottabad. This town, founded by the British, is home to many Pakistani military establishments. The successful US operation to kill Osama Bin Laden, not only shows the positive results that decisive action can have and how intelligence assets can be made best use of but also shows the limitations at the heart of the British approach. In the wake of the operation to kill Bin Laden questions were raised about whether the UK could mount such an operation. This is not because of a lack of military expertise and capabilities but because of self-imposed legal restrictions on how UK forces can operate.

Rules of Engagement

The UK forces are barred from operating in third countries which are not part of the area of their mandated operation, so would not have been acting 'legally' if they had entered Pakistan to capture or kill Osama Bin Laden. Furthermore, the British rules of engagement, known as Card Alpha, prevent the killing of terrorists unless they are holding a weapon and pose an immediate threat. Regulations also mean that even information gathered from intelligence is considered insufficient grounds for action to be taken against the terrorists. And suspicion that they may be about to commit an outrage is not enough to justify the killing of Taleban and Al-Qaeda operatives. This nullifies a key tool that should be available in the war against the terrorists in Afghanistan. What is more, the British authorities will not use, let alone pass on to other agencies, intelligence gleaned from methods that are considered to be torture. It is also against the UK's self-imposed restrictions to act on, or relay, information that may lead to people being assassinated in such a manner as Bin Laden was. The American extra-judicial execution of Osama Bin Laden was criticised by Dr Rowan Williams, the Archbishop of Canterbury, just like the Anglican Church leaders in Palestine criticised the actions of Montgomery and his soldiers in Palestine over seven decades ago.

Special operations are not alone in being hamstrung by the UK's overly restrictive rules of engagement. The war fighting capacity of the British army is being restricted by rules preventing them from adequately fighting back. This policy has become known as 'courageous restraint'. This approach has run the risk of only half defeating the Taleban leaving them an effective force that will be able to repeat their attacks against the soldiers of the British army. There have even been instances of soldiers discussing the legality of killing insurgents as they go about their deadly work of planting IEDs. And those who are suspected of being spotters for the Taleban, although unarmed, are directing fire onto the British forces; but these too are beyond the bounds of being targeted by offensive military action. Furthermore, those suspected of being members of the Taleban often have to be released by the troops.

In Palestine in the 1930s Montgomery recognised the need to detain the guerrillas, a policy which led directly to a reduction in violence. Yet in Afghanistan the troops could only detain a suspect for a maximum of four days after which half would be released. Leaving suspects to continue the fighting is no way to win a war. Before the former Secretary of State for Defence, Liam Fox, entered office he spoke of this disgraceful situation, saying; "Given the danger these people pose to our armed forces and the risks involved in their capture, it is outrageous if they are then released."[127] However, this was not addressed when the new government took office.

It needs to be borne in mind that the Taleban fighters are not entitled to all the rights that legitimate soldiers are granted by the Geneva Convention. They are not in uniform and are taking part in an unlawful rebellion against a lawful and elected government that is under the protection of the UN. Furthermore, the Taleban are fighting the United Nations Security Council authorised International Security Assistance Force (ISAF) which is there to help the legitimate Afghan government restore and maintain security. If the British army's rules of engagement continue to grant the Taleban fighters 'rights' to which they are not entitled means that efforts to combat them are undermined. Having become involved in Afghanistan the UK's military leadership has the moral duty to put the issue of enforcing security by establishing military control above any concerns about the 'human rights' of the Taleban's illegal combatants. In the long run this will also prove to be more beneficial to saving British lives. Having rules of engagement that are too restrictive towards the actions that can be taken against Taleban suspects also encourages them to perceive a lack of political resolve to force a close to the conflict.

Delivering Military Control

Ultimately, the success of a guerrilla war depends upon the ability to gnaw away at the strength and resolve of one's opponents, destroying their will to win and forcing them to take the political decision to withdraw. The war in Afghanistan will not be won like a conventional conflict where the capturing of an enemy capital was a great prize. The ISAF forces have Kabul, but this is not delivering peace. The strength of the Taleban needs to be eliminated, not bypassed and certainly not bought off.

The Taleban have been able to penetrate the British lines because there are not enough troops to hold the captured ground. In face of planned cuts in service personnel it is unlikely that sufficient troops will be made available to hold the captured ground. That should be the task of the Afghan National Army and the police. The British military leadership should have concentrated solely on using their strength to take the fight to the Taleban. British forces should have been locating the insurgents and then engaging their units in combat from the very start. This is the surest way to end the Taleban and Al-Qaeda linked insurgency.

Lessons to be learned

Montgomery did his utmost in Ireland and Palestine to locate the insurgents, engage them in combat and keep them there until the battle had been won. As British soldiers succeed in combat with the Taleban this should have been the UK's primary focus. Achieving military control is a much simpler and more obtainable policy.

Following on from the Soviet experience, there must have been a great deal of trepidation before entering the conflict in Afghanistan. Furthermore, the scenario surrounding Russian entry was very different. The word Al-Qaeda means 'the base' and when most of Afghanistan was ruled by the Taleban it became a base for repeated attacks on people in places as far afield as America and Africa. Their rule was ended a month after the 9/11 attacks. In time, however, they began an insurgency against the elected Afghan government which followed the Taleban's rule.

The USSR became involved in Afghanistan for very different reasons. The Russians invaded in 1979 to support an extremely unpopular and brutal communist government which attempted to create an atheist state. It also alienated the population by attempting to introduce land reforms. The Soviet involvement just added nationalism to the grievances of the Afghan people. An intense guerrilla war followed. The Soviets withdrew nearly a decade after their military involvement began.

The current regime in Afghanistan, although far from perfect, has more legitimacy than the Soviet puppet regime. The Taleban are also tainted by their taxing and persecution of the Afghan people under their control. The fact that the Taleban represent just one branch of the Muslim faith makes them deeply divisive. They are Sunni extremists and as such they have a deep hatred for those who do not share their interpretation of Islam, such as those from the Shia tradition – who they do not consider to be true Muslims – as well as those who follow a more moderate line. In a diverse nation the Taleban predominantly come from only one ethnic group. They primarily belong to the Pashtun ethnic and linguistic group and cannot unite the whole of Afghanistan in opposition to the ISAF military presence in Afghanistan. In fact the myriad of tribal and ethnic groups have a long history of warring amongst themselves.

What is more, parallels with the revolt against Soviet occupation are also undermined by the fact that throughout the 1980s the rebels, known as the Mujahedeen were aided by many Western and Muslim nations. The anti-communist guerrillas received the latest weaponry such as the Stinger surface-to-air missiles. The balance of technology in the current fighting in Afghanistan is now very different with British and ISAF forces having a clear technological advantage which can be brought to bear against the Taleban guerrillas when the political will encourages such an approach.

Chapter 16

CONCLUSION

'The rebellion in Palestine provides perhaps more than anything else an example of the consequences of delaying the application of force to meet force. The failure of a policy of conciliation led in the end to the despatch of a Field Force from England and the adoption of more severe repression than might perhaps have been needed had it been applied from the beginning.'
Report on the Military Lessons of the Arab Rebellion in Palestine

It is paradoxical that a greater degree of clemency was shown towards Irish Republicans, who threatened the very territorial integrity of the United Kingdom, than was shown towards the rebels in Palestine. The Arab Revolt of 1936 – 1939 was in defiance of British Imperial rule and her mandated obligations but it did not directly threaten the UK. Furthermore, the repressive measures used by the elected British authorities in Ireland were by no means as severe as those employed in Palestine which was truly a faraway land that should have been of less concern to its politicians.

Despite there being a number of differences between the approach of the UK to the IRA in Ireland and the Arab gangs in Palestine there were similarities in the way that the British authorities approached the political side of the conflict. The

British way of combatting these guerrilla wars and their challenge to the authority of the Crown was to prosecute the war by bringing the fight to the insurgents with the outcome that the rebels were brought to the point of defeat. The British government would then offer them a compromise deal that was sympathetic to the insurgent's aims and objectives. This happened during the tensions in Ireland in the earlier part of last century and in the fighting in Palestine. In both those cases the leaders of the rebel forces showed that they shared an extremist and belligerent attitude.

In Ireland the Republican leadership refused a number of compromise settlements. However, they were eventually forced to accept a peace deal which was far removed from their original uncompromising demands and submit to a deal that was almost identical to the ones the British had offered before. Furthermore, events had divided Ireland so deeply that there would be no hope of reaching a concord with the Unionists in the north-east of the island. In Palestine, the Arab Higher Committee rejected an offer that was to all intents and purposes a political victory for them and ultimately they ended up with nothing. This refusal to listen to reason was to have a detrimental effect not only on their cause but also on the Palestinian people for decades to come.

The cultural attitudes of the different populations of Ireland and Palestine would have played a part in explaining why the conflicts had different conclusions. The Irish are a European people and as such the IRA and their Sinn Féin leadership were, in relation to other guerrilla armies, highly organised and efficient. Furthermore, as Ireland was an integral part of the liberal and, by the standards of the day, democratic United Kingdom its citizens were, therefore, less likely to accept what they would have perceived to be maltreatment from the Crown forces. As the repressive measures intensified so did the resentment; this would have meant that the conflict would flare-up again when the troops were withdrawn even if it had been temporarily suppressed.

In contrast to the war in Ireland the Arab Revolt was poorly co-ordinated and was a chaotic conflict that was susceptible to having military control forced upon it. Furthermore, both the history and the political culture of the Middle East and its peoples contrasted with the liberal democratic values that were espoused, if not always followed, as part of the Anglo-Saxon and Western-European political inheritance. As such the Palestinian Arab population, a people who were familiar with being ruled by undemocratic and authoritarian means imposed upon them by an outside power – notably the Turkish Ottoman Empire – were more willing to accept the rule of the dominant power and in the late 1930s that power was the United Kingdom and not the Arab gangs. So when Montgomery proved the authority of the British forces in action the population swung behind the winning side. What is more, after his extensive tour of Palestine Montgomery concluded that the Arab Revolt was not a nationalist movement.

Nationalism, or more specifically the desire by peoples in many different countries to be self-governing and not ruled by those that are perceived to be of a different race, was the most important ideological force during the twentieth century. At times this philosophy could be a cause of much civil strife and destruction. However, at times liberal nationalism and the desire for national freedom can be a positive force as exemplified by the still relatively recent struggle against both Nazi and Communist tyranny on the Continent of Europe.

Without recourse to greatly repressive measures nationalistic yearnings are very difficult to defeat. Montgomery understood this and in Ireland he supported a solution which accommodated many of his enemy's nationalistic demands. In

Palestine he knew that there were other motives behind the fighting and therefore the response was quite different and consisted of a ruthless crackdown on the rebels and their supporters which showed them, and the local population, who was in charge. This effective application of force ended the banditry which was the Arab Revolt.

That is the main reason why the two different conflicts studied in this book had two very different outcomes. What is more, if adequate repressive measures were taken earlier by Montgomery's predecessors then the situation would not have become so acute in the first place. And at the heart of this was the application of the will to win. If the United Kingdom enters a conflict but is not prepared for the worst case scenario, as recently happened in both Helmand province and Iraq, its armed forces must adapt quickly. And if the Ministry of Defence and the military's top brass do not adopt the desire to prosecute a war to the fullest until military control is established then peace and law and order on British terms will not be achieved. Furthermore, if they are unwilling to apply the appropriate measures then – like Montgomery's conclusions in Ireland – the British political leadership should withdraw the soldiers instead of staying-on in a growing maelstrom of violence where the troops merely become targets for insurgent attacks. And run the risk of provoking a nationalist response from the citizens whose future the soldiers are sent there to secure.

Montgomery would have recognised that in southern Iraq the so-called Mahdi Army, which was a Shia militia under the control of the demagogic figure Muqtada al-Sadr, fought against the British army because they opposed the UK's presence in their land for both sectarian and nationalistic reasons. In Afghanistan the opponents of the British were driven partly by criminality and by the desire to rebel against the government of that deeply divided land. The Taleban are little more than religiously motivated bandits who are involved with organised crime and do not have the support of most of the population in their own country. Therefore, the conflict in Afghanistan is not a nationalistic rebellion against foreign occupiers. Montgomery would recognise this and plan a strategy that would seek to militarily defeat and eliminate the Taleban and their allies. Furthermore, his talents would be well suited to the fighting there.

The blinkered and dogmatic strategy to win hearts and minds placed British lives at risk and failed to draw the appropriate conclusions that are that in a conflict as intense as the one in Afghanistan the first part of any nation-building programme is to supress the violence. Taking the moral high-ground is a luxury that the lives of Britain's servicemen cannot afford.

Furthermore, it is both woeful and damning that, despite the many warnings and the clear loss of life, the British army leadership and the Ministry of Defence were slow to supply vehicles which adequately protected the troops. This sorry scenario occurred in both Iraq and Afghanistan, where the soldiers were repeatedly targeted by bomb attacks. It is notable that the British army in the 1920s and the 1930s was far more adaptable and responses to the needs of the soldiers than their modern day counterparts. During the fighting in Ireland and Palestine it was the case that as soon as the higher echelons of the military saw that their vehicles made the troops vulnerable they made sure that both the army and the police were supplied with armoured cars which were capable of protecting their men. They did not try to deny the problem or procrastinate like the MoD recently did; they made sure that the appropriate equipment was procured.

Montgomery's generalship during the Second World War has been criticised for being overly cautious. That verdict does ignore the fact that some of his operations were audacious; but his so-called cautiousness was simply waiting for the troops to be prepared and the right equipment made available to them. This approach would guarantee success and keep casualties down to a minimum. This approach should have been adopted before British forces went into Iraq in 2003 and again before the deployment to Helmand province in 2006.

Intervention can work; it did in Sierra Leone, Bosnia and Herzegovina and Kosovo and it can work in Afghanistan but there needs to be adequate security measures which entail taking the offensive to the Taleban. There are numerous failing and failed states around the globe which can become a safe haven for terrorists especially Al-Qaeda inspired groups. Hence they may pose a threat to the strategic interests of Britain and her allies. What is more, if Britain continues to follow the UN's Responsibility to Protect agenda then the UK may continue to be embroiled in asymmetric conflicts around the globe for the foreseeable future. Therefore, even if the on-going conflict in Afghanistan, which still has to be won, is left to one side there is a greater need than ever to learn the lessons from Montgomery and the first war on terror.

Montgomery would have known what needed to be done and how to do it.

Appendix 1

TIMELINE: MONTGOMERY'S CAREER AT A GLANCE

'Yet man is born unto trouble, as the sparks fly upward'
Book of Job 5:7; quoted by Bernard Law Montgomery in his *Memoirs*

1887
Birth of Bernard Law Montgomery
Monty was born on 17th November 1887, the son of a reverend of Irish ancestry. Montgomery, despite rising far in his career, was not from an especially privileged background; a point he was at pains to emphasise to the Labour government when he had to work with them during his time as the professional head of the British armed forces

EARLY YEARS IN THE MILITARY

1907
The Royal Military Academy, Sandhurst
Montgomery enters the British Army's initial officer training centre, it is styled as a national centre of excellence for leadership

1908
The Royal Warwickshire Regiment
In September 1908 Montgomery joins the Royal Warwickshire
Regiment
The North-West Frontier
In December he arrived with the 1st Battalion of the Royal
Warwicks on the North-West Frontier of India, now Pakistan, facing
Afghan tribesmen

1910
Promotion
In April 1910 Montgomery was promoted to the rank of Lieutenant,
his stellar rise in Britain's armed services was underway
Bombay in India
In October Montgomery and his battalion were posted to Bombay,
now known as Mumbai, in India

1913
Promotion and service back in Britain
Monty left India in the autumn of 1912 and in January 1913 he
became the Assistant Adjutant of the 1st Battalion of the Royal
Warwickshire Regiment. This gave him responsibility for some of
the battalion's organisation

THE FIRST WORLD WAR

1914
Montgomery is part of the British Expeditionary Force
In August 1914 Montgomery and the Royal Warwickshire Regiment
are sent to France to face the German army. Monty saw battle that
very same month
Seriously injured in combat
On 13th October, after fighting in France and Belgium where he
distinguished himself with a number of brave actions, Montgomery
was seriously injured by a sniper during British attacks on the
Germans when leading his platoon in Belgium. Captain
Montgomery was awarded the Distinguished Service Order for,
according to the *London Gazette* published on 1st December 1914,

'Conspicuous gallant leading on 13th October, when he turned the enemy out of their trenches with the bayonet. He was severely wounded.' [128]

1915
Training the British volunteer army
In February, after recovering from his near life threatening injuries, which included being shot several times through the lung and in the knee, he was still not fit for overseas service so Montgomery was given the task of training the 91st Infantry Brigade. He was given the rank of Brigade Major

1916
Back to the Front
After being declared fit to be sent back abroad, Montgomery was posted back to France in January 1916
Battle of the Somme
On 26th July Montgomery was hit during an artillery attack but not hurt seriously enough to be withdrawn from combat

1917
Promoted to Major
He received the rank of Major and became a staff officer. Monty excelled in his organisation and training roles

1918
Helping plan and organise the successful British offensives
He received a further promotion in July 1918 when Monty was made a Brevet Lieutenant Colonel. Montgomery, from August to the close of the war on 11th November, helped organise and plan the successful British advances that drove back the German army
Awards
On top of his Distinguished Service Order, Montgomery was also Mentioned in Dispatches on eight occasions, a highly prestigious amount, and he received the French Croix de Guerre; an award given to those who distinguish themselves by acts of heroism in combat

BETWEEN THE WORLD WARS

1919
Command of 17th Battalion Royal Fusiliers
On 5th September he was promoted to Lieutenant Colonel and was given command of part of the British occupation forces of Germany, known as the British Army of the Rhine

1920
Staff College in Camberley
In January Montgomery entered the British Army Staff College in Camberley after being nominated to join the course there

1921
County Cork, Ireland
Montgomery arrived in January 1921 to take up the position of Brigade Major of the 17th (Cork) Infantry Brigade in Ireland

1922
Appointed as Brigade Major of the 8th Infantry Brigade,
Montgomery left Ireland in May to take up his new position based in Plymouth on the UK mainland

1923
Chief of Staff of a Territorial Army Division
Montgomery was appointed to a position that was tantamount to being the Chief of Staff of a Territorial Army division

1925
Royal Warwickshire Regiment
Montgomery re-joined his old regiment

1926
Military Instructor
Montgomery became an Instructor at the Staff College based in Camberley

1930
Works on Military Theory
In 1930 Montgomery was commissioned by the War Office to write the British Army's *Infantry Training Manual*. Throughout the 1920s and the 1930s Montgomery was a prolific author of articles on the successful execution of his profession – war

1931
Command of the 1st Battalion Royal Warwickshire Regiment
Monty was promoted to full Lieutenant Colonel and given command of the 1st Battalion of the Royal Warwickshire Regiment
Palestine
Montgomery was the overall commander of the British Army in Palestine and as he was the senior officer there he was effectively the military governor of the British Mandate
Egypt
Monty and his battalion were posted to Egypt

1934
India
In 1934 the battalion and their Lieutenant Colonel arrive at their new posting in India
Indian Army Staff College
In June 1934 Montgomery was given the position as the Senior Instructor at the Indian Army Staff College

1937
Promotion to Brigadier
Montgomery was given command of the 9th Infantry Brigade and promoted to the rank of Brigadier. This brigade was part of the 3rd (Iron) Division, now known as the 3rd Mechanised Division

1938
The war in Palestine
Promoted to the rank of Major General, Montgomery took command of the 8th Division in northern Palestine and set about quashing the Arab Revolt

1939
Command of the 3rd (Iron) Division
In August Monty took command of this important division which was to be part of the British Expeditionary Force that would be sent to France in the event of war with Germany

SECOND WORLD WAR

1940
Montgomery's 3rd Division beat off a German attack
On 15th May the Iron Division fight off German attacks but as the other fronts collapsed that month Monty's troops were ordered to withdraw to cover the retreat to Dunkirk
Dunkirk
In late May and early June Montgomery commanded II Corps and successfully withdraw from the continent. Monty was praised for his professional handling of the crisis that was not of his making
Promotion
In July Montgomery was promoted to the rank of Lieutenant General and took command of V Corps which was covering the region of Wessex

1941
Commander in Chief South-East Command
After assuming command of another army Corps, XII Corps, in the South-east of England where any German invasion was expected to take place, Montgomery in November 1941 was given the command of the British army in the South-east. Montgomery improved the army's ability to defend the South coast emphasising the need for a mobile aggressive defence

1942
The War in North Africa
In August Montgomery was placed in command of the 8th Army facing Rommel and his German Africa Corps which had earlier driven the British forces back to the position of El-Alamein

Battle of El Alamein

After defeating Rommel in the Battle of Alam el Halfa, on 23rd October Montgomery launched his offensive against the axis forces. He predicted that the battle of El Alamein would last 12 days, it lasted twelve days and the German and Italian forces were routed. Montgomery and the 8th Army pursued them across North Africa fighting a number of other battles and engagements on the way

1943

Operation Husky

Montgomery leads the British 8th Army in the allied invasion of Sicily. This operation, which was effectively planned by Montgomery, was launched on the night of 9th September and concluded with the Anglo-American forces in control of the island

Invasion of Mainland Italy

On 3rd September Montgomery led the 8th Army in the allied invasion of mainland Italy. After linking up with the US 5th Army, which had landed at Salerno, the 8th Army took the right of Italy and pushed forward breaching the Gustav line. Montgomery left this theatre in late December 1943 to begin his planning and preparation for the opening of the allied second front in France

1944

Preparing for D-Day

In January Montgomery arrived back in Britain to prepare for the allied invasion of Normandy where he was to be the overall commander of British, Canadian and American forces. He embarked on an extensive series of training and morale boosting visits to the units involved in the forthcoming campaign in northern France including a host of troops from many other allied nations

D-Day – 6th June

Montgomery commanded the ground forces for the Battle of Normandy. He planned the campaign in Normandy to last for 90 days; it took 81 to defeat the German army.

Promotion to Field Marshal

On 1st September Montgomery was promoted to the rank of Field Marshal. Monty, accompanied by his two dogs named Hitler and Rommel, commanded the 21st Army Group as they advanced through France and Belgium and into the Netherlands. At one point the army in just as little as four days managed to push forward an astounding 250 miles

Operation Market Garden

On 17th September Montgomery launches his attempt to outflank the German defences on the Siegfried Line and penetrate into the Ruhr

Battle of the Bulge

On 16th December the Germans launch what became known as the Battle of the Bulge; this splits the American forces under Omar Bradley and General Dwight D Eisenhower, the Supreme Allied Commander, gives Montgomery command of the US troops on the northern shoulder of the German advance. Monty has been credited with stabilising the front line, organising an effective defence and leading a counter attack which together with other American forces advancing from the south eliminated the bulge

1945

Advance to the Rhine

In a number of operations throughout the winter of early 1945 Montgomery pushed through the German defences to advance to the Rhine

Crossing the Rhine

On 24th March Monty's 21st Army Group crossed the Rhine in Operation Plunder and Operation Varsity in what Eisenhower intended to be the main allied thrust across that great river

Advance across Germany

In April Montgomery's forces and those of General Omar Bradley completed a double-envelopment of Germany's main industrial base, the Ruhr. Monty's 21st Army Group continues its advance across the North German Plain

British forces reach the Baltic Sea

On 2nd May Montgomery's forces reach the German port city of Lübeck on the Baltic coast six hours before the Russian's arrived, thus preventing the Red Army from entering Denmark

Taking the German Surrender

On the order of Grand Admiral Dönitz, the last leader of Nazi Germany, the offer is made to Montgomery on 3rd May to surrender all Germany forces in the north to his command, including those facing the Red Army. Montgomery refused to take their surrender as this would have allowed many Germans to escape Russian captivity. The German leadership complained about this decision but Montgomery told them that they "should have thought of all these things before they began the war, and particularly before they attacked the Russians in June 1941." On 4th May Nazi forces in North-west Germany, Denmark and the Netherlands surrender to Montgomery at his Headquarters

AFTER THE SECOND WORLD WAR

1945
Military Commander of the British Zone in Germany
Montgomery became a member of the Allied Control Council in Germany and the commander of the British Zone of Occupation in that country. Monty held this position until May 1946 when he left to take up a new position in Whitehall
Awards
Amongst other honours from a multitude of countries Montgomery was awarded by Stalin the Order of Victory, the Soviet Union's highest award

1946
Ennobled
Montgomery was given a peerage in 1946 becoming the Rt Hon. Field Marshal Viscount Montgomery of Alamein
Appointed as Chief of the Imperial General Staff
In June 1946 Montgomery became the professional head of the British armed forces known as the Chief of the Imperial General Staff. He served in this role until the autumn of 1948

1947 – 1948
War and Withdrawal from Palestine
As violence again erupted in Palestine Montgomery as Chief of the Imperial General Staff ordered that repressive measures be used to restore peace. However, in the face of violence from Palestine's Arab

community and from the Holy Land's American and Soviet backed Jewish population Britain withdraws from Palestine in 1948

1948
International Defence Cooperation
Monty become the Western Union Defence Organisation's Chairman of the Commanders-in-Chief Committee

1951
Deputy Supreme Commander of NATO
In April Montgomery became the North Atlantic Treaty Organisation Deputy Supreme Commander, first serving under General Eisenhower. Montgomery held this post until 1958

1958
Publishing of Montgomery's Memoirs
Montgomery retired in 1958. That year he also published his memoirs. In these he notably criticised his former commander and friend Dwight D Eisenhower, then President of the United States, for decisions Ike made during the allied advance to the Rhine. According to Montgomery Eisenhower's decisions caused the war to drag on into 1945 and prevented the Allies from ending the Second World War in 1944. Their friendship came to an end

1976
The passing of Viscount Montgomery of Alamein
Bernard Law Montgomery died on 24th March 1976, he was 88 years old

Appendix 2

ENDNOTES

[1] Hamilton, Nigel, *Monty: The Making of a General 1887 – 1942*, page 52

[2] Hamilton, Nigel, *Monty: The Making of a General 1887 – 1942*, pages 52 - 53

[3] *London Gazette*, Issue 28992 published on the 1st December 1914, page 34

[4] Bernard Law, Viscount Montgomery of Alamein, *The Memoirs of Field-Marshal Montgomery*, Collins 1958, page 36

[5] Bernard Law, Viscount Montgomery of Alamein, *The Memoirs of Field-Marshal Montgomery*, Collins 1958, page 35

[6] Bernard Law, Viscount Montgomery of Alamein, *The Memoirs of Field-Marshal Montgomery*, Collins 1958, page 35

[7] Liddell Hart Papers, King's College London

[8] Letter from Bernard Law Montgomery writing to Major Arthur Percival, Percival Papers, Imperial War Museum, 14th October 1923

[9] Leeson, Dr David, Death in the afternoon: the Croke Park massacre, 21 November 1920, *Canadian Journal of History,* April 2003, pages 43-67

[10] Cottrell, Peter, The Anglo-Irish War, Osprey Publishing, 2006, pages 54, 70 and 71

[11] Cottrell, Peter, The Anglo-Irish War, Osprey Publishing, 2006, page 47

[12] Widders, Robert, *Spitting on a Soldier's Grave*, Troubador Publishing

[13] Cottrell, Peter, The Anglo-Irish War, Osprey Publishing, 2006, page 18

[14] Cottrell, Peter, The Anglo-Irish War, Osprey Publishing, 2006, page 20

[15] Sir Harman Greenwood, Pamphlet on Sinn Féin Organisation, *Sinn Féin and the Irish Volunteers*, National Archives, WO 32/4308

[16] Barry, Tom, *Guerilla Days in Ireland*, The Irish Press, 1949, page 208

[17] Report on Sinn Féin Organisation, National Archives, WO 32/4308

[18] Cottrell, Peter, The Anglo-Irish War, Osprey Publishing, 2006, page 46

[19] Proclamation of Martial Law, National Archives, WO 32/9536

[20] Barry, Tom, *Guerilla Days in Ireland*, The Irish Press, 1949, pages 69 – 70

[21] Hamilton, Nigel, Monty: The Making of a General 1887 – 1942, Hamish Hamilton Ltd, 1981, pages 156 - 157

[22] Barry, Tom, *Guerilla Days in Ireland*, The Irish Press, 1949

[23] Barry, Tom, *Guerilla Days in Ireland*, The Irish Press, 1949

[24] Major B L Montgomery, *17th Infantry Brigade: Summary of Important Instructions*, placed in the Imperial War Museum by General Strickland

[25] Barry, Tom, *Guerilla Days in Ireland*, The Irish Press, 1949, page 154

[26] Letter from Bernard Law Montgomery writing to Major Arthur Percival, Percival Papers, Imperial War Museum, 14th October 1923

[27] Letter from Bernard Law Montgomery writing to Major Arthur Percival, Percival Papers, Imperial War Museum, 14th October 1923

[28] Barry, Tom, *Guerilla Days in Ireland*, The Irish Press, 1949

[29] Letter from Bernard Law Montgomery writing to Major Arthur Percival, Percival Papers, Imperial War Museum, 14th October 1923

[30] Letter from Bernard Law Montgomery writing to Major Arthur Percival, Percival Papers, Imperial War Museum, 14th October 1923

[31] Barry, Tom, *Guerilla Days in Ireland*, The Irish Press, 1949, pages 115 – 117

[32] Memorandum from the General Officer Commanding-in-Chief of the British Forces in Ireland, 23rd May 1921, National Archives, WO 32/9572

[33] Memorandum from the General Officer Commanding-in-Chief of the British Forces in Ireland, 23rd May 1921, National Archives, WO 32/9572

[34] Barry, Tom, *Guerilla Days in Ireland*, The Irish Press, 1949, pages 225 to 226

[35] Measures to Restore Law and Order, 24th May 1921, National Archives, WO 32/9572

[36] Barry, Tom, *Guerilla Days in Ireland*, The Irish Press, 1949, page 226

[37] Measures to Restore Law and Order, 24th May 1921, National Archives, WO 32/9572

[38] Letter from Bernard Law Montgomery writing to Major Arthur Percival, Percival Papers, Imperial War Museum, 14th October 1923

[39] Cottrell, Peter, The Anglo-Irish War, Osprey Publishing, 2006, page 80

[40] Letter to the Secretary of State for Defence from the Commander of the Imperial General Staff, 16th August 1921, National Archives, WO 32/9572

[41] Cottrell, Peter, The Anglo-Irish War, Osprey Publishing, 2006, page 85

[42] Michael Reynolds, *Monty and Patton: Two paths to Victory*, Spellmount Ltd, pages 68 - 69

[43] Hamilton, Nigel, Monty: The Making of a General 1887 – 1942, Hamish Hamilton Ltd, 1981

[44] Bernard Law, Viscount Montgomery of Alamein, *The Memoirs of Field-Marshal Montgomery*, Collins 1958

[45] Chalfont Alun, *Montgomery of Alamein*, Weidenfeld & Nicolson, 1976

[46] Butler, Ewan, Barry's Flying Column, Leo Cooper Ltd 1971 and Hamilton, Nigel, Monty: The Making of a General 1887 – 1942, Hamish Hamilton Ltd, 1981

[47] Cottrell, Peter, The Anglo-Irish War, Osprey Publishing, 2006

[48] Letter from Bernard Law Montgomery writing to Major Arthur Percival, Percival Papers, Imperial War Museum, 14th October 1923

[49] Letter from Bernard Law Montgomery writing to Major Arthur Percival, Percival Papers, Imperial War Museum, 14th October 1923

[50] Winston Churchill, *The Aftermath*, Thornton 1929, page 297

[51] Barry, Tom, *Guerilla Days in Ireland*, The Irish Press, 1949, pages 207 to 208

[52] Letter from Bernard Law Montgomery writing to Major Arthur Percival, Percival Papers, Imperial War Museum, 14th October 1923

[53] Hamilton, Nigel, *Monty: The Making of a General 1887 – 1942*, page 249

[54] Bernard Law, Viscount Montgomery of Alamein, *The Memoirs of Field-Marshal Montgomery*, Collins 1958, page 41

[55] Hamilton, Nigel, *Monty: The Making of a General 1887 – 1942*, page 249

[56] Carver, Michael, *Churchill's Generals*, Edited by John Keegan, 1991

[57] Letter from Bernard Law Montgomery to the Chief of the Imperial General Staff, 4th December 1938, National Archives, WO 216/111

[58] Bernard Law, Viscount Montgomery of Alamein, *The Memoirs of Field-Marshal Montgomery*, Collins 1958

[59] Brief Notes on Palestine, Major-General Bernard Law Montgomery, National Archives, WO 216/46

[60] Hughes, Dr Matthew, The Banality of Brutality: British Armed Forces and the Repression of the Arab Revolt in Palestine, 1936–39, English Historical Review (2009) CXXIV (507) page 327

[61] Statement of HM Government, 7th September 1936

[62] Military Lessons of the Arab Rebellion in Palestine, National Archives, WO 191/70

[63] Letter from Bernard Law Montgomery to the Chief of the Imperial General Staff, 4th December 1938, National Archives, WO 216/111

[64] Military Lessons of the Arab Rebellion in Palestine, National Archives, WO 191/70

[65] Letter from Bernard Law Montgomery to the Chief of the Imperial General Staff, 4th December 1938, National Archives, WO 216/111

[66] Military Lessons of the Arab Rebellion in Palestine, National Archives, WO 191/70

[67] History of Disturbances in Palestine 1936 – 1939, National Archives, WO 191/88

[68] History of Disturbances in Palestine 1936 – 1939, National Archives, WO 191/88

[69] History of Disturbances in Palestine 1936 – 1939, National Archives, WO 191/88

[70] Barker, James, *History Today*, Monty and the Mandate in Palestine, Volume: 59, Issue: 3

[71] History of Disturbances in Palestine 1936 – 1939, National Archives, WO 191/88

[72] History of Disturbances in Palestine 1936 – 1939, National Archives, WO 191/88

[73] Baxter, Colin F, *Field Marshal Bernard Law Montgomery, 1887 – 1976: A Selected Biography*, Greenwood Press, 1999

[74] Morris, Benny, *Righteous Victims : A History of the Zionist-Arab Conflict 1881-1999*, page 150 – 151

[75] Barker, James, *History Today*, Monty and the Mandate in Palestine, Volume: 59, Issue: 3

[76] A collection of memorandums by Major-General Bernard Law Montgomery, on the general situation in Palestine, National Archives, WO 216/111

[77] Report on Military Control in Palestine 1938/39, National Archives WO 191/89

[78] Hughes, Dr Matthew, The Banality of Brutality: British Armed Forces and the Repression of the Arab Revolt in Palestine, 1936–39, English Historical Review (2009) CXXIV (507) page 333

[79] History of Disturbances in Palestine 1936 – 1939, National Archives, WO 191/88

[80] The Development of the Palestinian Police Force Under Military Control, June 1939, National Archives, WO 191/90

[81] Letter from Bernard Law Montgomery to the Chief of the Imperial General Staff, 4th December 1938, National Archives, WO 216/111

[82] Letter from Bernard Law Montgomery to the Chief of the Imperial General Staff, 4th December 1938, National Archives, WO 216/111

[83] Letter from Bernard Law Montgomery to the Chief of the Imperial General Staff, 4th December 1938, National Archives, WO 216/111

[84] Letter from Bernard Law Montgomery to the Chief of the Imperial General Staff, 4th December 1938, National Archives, WO 216/111

[85] Barker, James, *History Today*, Monty and the Mandate in Palestine, Volume: 59, Issue: 3

[86] A collection of memorandums by Major-General Bernard Law Montgomery, on the general situation in Palestine, National Archives, WO 216/111

[87] Letter from Bernard Law Montgomery to the Chief of the Imperial General Staff, 4th December 1938, National Archives, WO 216/111

[88] A collection of memorandums by Major-General Bernard Law Montgomery, on the general situation in Palestine, National Archives, WO 216/111

[89] Hughes, Dr Matthew, The Banality of Brutality: British Armed Forces and the Repression of the Arab Revolt in Palestine, 1936–39, English Historical Review (2009) CXXIV (507) page 352

[90] Morris, Benny, *Righteous Victims : A History of the Zionist-Arab Conflict 1881-1999*, page 151 – 152

[91] Hughes, Dr Matthew, The Banality of Brutality: British Armed Forces and the Repression of the Arab Revolt in Palestine, 1936–39, English Historical Review (2009) CXXIV (507) pages 323 – 327

[92] Hughes, Dr Matthew, The Banality of Brutality: British Armed Forces and the Repression of the Arab Revolt in Palestine, 1936–39, English Historical Review (2009) CXXIV (507) pages 328

[93] Hughes, Dr Matthew, The Banality of Brutality: British Armed Forces and the Repression of the Arab Revolt in Palestine, 1936–39, English Historical Review (2009) CXXIV (507) pages 329 - 330

[94] Hughes, Dr Matthew, The Banality of Brutality: British Armed Forces and the Repression of the Arab Revolt in Palestine, 1936–39, English Historical Review (2009) CXXIV (507) pages 336 - 337

[95] Hughes, Dr Matthew, The Banality of Brutality: British Armed Forces and the Repression of the Arab Revolt in Palestine, 1936–39, English Historical Review (2009) CXXIV (507) pages 337 – 338

[96] Morris, Benny, *Righteous Victims : A History of the Zionist-Arab Conflict 1881-1999*, page 157

[97] Hughes, Dr Matthew, The Banality of Brutality: British Armed Forces and the Repression of the Arab Revolt in Palestine, 1936–39, English Historical Review (2009) CXXIV (507) page 352

[98] History of Disturbances in Palestine 1936 – 1939, National Archives, WO 191/88

[99] History of Disturbances in Palestine 1936 – 1939, National Archives, WO 191/88

[100] Brief Notes on Palestine, Major-General Bernard Law Montgomery, National Archives, WO 216/46

[101] Levenberg, Haim, *Military Preparations of the Arab Community in Palestine: 1945–1948*, Frank Cass and Co Ltd, 1993

[102] Morris, Benny, *Righteous Victims : A History of the Zionist-Arab Conflict 1881-1999*

[103] Khalidi, Walid, *From Haven to Conquest: Readings in Zionism and the Palestine Problem until 1948*, The Institute for Palestine Studies, 1971

[104] Rashid Khalidi in *The war for Palestine: rewriting the history of 1948*, Edited by , Eugene L Rogan and Avi Shlaim, Cambridge University Press, 2001

[105] Brief Notes on Palestine, Major-General Bernard Law Montgomery, National Archives, WO 216/46

[106] A collection of memorandums by Major-General Bernard Law Montgomery, on the general situation in Palestine, National Archives, WO 216/111

[107] History of Disturbances in Palestine 1936 – 1939, National Archives, WO 191/88

[108] The Development of the Palestinian Police Force Under Military Control, June 1939, National Archives, WO 191/90

[109] History of Disturbances in Palestine 1936 – 1939, National Archives, WO 191/88

[110] A collection of memorandums by Major-General Bernard Law Montgomery, on the general situation in Palestine, National Archives, WO 216/111

[111] Brief Notes on Palestine, Major-General Bernard Law Montgomery, National Archives, WO 216/46

[112] Military Lessons of the Arab Rebellion in Palestine, National Archives, WO 191/70

[113] History of Disturbances in Palestine 1936 – 1939, National Archives, WO 191/88

[114] Military Lessons of the Arab Rebellion in Palestine, National Archives, WO 191/70

[115] Hughes, Dr Matthew, The Banality of Brutality: British Armed Forces and the Repression of the Arab Revolt in Palestine, 1936–39, English Historical Review (2009) CXXIV (507) page 314

[116] A collection of memorandums by Major-General Bernard Law Montgomery, on the general situation in Palestine, National Archives, WO 216/111

[117] Hamilton, Nigel, Monty: The Making of a General 1887 – 1942, Hamish Hamilton Ltd, 1981, page 307

[118] North, Dr Richard, *Ministry of Defeat*, Continuum, 2009

[119] A collection of memorandums by Major-General Bernard Law Montgomery, on the general situation in Palestine, National Archives, WO 216/111

[120] Basra residents blame UK troops, *BBC Website*, 14th December 2007

[121] House of Commons Defence Committee, Fourth Report of Session 2010 – 2012: *Operations in Afghanistan*, 6th July 2011

[122] Brigadier James Cowan, BBC *Newsnight,* 8th February 2010

[123] House of Commons Defence Committee, Fourth Report of Session 2010 – 2012: *Operations in Afghanistan*, 6th July 2011, page 26

[124] Colonel Chris Claydon, Head of Counter IED, commenting on BBC *Newsnight*, 21st October 2009

[125] House of Commons Defence Committee, Fourth Report of Session 2010 – 2012: *Operations in Afghanistan*, 6th July 2011, page 24

[126] House of Commons Defence Committee, Fourth Report of Session 2010 – 2012: *Operations in Afghanistan*, 6th July 2011, pages 52 – 53

[127] Troops 'release half of Taliban prisoners after four days', *The Daily Telegraph*, 27th September 2009

[128] *London Gazette*, Issue 28992 published on the 1st December 1914. Page 34

Appendix 3

ABOUT THE AUTHOR

The author, Robert Oulds M.A., has a keen interest in military affairs, politics and history. As matters relating to military operations are closely intertwined with politics the author's involvement with both national and transnational affairs gives him a good grounding in international relations. And it gives him a useful understanding of the wider strategic significance of major questions regarding Britain's involvement in the world.

Robert Oulds is the longstanding Director of the Bruges Group, the respected think tank which for the last 20 years has been at the forefront of the debate about the UK's relationship with the wider world. Their research, which informs both members of the press and politics, is often reported in the media. And Robert Oulds regularly appears on the television and the radio debating topical issues. The President of the Bruges Group is the former Prime Minister Margaret Thatcher.

As such he is very familiar with the public policy process and how this impacts upon many areas of national and international affairs. His meticulous research skills have also been honed by his authorship of a great deal of material on many political and international issues, and this gives him the skill of making complex strategic issues accessible to the general public. This will allow him to uncover for the first time the full story behind Montgomery and the First War on Terror and what it can teach us today.

Since 2002 the author has also served his community as a local government Councillor in a London Borough. This led him to become a Chairman of Planning and he also became a Cabinet Member with responsibility for Education and Children's Services. His involvement in politics also led to him becoming a Chairman of a Parliamentary Constituency Association.

Robert Oulds actively recognises the deep debt of gratitude which we owe in this country to our armed forces. As such he is a Standard Bearer and Treasurer for his local branch of the Royal British Legion (RBL). This is an organisation established to help the welfare of ex-Servicemen and campaign on issues relating to the armed forces. The RBL are also the custodians of the nation's Remembrance services; and they also organise and run the annual Poppy Appeal which raises funds for the aid of our soldiers, sailors and airmen and women as well as their dependents.

Robert Oulds' Grandfather served as a soldier under the main protagonist in this book, Bernard Law Montgomery, in North Africa, Sicily and at Arnhem during the Second World War.

INDEX

Abd al-Halim al-Jaulani 179

Abdullah el Asbar 137, 155

Afghanistan 8, 9, 10, 11, 13, 14, 21, 22, 23, 24, 128, 219, 228, 231 - 242, 245 - 263, 267, 269

Al-Qaeda 13, 231, 232, 233, 234, 248, 259, 261, 262, 269

Arm Cathartha na hÉireann 54

Baldwin, Stanley 137, 138

Balfour Declaration 132, 133

Barry, Tom 33, 78, 88, 91, 101, 114, 121

'Black and Tans', see Royal Irish Constabulary Special Reserve

British Army Staff College 27, 123, 128, 129

British Defence Doctrine (BDD) 8, 202, 209, 211, 212, 226

Brugha, Cathal 41

Cherat 23,

Clausewitz, Carl von 16, 18, 29, 204, 220

Collins, Michael 32, 41, 58

Costello, Michael 78, 89

County Cork 32, 33, 42, 50, 61, 75, 77, 78, 79, 84, 87, 88, 89, 90, 93, 101, 113, 114, 115, 116, 120, 177, 209, 211

Croke Park 32, 33, 77

Dead Sea 147

de Valera, Eamonn 41, 42, 102, 103, 104

Dublin 32, 33, 34, 36, 39, 40, 42, 43, 45, 48, 49, 50, 54, 58, 60, 61, 64, 67, 709, 71, 72, 98, 101, 109

Easter Rising 1916 36, 39, 54, 75

Fawzi el Qawukji 137

Galilee 137, 147, 155, 157, 180

Griffith, Arthur 34, 42

Guevara, Ernesto 'Che' 19

Haganah 145, 146, 147, 157, 190, 191

Haj Mohammad Effendi Amin al Husseini (Grand Mufti) 136, 137, 149, 151, 162, 185, 193

Helmand Province 22, 219, 232, 235, 236, 241, 242, 243, 244, 246, 252, 253, 267, 269

Improvised Explosive Device (IED) 228, 238, 239, 241, 243, 244, 246, 258

Iraq 10, 11, 12, 13, 14, 95, 136, 138, 144, 195, 219, 229, 230, 231, 232, 233, 245, 246, 253, 256, 257, 258, 267, 268, 269,

Irish Republican Army (IRA) 7, 9, 29, 31, 32, 33, 40, 41, 45, 46, 47, 51, 52, 53, 57 - 70, 73, 75, 76, 77 - 96, 99, 100, 101, 102, 105, 106, 108 - 122, 127, 207, 208, 209, 210, 211, 216, 217, 221, 222, 225, 227, 228, 264

Irish Republican Brotherhood (IRB) 54, 55, 56, 107

Irish Volunteers 56, 57

Islam 10, 134, 137, 138, 212, 220, 229, 233, 234, 239, 248, 251, 262

Jerusalem 136, 142, 150, 160, 161, 166, 169, 174, 177, 182, 183, 195

Kai-Shek, Chiang 19

Khyber Pass 23,

Lambart, Frederick 44

Land Rovers 243

Libya 10

Lloyd George, David 43, 72, 95, 102, 103, 107, 119

Na Fianna Éireann 53

NATO (North Atlantic Treaty Organisation) 7, 13, 202, 231, 232, 233, 237, 239, 245, 246, 247, 248, 249, 250, 255

Obama, Barrack 255, 256

O'Connor,, Richard 139, 168

Pakistan 9, 13, 22, 23, 24, 128, 234, 247, 248, 250, 258, 259,

Palestine 7, 9, 10, 12, 13, 14, 45, 51, 125, 126, 129, 131 - 201, 205, 206, 207, 208, 210, 211, 215, 216, 217, 218, 220, 229, 232, 238, 24, 253, 254, 257, 259, 260, 262, 264, 265, 266, 267, 268

Percival, Arthur 31, 78, 115, 118, 120,

Redmond, John Edward 34, 37, 42

Royal Air Force 143, 147, 176, 193

Royal Irish Constabulary (RIC) 40, 41, 48, 49, 50, 69, 70

Royal Irish Constabulary Special Reserve 'Black and Tans' 49, 50, 70, 78, 102, 113, 171, 209

Royal Warwickshire Regiment 21, 22, 25, 111, 123, 124, 125

Scimitar, FV107 ARV 243,

Sheikh Attieh 137, 155

Sin Fein 34, 35, 36, 37, 40, 41, 42, 55, 57, 58, 66, 72, 81, 87, 96, 99, 102, 106, 109, 222, 225, 228, 265

Special Air Service (SAS) 23, 224, 225,

Taleban 8, 11, 13, 22, 24, 127, 218, 230, 231, 232, 233, 234, 235, 236, 239 - 261, 265, 266, 267

Tegart, Sir Charles 171, 172, 173, 177,

Tegart's Wall 171, 172

Trans-Jordan Frontier Force 143, 147, 176,

Tudor, Henry 45,

War on Terror 8, 9, 214, 246, 258, 269, 287

Wavell, Sir Archibald 139, 161, 198

Wilson, Sir Henry Huges 44, 94, 95, 96, 97, 99, 104, 105, 116

Zedong, Mao 19, 20, 239

Zionism 132, 133, 157

Bretwalda Books Ltd